PENGUIN BOOKS

PURITY OF DICTION IN ENGLISH VERSE

AND

ARTICULATE ENERGY

Donald Davie, born in 1922, was educated at Barnsley Grammar School and Cambridge, and served in the Royal Navy from 1941 to 1946. His first books of both poetry and criticism appeared in the 1950s, when he was teaching at Trinity College, Dublin. Subsequently he taught in Cambridge and at the University of Essex and, after 1968, at Stanford University, California, and Vanderbilt University, Tennessee. He retired to his native land in 1988 and lives in Devon. He has written three books about Ezra Pound, has translated from the Russian, and has adapted a Polish classic, the *Pan Tadeusz* of Mickiewicz, from an American prose translation. He is in the process of bringing out a collected edition of his works in both verse and prose; four volumes have so far appeared. He has also published his memoirs, *These the Companions*.

PURITY OF DICTION IN ENGLISH VERSE

AND

ARTICULATE ENERGY

Donald Davie

PENGUIN BOOKS

PENGUIN BOOKS

Published by the Penguin Group
Penguin Books Ltd, 27 Wrights Lane, London W8 5TZ, England
Penguin Books USA Inc., 375 Hudson Street, New York, New York 10014, USA
Penguin Books Australia Ltd, Ringwood, Victoria, Australia
Penguin Books Canada Ltd, 10 Alcorn Avenue, Toronto, Ontario, Canada M4V 3B2
Penguin Books (NZ) Ltd, 182–190 Wairau Road, Auckland 10, New Zealand

Penguin Books Ltd, Registered Offices: Harmondsworth, Middlesex, England

Purity of Diction in English Verse
First published by Chatto and Windus 1952

Articulate Energy
First published by Routledge & Kegan Paul 1955
Reprinted with a Postscript 1976

Published together in one volume with a Foreword in Penguin Books 1992
Published simultaneously by Carcanet Press
1 3 5 7 9 10 8 6 4 2

Filmset in Monophoto Garamond
Printed in England by Clays Ltd, St Ives plc

Contents

ARTICULATE ENERGY: AN INQUIRY INTO THE SYNTAX OF ENGLISH POETRY

Foreword to the 1992 edition

Purity of Diction in English Verse was my first book; it came out in 1952. The sequel, *Articulate Energy*, followed in 1955. To have them back in print after many years – for the first time as two stages in one investigation – tempts me to feel triumphant: history has vindicated me! More soberly, I am glad to foresee an end to the complaints that have reached me, over the years when both books were out of print, to the effect that library copies had disintegrated from overuse, or else had apparently been stolen from the shelves. The demand has been constant; the supply hasn't.

The first book was written largely in Plymouth, the second in Dublin; though both relied – heavily to begin with, less heavily as time went on – on what I had learned in Cambridge. The critic is supposed, unlike the poet or the novelist, to be impervious to the localities he writes in. He has to be – so it is assumed – clinical, detached, Olympian. I can only report that in the first of these books there wouldn't have been a chapter on Charles Wesley, had there not been in my in-laws' terrace house in Plymouth a copy of *The Methodist Hymn-book*; nor, in the second, would Berkeley have been the one and only philosopher appealed to, had not the book been written in George Berkeley's Alma Mater, Trinity College, Dublin. The sights and sounds and smells of Dublin Bay and Plymouth Sound hang around these books in a way that cannot be demonstrated. Indeed, the young man who wrote these essays was the same who, in poems of the same time, was wrestling the actualities of Plymouth and of Dublin into a significance that satisfied him. For him then, as for me now rereading him, essay and poem were equivalent and almost interchangeable attempts to grapple with the one same reality.

That reality was post-war – more insistently so, for obvious reasons, in Plymouth than in Dublin. The sense of this has faded for me over the years, and now I must exert myself to recall it. It was a matter of 'picking up the pieces'. What I and my friends of those days took for granted was that the Second World War had invalidated even those radically diminished principles and sentiments that had survived the war of 1914–18. In poetics the assumptions of the 1920s and 1930s had to be questioned, no less than those of the 1880s and 1890s which our fathers in the art in the inter-war years had exploded and derided. We had to go back to basics. And that – 'Back to Basics' – is the flag that flew, and I think still flies, over both these books.

As the generations that have known world war die out, so those 'basics' begin to seem prescriptive and constricting. Those who resent them don't characteristically assail them one by one, but rather contend that 'basics' in that sense do not and cannot exist. Since poetry itself has no secure basis in human experience, so (they say) whatever at any given time is declared to be basic to it can be shown to be on the contrary conditioned by historical time, by the needs and purposes of a governing class for instance. I have seldom contended with those who argue in this way, because the alleged bone of contention – the poem or body of poems – is never subjected to as intense a scrutiny from their standpoint as it is from mine.

'Scrutiny' – it was the watchword of my first teacher F. R. Leavis, who alas in his later writings abused the notion, and discredited it. 'Just what is going on here?' – not on the page (for there nothing is 'going on'), but in the minds of us who read that page. That is what we scrutinize, if we are critics. And such scrutiny uncovers some who read too much from the page, as well as the many who read too little. But when is 'much' *too* much? To answer that we have to go outside literary criticism, to common sense or else to philosophy. And philosophy, in my experience, is very much the worse option, because characteristically it answers only by abdicating; philosophically, there is never any 'much' that can be called 'too much'. Common sense on the other hand – the common sense of 'old sweats', ex-servicemen – knows very well, because self-preservation has taught it, where bravery topples over into foolhardiness, caution into timidity, subtlety into sterile ingenuity. In these my first books, I was aware (or at least I am now aware, rereading them) of trusting to that old sweat's common sense.

Theory, therefore – at least as 'theory' is nowadays understood in literary studies – will find little to nourish it in these pages. And yet these two books seem to me the most theoretical that I have written. Those who ask for more theory – less tentative, more sweeping – are those who have never experienced war, nor expect to experience it in their lifetimes, nor can imagine what it is like. Recovering a wartime usage, I might say that these pages present poetry in 'an austerity package'. When every other commodity could be offered only under the acknowledged and overriding necessity of austerity (because of the successful U-boat onslaught on Allied shipping), the commodity called poetry had, simply as a matter of honour, to submit to the same controls. When peacetime came, those wartime stringencies could not be set aside nor forgotten. Others besides me believed this, though the 'basics' that they found themselves driven back upon were different from mine. Contemporaries like Kingsley Amis and Philip Larkin were far more prohibitive than I was: towards artistic liberties that they condemned, I found I could be indulgent. Still, I agreed with them that stringency was called for. I do not think it less called for now than it was forty years ago.

Exeter, Devon — Donald Davie

PURITY OF DICTION IN ENGLISH VERSE

To Doreen

Introduction

SOME time ago I began to read the works of some English poets who lived in the middle and towards the close of the eighteenth century. I was surprised and pleased to find how much I enjoyed them; but I found it hard to rationalize the enjoyment they gave me. With most of my contemporaries, I thought that the surest sign of poetic greatness was the ability to organize experience by apt and memorable metaphor. Suitably qualified, this is still my belief. But to make those qualifications, and to account for the respect I felt, I have had to go a long way round. My difficulties hinged on the question: whether it is true that in the eighteenth century literary English was metaphorically impoverished. In the last hundred years most literary historians have found this metaphorical poverty falling, like a shadow, over most English poetry written between the death of Pope and the publication of *Lyrical Ballads*. I have come to believe that what seems poverty is sometimes economy; and that this economy in metaphor produces effects which I call 'poetical', to which, it seems to me, most readers of our day are blind. The effects seem to me to be morally valuable; otherwise I should not care to write of them.

I have spent much time trying to understand what is meant by the 'diction' of poetry. But I am interested in the problem of diction only so as to use that notion, where no other will meet the case, in appreciating certain poetry of the past and the present. I derive from this poetry a pleasure which I can only describe by saying that the diction is pure. I feel, when I read some other poetry, a peculiar discomfort which I can define only by saying that the diction is impure. I want to understand what I mean when I make these judgements. I want to know how the poet goes about to produce this kind of pleasure, and what is its moral value for the reader. I do not offer the notion of purity in diction as an ultimate criterion of the worth of poetry. I know some valuable poems, especially of the nineteenth century, which suffer, as I think, from an impure diction; and I regret the discomfort which this causes, while admitting a counterbalance of virtues (that is, useful pleasures) of another order or another kind. Again, I find many great poems to which the notions of purity or impurity in diction seem merely irrelevant. I do not argue for a new criterion, only for an old one which has fallen out of use. This criterion is not equally relevant to all sorts of English poetry or in all phases of the English poetic tradition. I am interested in it because I think it relevant, indeed indispensable, to the poetry of Goldsmith's contemporaries, and to that of my own.

Of the essays which follow, those in Part I are devoted to defining and exemplifying the principles of purity in diction, with reference for the most part to poetry of the later eighteenth century; in the remainder I attempt to apply these principles to some later poetry, or to show how later criticism could find no room for them. The essays in Part II are self-contained, more provocative and probably more questionable in their conclusions than those in Part I, where I try to follow a consecutive argument through several chapters.

PART I

I

The Diction of English Verse

A FRIEND asks me what I stand to gain from talking about 'the diction of verse', instead of 'the language of poetry'. For him these are two ways of saying one thing, and my way is only the more pretentious. Now it seems to me that it would be pretentious to talk about the 'diction' of Gerard Manley Hopkins, and faintly precious, even, to talk of his 'verse'. If 'diction' is a selection from the language of men, then Hopkins may be said to use a poetic diction in the ridiculous sense that 'hogshead', or any other word one may call to mind was never used by him in any of his poems, and that he therefore used a selection of the language which excluded 'hogshead', or whatever word it is. But the point is that in reading the poems of Hopkins one has no sense of English words thrusting to be let into the poem and held out of it by the poet. One feels that Hopkins could have found a place for every word in the language if only he could have written enough poems. One feels the same about Shakespeare. But there are poets, I find, with whom I feel the other thing – that a selection has been made and is continually being made, that words are thrusting at the poem and being fended off from it, that however many poems these poets wrote certain words would never be allowed into the poems, except as a disastrous oversight. These different feelings we have when we read English poetry justify us in talking of the language of the one kind of poet, and the diction of the other kind, of the poetry of the one and the verse of the other.

We cannot help feeling that verse is somehow less important and splendid than poetry, just as diction is less splendid than language. And I think this is right. To begin with, nearly all bad poets (we have to except the lunatic fringe) use a poetic diction. And usually we cannot deny that what they write is verse, although we would strenuously deny that it is poetry. Everyone knows why bad poets use a poetic diction: the worst poets of all have no sense for words. But most poets are sufficiently sensitive to recognize the words which are fashionable. There are fashions in words for poetry, as in words for conversation, and out of the words that are fashionable every age constructs willy-nilly its own poetic diction, which the bad poets (unconsciously for the most part) adopt. An example of such a fashionable word in our own time is 'improbable' – 'the trees' improbable green', 'Islands improbably remote'. It is relatively easy to recognize bad poetic diction. It is more difficult to understand that poetic diction can be good, to recognize good diction, and to distinguish it from the bad.

Presumably, if a bad diction is the result of selecting from the language at random, according to the whim of fashion, then good diction comes from making a selection from the language on reasonable principles and for a reasonable purpose. All poets when they write have one purpose: they want to create an effect upon the mind of the reader. These effects are various, and the poets dispute about which effects are legitimate and worth while. When the poets and critics are very sure about what effects are legitimate, then they can construct a very elaborate structure of poetic diction, as it were departmentalized, according to the different effects which the poet may legitimately seek to produce. Such an elaborate structure was outlined by George Puttenham in the sixteenth century. Puttenham will tell the poet what sort of words, images, measures and rhymes he must adopt in order to produce any one of the effects which Puttenham considers legitimate. Since Puttenham's day this elaborate structure has been broken down more and more, as the poets in practice have blurred the distinctions upon which that structure rested. By the time that Goldsmith and Wordsworth write of poetic diction, they only occasionally remember that there is more than one sort of poetry. Goldsmith in his essays often pulls himself up short to pay his respects to Ossian, remembering that, besides his own poetry of sentiment, aiming at the effect of pathos, there is a poetry of passion, aiming at the sublime. But Wordsworth only once remembers, in his Appendix to the Preface to the *Lyrical Ballads*, to limit all his remarks to 'works *of imagination and sentiment*, for of these only have I been treating'. Both Goldsmith sometimes and Wordsworth usually seem to be laying down the law about diction for all sorts of poetry seeking all sorts of effects. Coleridge, when he tried to reply to Wordsworth in the last chapters of *Biographia Literaria*, attempted to rebuild some of the elaborate structure of Puttenham. He talks about different departments of language and different styles working in these departments. But Coleridge's distinctions and classifications have the air of being made *ad hoc*, and English criticism has preferred in this respect to follow Wordsworth. Nowadays there seems to be nothing to choose between a slack catholicism, which implies that every poem in its kind is as good as every other poem in another kind, and a dogmatic purism, which says, 'This good poem is written in this way. Therefore all good poems must be written in this way.'

Words like 'lyric', 'satire', 'epic' are remnants of an old elaborate structure in which we no longer believe. And as forty years ago it often seemed that all poems had to be lyrics, so now it often seems that they must all be satires. It is not to be expected that the old elaborate classifications will be restored in their old strength and minuteness. And perhaps it is just as well. For it may be doubted whether a modern poet could write with the conscious art of Spenser. And even in Spenser's day the schemes of diction seem to have produced pedantic and self-opinionated readers. On the other hand it may be doubted whether criticism can improve unless it can breathe life into some of the old classifications.

Related to this distinction by genres is distinction by tone. Goldsmith provides an example:

Homer has been blamed for the bad choice of his similes on some particular occasions. He compares Ajax to an ass, in the *Iliad*, and Ulysses to a steak broiling on the coals, in the *Odyssey*. His admirers have endeavoured to excuse him, by reminding us of the simplicity of the age in which he wrote; but they have not been able to prove that any ideas of dignity or importance were, even in those days, affixed to the character of an ass, or the quality of a beef collop; therefore they were very improper illustrations for any situation in which a hero ought to be represented.

It is important to realize how we differ from Goldsmith on this count. We cannot deny that there is such a thing as bathos; and I think we must agree that when we compare an eminent man to a broiling steak we run a risk of bathos. We only question whether the prime object of Homer or the epic poet in general is the dignifying of his heroes; or else perhaps we have different ideas of human dignity. J. M. Synge condemned poetic diction in the Preface to his *Poems and Translations*, poems which were experiments, as it must seem to us, in poetic diction of an unusually elaborate and eccentric kind. In making a diction out of the talk of Irish peasantry, Synge deliberately exploited the bathetic, because he believed 'that before verse can be human again it must learn to be brutal'. Goldsmith, however, believed that man was human and dignified when he was least brutal, and so it was right for him to complain that human dignity was affronted when compared with the brutish ass. When brutal or vulgar references were inescapable, the eighteenth-century poet preserved a lofty tone by circumlocution. Every poet does the same when he is working in a lofty vein. Only Wordsworth sometimes refused – often with ludicrous results.

But diction varies in another way. Not only does any given diction vary according to genre (i.e. according to the effect the poet wishes to produce) and according to tone, but one scheme or structure of diction will vary from another because of the different cultures from which they spring. Synge differs from Goldsmith about diction because he has a different scheme of morality. Thus it is possible to speak of a courtly-humanist diction (Spenser perhaps) and of a bourgeois-pious diction (Samuel Johnson). It seems as if the poet's choice of diction is determined in part, at any rate, by the structure and the prevailing ideologies of his society. If this is so, then the only diction which can be right for a modern poet is the sort of diction which his own society throws out, that is to say the diction which we have already seen coming out of changes in fashion.

It can be argued, though, that here the good artist of modern times differs from the masters of the past. André Malraux sees the world of the modern artist as 'le musée imaginaire', upon the walls of which hang examples of all the styles of the past. These styles the modern artist has learnt to appreciate independently of the different cultures of which they were the flowers; and he can choose among them at will, seeking the one he shall use as a model. I think this is largely true, though the artist is still determined by his society to some extent. Yeats must have found in the Irish culture of his time some points of contact with the noble culture of Japan or the courtly culture of Spenser. Otherwise, I believe, he could not have adopted, even though he modified, the styles of the Japanese theatre and of Spenser's poetry. Still it must be admitted that the poet today has a greater freedom of choice than the poet of the sixteenth century or even of the eighteenth. It is a freedom for which he has to pay dearly, since it is part and parcel of his isolated position in his civilization. But I have to believe that he has this wider measure of freedom in order to explain the strain of serious parody which runs through so much of the best poetry of our age. For the best modern poems often read as if they were good translations from another language.

But the contemporary poet will not ask what words, arranged in what ways, are suitable for elegy; what other words and arrangements are proper to the ode. He will not ask whether his diction should be courtly and humanist, or heroic and pagan, or bourgeois and pious, or whatever else. He wants to know why he should use a diction at all, why he should exclude from his poetry any of the language with which he is familiar. For him it is axiomatic that 'there are no poetical and no unpoetic words'. Now, certainly all words are potentially poetical; the achievement of Shakespeare is proof of that. On the other hand it is plain from Goldsmith's essay that for him the language was divided into poetical and unpoetical words. There was a disputed margin in which occurred words and arrangements which were poetical in some genres, unpoetical in others; but Goldsmith never doubts that some expressions are inherently more poetical than others, and of course it is plain that this conviction governed his practice. It may be agreed that our sense of this principle at work in his verse causes us to rate it below Shakespeare's. But it does not follow that Goldsmith achieved what he did in verse in spite of an erroneous opinion. It may have been the condition of his doing what he did. Perhaps it was not erroneous for him. There may be some poets for whom 'there are no poetical and no unpoetical words'; it may be equally true that, for other poets, some words are poetical while others are not.

It may even be true (I think it is) that the poet who works in Goldsmith's way can compass certain effects, or at least one effect, which is not possible even for a Shakespeare. Shakespeare does many things that Goldsmith cannot do; but Goldsmith does at least one thing that Shakespeare cannot do. This one effect, which can be compassed by verse and not by poetry, has already been described – as a sense of 'words thrusting to be let into the poem, but fended off from it'. It remains to be seen at a later stage what moral value can be derived from this effect by the reader who enjoys it.

The poet who creates a style should not, perhaps, be said to write *in* that style. At any rate, there is no Miltonic diction in Milton; there is only Milton's style. For Miltonic diction we go to Thomson. There is no Chaucerian diction in Chaucer; for that we go to some poems by Dunbar. Anyone who thinks otherwise is that famous reader who found Gray's *Elegy* 'full of quotations'.

Not Chaucer nor Milton nor Pope can be said to employ a diction. They create styles, which is a different matter; and it is a sort of historical accident that later poets should have drawn upon their styles to make up a poetic diction.

Even so, there is a difference between imitating a style and observing a diction, for only bad poets, I think, use a diction taken over, lock, stock and barrel, from the style of a previous poet. At this point the discussion has been bedevilled by Wordsworth. As every schoolboy knows, Wordsworth disliked poetic diction and decided, instead, to write in a selection of the language really used by men. But nearly every schoolboy knows, too, that this is what diction is – a selection from the language commonly used. It is a fact that when we read criticism by such poets as Johnson and Goldsmith (who use a diction which we think we can recognize), we find that they appeal, not to literary precedent alone, but to spoken usage:

> Gray thought his language more poetical as it was more remote from common use: finding in Dryden *honey redolent of Spring*, an expression that reaches the utmost limits of our language, Gray drove it a little more beyond apprehension by making *gales* to be *redolent of joy and youth*.

Here there is certainly appeal to the practice of a past master; but there is, at least equally, an appeal to 'common use'.

It may be questioned, perhaps, whether this 'common use' to which Johnson appeals is indeed spoken usage and not, rather, the usage of prose writing. And it is certainly important to ask whether he appeals equally to the spoken usage of Gin Lane, of Grub Street, of the Cumbrian fells and of Mrs Thrale's drawing-room. But to any sympathetic reader of Johnson's verse, and the verse of his age, such questions turn out to be (except for some rather peculiar cases[1]) only quibbles. Everyone must agree with

1 There is the peculiar and interesting case of Dr John Byrom of Manchester. Some of his attractive poems are prosaic in the most obvious sense, being versified excerpts from the prose of William Law; while others are conversational in the sense that they appeal to spoken usage far from the discipline of

Coleridge that poetic language, however conversational in origin, must be arranged with a care unusual in any but the most studied speaking;[1] and hence the distinction between prosaic and conversational elements in poetic diction is blurred from the start. Moreover, the eighteenth century is the age of great letter-writing, that is, of a form of writing which depends upon blurring the distinction between conversation and written prose. And so, to cut a long story short, it must appear that the 'common use' to which Johnson appeals is to be found in the letters written in his age.

This tie between the writing of poetry and the writing of letters makes it possible, and necessary, to speak of Johnson's diction as 'bourgeois'. On the one hand the poets under discussion often regarded themselves as spokesmen of the middle classes, which they valued as the most stable element in the commonwealth.[2] And on the other hand the great letters of the age were written by members of the bourgeoisie, in drawing-rooms like Mrs Thrale's at Streatham. There is a notable difference between the letters of Mrs Boscawen, for instance, and those of Lady Mary Wortley Montagu. Lady Mary's comments on *The Rambler* show her well aware of the difference between her age and Johnson's. For the difference between her letters and Mrs Boscawen's is the same as that between *The Spectator* and *The Rambler*; Addison was a mannerly man and in that he was moral, Johnson was

---

even conversational prose. I know no other poet of the period in respect of whom it is feasible to make this distinction between conversational and prosaic diction.

1 There have been poets, especially in recent years, who have done without some or all of the resources of logical syntax; and these poets have drawn upon very unstudied speech-usages, as far as possible from literary prose. John Byrom was one of these, and their work lies out of the present discussion. It seems just to speak of Johnson and Wordsworth, for example, as appealing to 'conversational' usage, so long as we keep 'colloquial' for the more daring usages exploited by these others.

2 See, for instance, chapter xix of *The Vicar of Wakefield*; and cf. Hume's essay 'On the Middle Station of Life'.

unmannerly but moral none the less. The 'common use' to which Prior appeals is in the letters of Lady Mary; the court of appeal for Johnson is in Mrs Thrale's letters, or Mrs Boscawen's. People write of the diction of eighteenth-century poetry as if it were one thing governing almost all writing from Dryden to Crabbe; and certainly Dryden, Johnson and Crabbe can be shown to draw upon a common stock of artifice and convention. But there is an important difference between the use of this common stock by Dryden on the one hand and Johnson on the other. We define this difference when we call Johnson's diction 'bourgeois' and 'pious'.

The two terms go together. The culture of Prior, Lady Mary and Addison differed from that of Goldsmith, Mrs Boscawen and Johnson, chiefly in this: that conversation and letters in the later period are far readier to discuss questions of personal conduct, not under cover of a code of manners, but directly, by appeal to the moral absolutes of Christian tradition.[1] This greater readiness appears also in the poetry. This Christianity of the later age is not so much a conviction as a will to conviction; to a conviction which the poets can sometimes grasp, chiefly through sympathy with human sentiment, but which for the most part they can only desperately hope for and will into being. They seem to have no faculties for apprehending spiritual reality immediately and in itself, but only as mediated in a struggling way through the natural and especially the human creation. This attitude I call 'pious', and it appears in their verse as a strenuous determination to moralize the instance, making continual play with certain moral absolutes until each circumstance they write about can be lifted to a level of moral judgement and sympathy. Jane Austen called Cowper and Johnson 'her favourite moral

1 By Cowper's day this change in conversational habit was consciously advocated. See his poem 'Conversation'; and cf. Mrs Boscawen (C. Aspinall-Oglander, *Admiral's Wife*, Longmans, 1940, p. 34) for an example of the intimate letter moving easily into assured and quite complicated moral judgement.

writers'. We can hardly call them that, for we are likely to agree with Lady Mary that *Pamela* may do more harm than all the poems of Rochester; and Dr Johnson's admiration of Richardson testifies, we may think, to a coarsening of the moral sense. What distinguishes him from Lady Mary is not a finer moral sense but a more urgent moral concern. And it seems fair to call this his 'piety'.

We are saying that the poet who undertakes to preserve or refine a poetic diction is writing in a web of responsibilities. He is responsible to past masters for conserving the genres and the decorum which they have evolved. He is responsible to the persons or the themes on which he writes, to maintain a consistent tone and point of view in his dealings with them. He is responsible to the community in which he writes, for purifying and correcting the spoken language. And of course he is responsible, as all poets are, to his readers; he has to give them pleasure, and also, deviously or directly, instructions in proper conduct.

It follows that the poet who uses a diction must be very sure of the audience which he addresses. He dare not be merely the spokesman of their sentiments and habits, for he must purify the one and correct the other. Yet he dare not be quite at odds with his age, but must share with his readers certain assumptions. I am not sure if it matters how large or how small his audience is. Cowper in the last book of *The Task*, like Wordsworth in his *Poems Dedicated to National Independence and Liberty*, seems to address the whole English nation. Johnson and Goldsmith do not give this impression. On the other hand, none of these poets can have thought of himself as addressing only a coterie of personal friends and other poets, as most modern poets have to think. At this point, discussion of diction becomes discussion of the poet's place in the national community, or, under modern conditions (where true community exists only in pockets), his place in the state. This aspect of the matter will become clearer when we ask how the poet, in his choice of language, should be governed, if at all, by principles of taste. And this is inseparable from the question of what Goldsmith and others understood by chastity and propriety in language.

II

The Chastity of Poetic Diction

According to Goldsmith,[1] chastity in writing is the best safeguard against frigidity; and frigidity is 'a deviation from propriety owing to the erroneous judgement of the writer, who, endeavouring to captivate the admiration with novelty, very often shocks the understanding with extravagance'. This extravagance, he claims, betrays itself most often in the use of metaphor, and in two ways, in metaphors which are mixed and in metaphors which are laboured into conceits. It follows that hyperbolical and highly metaphorical language runs most risk of frigidity; and chastity therefore appears most often as restraint and economy in the use of metaphor.

Goldsmith allows that in certain genres the language may and should be less chaste than in others. Goldsmith gives no full account of the genres, and in practice he distinguishes only between the poetry of passion and the poetry of pathos. Chastity is more important in the poetry that aims at pathos:

> Passion itself is very figurative, and often bursts out into metaphors; but, in touching the pathos, the poet must be perfectly well acquainted with the emotions of the human soul, and carefully distinguish between those metaphors which rise glowing from the heart, and those cold conceits which are engendered in the fancy.

So Goldsmith can say:

1 I base this account of Goldsmith's doctrine on the three essays: 'XV, Poetry distinguished from other writing'; 'XVI, Metaphor'; and 'XVII, Hyperbole'. These essays are not very distinguished writing, and may be all the more representative of views commonly held by the readers of Goldsmith's age.

> The Ode and Satire admit of the boldest hyperboles: such exaggerations suit the impetuous warmth of the one; and, in the other, have a good effect in exposing folly, and exciting horror against vice.

The most important features, then, in this view of 'chastity' seem to be: first, that it is an effect attained through judgement and taste, not by imagination or passion or inspiration; second, that it is connected with sparing use of metaphor; and finally, that what is chaste in one genre may be flat in another.

When Goldsmith attempts to apply these principles, he can condemn a soliloquy from *Hamlet* on the score of mixed metaphor. But merely as principles they strike me as thoroughly sound; and Wordsworth's more famous discussion of diction seems weakest where it strays most from what Goldsmith lays down.

Wordsworth talks of 'chastity' in language, in the Appendix to his Preface, when he comments on two lines from Cowper:

> But the sound of the church-going bell
> These valleys and rocks never heard.

Wordsworth remarks:

> The epithet 'church-going' applied to a bell, and that by so chaste a writer as Cowper, is an instance of the strange abuses which poets have introduced into their language, till they and their Readers take them as matter of course, if they do not single them out expressly as objects of admiration.

It seems as if 'chastity' meant much the same to Wordsworth and to Goldsmith. Wordsworth thinks an expression unchaste when it departs from the language of prose; Goldsmith thinks so when it departs from 'common use', the language of prose and careful conversation. One could even say that for both critics 'chastity' means, once again, economy in metaphor, for the discomfort we feel about Cowper's line derives from an unwanted metaphor, the ludicrous image of the bell itself trundling along the road to church. Of course the image is inadvertent, and of course we do not take it seriously; but it is present, and offensive, as we read.

Wordsworth's comments on the two stanzas he quotes from Cowper are very just. From them Wordsworth proceeds to lay down his principle:

– namely, that in works *of imagination and sentiment*, for of these only have I been treating, in proportion as ideas and feelings are valuable, whether the composition be in prose or in verse, they require and exact one and the same language.[1]

From what we have said it will appear that this formulation differs little from the warning of Goldsmith:

in touching the pathos, the poet must . . . carefully distinguish between those metaphors which rise glowing from the heart, and those cold conceits which are engendered in the fancy.

Where it differs, it differs for the worse; and chiefly in this – that what in Goldsmith was flexible, with Wordsworth is a rigid rule.[2]

It is easy to see why Goldsmith could be flexible where Wordsworth could not. Goldsmith could confidently leave to his readers a margin for the exercise of judgement and taste. Wordsworth had no such confidence:

TASTE, I would remind the reader, like IMAGINATION, is a word which has has been forced to extend its services far beyond the point to

1 Thomas Hutchinson (ed.), *The Poetical Works of William Wordsworth* (OUP, 1905), p. 944.

2 In practice, for instance, Wordsworth forgets the qualification in respect of the genre – 'works *of imagination and sentiment*, for of these only have I been treating'. The other example in this Appendix, Johnson's paraphrase of Proverbs 6, may be called a work of imagination (though not, perhaps, in any Wordsworthian sense), but it is hard to see by what stretch it can be described as a work of 'sentiment'. And I think that, in dismissing this admirable piece as 'a hubbub of words', Wordsworth is as flagrantly wrong as, on Cowper, he is plainly right.

which philosophy would have confined them. It is a metaphor, taken from a *passive* sense of the human body, and transferred to things which are in their essence *not* passive, – to intellectual *acts* and *operations*. The word Imagination has been overstrained, from impulses honourable to mankind, to meet the demands of the faculty which is perhaps the noblest of our nature. In the instance of Taste, the process has been reversed; and from the prevalence of dispositions at once injurious and discreditable, being no other than that selfishness which is the child of apathy, – which, as Nations decline in productive and creative power, makes them value themselves upon a presumed refinement of judging. Poverty of language is the primary cause of the use which we make of the word Imagination; but the word Taste has been stretched to the sense which it bears in modern Europe by habits of self-conceit, inducing that inversion in the order of things whereby a passive faculty is made paramount among the faculties conversant with the fine arts. Proportion and congruity, the requisite knowledge being supposed, are subjects upon which taste may be trusted; it is competent to this office; – for in its intercourse with these the mind is *passive*, and is affected painfully or pleasurably as by an instinct. But the profound and the exquisite in feeling, the lofty and universal in thought and imagination; or, in ordinary language, the pathetic and the sublime; – are neither of them, accurately speaking, objects of a faculty which could ever without a sinking in the spirit of Nations have been designated by the metaphor – *Taste*. And Why? Because without the exertion of a co-operating *power* in the mind of the Reader, there can be no adequate sympathy with either of these emotions: without this auxiliary impulse, elevated or profound passion cannot exist.[1]

Wordsworth here denies taste any say in the choice of language, for the pathetic strain no less than the sublime. It is denied any authority on the plausible grounds that it is passive while the appreciation of pathos requires active co-operation from the reader. The argument from the metaphorical origin of the word 'taste' is telling; but like all arguments from origins, it cannot be conclusive. It is only Wordsworth who decides that the conception 'taste' has remained true to its metaphorical origin as a

1 'Essay, Supplementary to the Preface' (1815).

passive faculty. Wordsworth, in fact, makes no distinction between 'taste' and 'fashion'.

Goldsmith holds by this distinction, and argues that taste is active, because informed by judgement. The acquisition and preservation of taste, according to Goldsmith, is a strenuous business:

In order to restrain the luxuriancy of the young imagination, which is apt to run riot, to enlarge the stock of ideas, exercise the reason and ripen the judgement, the pupil must be engaged in the severer study of science. He must learn geometry, which Plato recommends for strengthening the mind, and enabling it to think with precision. He must be made acquainted with geography and chronology, and trace philosophy through all her branches . . .

And so Goldsmith goes on, with a lifetime's regimen of study and discipline, all because 'taste is a natural talent' only in origin, and 'cannot be brought to perfection without proper cultivation; for taste pretends to judge, not only of nature, but also of art; and that judgement is founded upon observation and comparison'.

At the risk of being shallow, we may say that for Wordsworth judgement in the poet was limited to the choice between going and not going to live in Cumberland. The rest was done by mountains and lakes and shepherds. He believed in a culture of the feelings, not in cultivation of taste. Taste, in art as in nature, was for him a province of feeling.

We should be naïve if we took this disagreement between Goldsmith and Wordsworth as a difference of philosophical opinion about the hierarchy of human faculties. Neither of them has a philosopher's detachment. They differ because of the different conditions obtaining for each of them as practising poets. Goldsmith could leave to taste and judgement a margin of activity in appreciating poetry; he could do so because he thought he found, among readers, a sufficient number whose taste and judgement seemed reliable. Wordsworth dare leave no margin of operation for taste and judgement, because he thought he found, among readers of poetry, only vicious taste and unstable judgement. Wordsworth had no such confidence in his readers as Goldsmith had in his. When he lost confidence in his public, the poet was thrown back upon confidence in himself. When this confidence, too, was shaken, it masked itself as hysterical arrogance. This is one way of describing the Romantic Revival.

Wordsworth, of course, found a halfway house. If he had lost confidence in the readers of London and Cambridge, he still had confidence in the readers of Cumberland and Somerset. In the same way Jane Austen could still count upon the readers in rural rectories and small country houses, though she had lost confidence in the 'gad-about'[1] publics of London and Bath and Brighton. As England transformed itself into an industrial state, people were uprooted from native localities and from the social and cultural disciplines of settled communities. Hence the importance, for this literature, of the uprooted, nomadic and classless type of the governess and paid companion. Wordsworth and Jane Austen are trying to hand on to these new types the values of the older society. Edmund Bertram is educating the typical *déracinée*, Fanny Price, in the values of that rooted life which has been denied her. And the eldest of 'The Brothers', in Wordsworth's poem of that name, having broken from the community, is unable to return to it, and has to be instructed anew by the natural spokesman of the community, the village pastor. The

1 I think that, when Jane Austen allows a character to be described as 'a gad', she is embarking upon a question important for her, and putting a question mark against the moral stability of that character. *Sanditon*, the fragmentary last novel, seems particularly concerned with this question, and I cannot agree with Mr E. M. Forster about it, but think that, if it had been completed, it might have been one of Jane Austen's most interesting and important books. The rise of the seaside resort – Brighton, Worthing, Scarborough – was one of the most marked and significant social changes of Wordsworth's and Jane Austen's period. Cobbett shows himself concerned with it and suspicious of it; and there is a mildly satirical poem by Robert Bloomfield about Worthing.

case of Jane Austen is particularly clear, for to a reader conversant with *The Task*, Jane Austen appears to appeal continually to Cowper for a standard of the older kind by which to judge the conduct of her characters. These references are so closely veiled that they are missed by anyone who knows Cowper less well than Jane Austen's family knew him. Cowper constitutes, in fact, that 'moral positive' which is so elusive in Jane Austen's work, which so many of her readers have missed and joyfully gone without. From one point of view Wordsworth stands with her, for the sobriety of Goldsmith and Cowper, against the 'glare and glitter' of Gray and Beattie and Logan, the poets of the uprooted.

Only in this way can one explain why no considerable poet since Goldsmith and Cowper has taken, as a guide to his writing, the good sense of 'the best people'. The centre fell apart. In architecture and furnishing, as in literature, the people with the money to command the best began to command something else; and taste and judgement no longer went with power and wealth. Inferior art, such as the 'tales of terror', satisfied the depraved taste of the wealthy, the leisured and the eminent; and whereas, fifty years before, bad architecture and poetry had been dull, now they were vulgar. Because the poets could no longer trust the taste of their readers, they could be guided no longer, in their choice of language, by the conversational usages of those readers. In any case, that conversation must have deteriorated; for the literary forms which depended upon it, the familiar letter and the epistolary novel, fell suddenly below the level of serious art. It is not fantastic to surmise that Jane Austen in England and Pushkin in Russia first realized the social breakup when they tried to write the epistolary novel, and failed. With the stay of 'common use' thus taken away, the notions of chastity and purity in diction could have no meaning. Wordsworth tried to preserve the meaning by anchoring it to a hard-and-fast principle. But Coleridge showed that this was impracticable; and so the diction of the Romantic poets is extremely impure. Keats is a flagrant case – in all but his best work his language oscillates wildly between a colloquialism which is slang and a literary pomp which is exotic; and his own ideas about 'purity' were puerile.[1] Byron in *Don Juan*, like Mr Auden in our own day, found an ingenious solution in deliberately causing such oscillations, exploiting a sort of calculated impurity. As it happened, most of the Romantic poets affected the sublime rather than the pathetic, so that the impurity of their diction, though still a discomfort when one has learnt to love chastity, does not matter so much. But it must be said that, of all the nineteenth-century poets since Wordsworth, none has 'purified the language of the tribe'. They have enriched that language, and with some of them, such as Hopkins, the enrichment is so great that we can feel the question of purity impertinent; but the spoken tongue has suffered at their hands.

The critic who most nearly recognized the loss was Matthew Arnold, when he lamented the absence from English writing of 'the tone of the centre'. The argument is to be found in 'The Literary Influence of Academies'; and what is there said of 'Attic' prose, its value and its significance, seems to me equally applicable to chaste diction in poetry. A chaste diction is 'central', in Arnold's sense; it expresses the feeling of the capital, not the provinces. And it can do this because it is central in another way – central to the language, conversational not colloquial, poetic not poetical. The effect is a valuable urbanity, a civilized moderation and elegance; and this is the effect attainable, as I think, by Goldsmith, and not by Shakespeare. It seemed to Arnold that this matter was the responsibility of prose writers, something

1 'The purest English I think – or what ought to be the purest – is Chatterton's. The Language had existed long enough to be entirely uncorrupted of Chaucer's gallicisms and still the old words are used. Chatterton's language is entirely northern.' Keats confuses diction with language. Chatterton employed a very eccentric and impure diction. One can speak of pure and impure diction; to speak of pure or impure *language* is as ridiculous as it is to speak of a pure or impure *tree*.

from which the poets could be absolved; and all critics have agreed,[1] until Mr Eliot asserted that 'to have the virtues of good prose is the first and minimum requirement of great poetry'.[2] This comment must be taken along with the same critic's contempt of those persons 'who cannot understand that it is more

1 A good statement of a position close to Arnold's is made by J. S. Phillimore – 'Poetry is a wind that bloweth where it listeth: a barbaric people may have great poetry, they cannot have great prose. Prose is an institution, part of the equipment of a civilization, part of its heritable wealth, like its laws, or its system of schooling, or its tradition of skilled craftsmanship.' *Dublin Review*, vol. cliii (1913), p. 8; quoted by R. W. Chambers, *On the Continuity of English Prose from Alfred to More* (Oxford, 1932).

2 One has to agree with Dr Leavis (*Revaluation*, Chatto, 1936 p. 122) that the poetry of 'Ash Wednesday' has not 'the virtues of good prose'. But it is common for poets to know the way they ought to go before they can follow their own advice. And an apter example of Mr Eliot practising what he preaches comes from 'Little Gidding':

There are three conditions which often look alike
Yet differ completely, flourish in the same hedgerow:
Attachment to self and to things and to persons, detachment
From self and from things and from persons; and, growing between them,
  indifference
Which resembles the others as death resembles life,
Being between two lives – unflowering, between
The live and the dead nettle. This is the use of memory:
For liberation – not less of love but expanding
Of love beyond desire, and so liberation
From the future as well as the past.

'Ash Wednesday' is a poem in the symbolist tradition. Images or symbols are ranged about, and the meaning flowers out of the space between them. Poetry of this sort depends upon the dislocation of normal syntax, and so it can never be written in a pure diction. It seems to me that the most enduring work of both W. B. Yeats and T. S. Eliot is that in which they have reached a pure diction. For the other (Shakespearian) kind of verse writing in our age we have to go to some prolific and unequal poets of America: Hart Crane, Wallace Stevens and Allen Tate. The best poetry of Yeats and Eliot has the virtues of good prose; the best poetry of Crane, Tate and Stevens has not. On the other hand minor modern poets on both sides of the Atlantic have employed successfully for their limited ends a personal diction deliberately

important, in some vital respects, to be a *good* poet than to be a *great* poet'. And in the rest of this book I shall be concerned with poets who are 'good' rather than 'great', to show how their work has the virtues of good prose and yet is good poetry. I shall think that their poems have the virtues of prose if I can establish that their diction is chaste; and I shall think them good poetry if I can show that, when necessary, they have the metaphorical richness and force we associate with poetry of quite another sort.

impure, eccentric and mannered; Robert Graves, Marianne Moore and John Crowe Ransom are examples. To compare Eliot's verse above with Yeats's 'A Prayer for my Daughter' is to see how two poems can be equally chaste, while differing widely in tone; Yeats is lofty, Eliot is what Puttenham would call 'mean'.

III

The Language of the Tribe

(i) *Live and Dead Metaphors*

THE best account of metaphor known to me is a fine and subtle essay by Owen Barfield.[1] Mr Barfield remarks that simile, metaphor and symbol are all devices for seeming to say one thing (B) while really saying another (A). This process is called in German '*Tarnung*', anglicized by Mr Barfield as 'tarning', and it is essential not to poetic language alone but to all language. For the greater part of any language consists of so-called 'dead' metaphors, that is, of words produced by tarning, but so long ago that they are used with no consciousness of the tarning behind them. Something similar occurs in law. For instance, the sort of tarning known as 'personification' corresponds to 'the personification of limited companies by which they are enabled to sue and be sued at law'. A more complicated tarning in law produces the fictitious characters John Doe and Richard Roe. This is now a sort of dead metaphor in the courts; but when the device was first introduced 'John Doe' was a live metaphor. And so:

> The long analogy which I have been drawing may be expressed more briefly in the formula – metaphor: language: meaning:: legal fiction: law: civil life.[2]

For just as law is consistent, inflexible and determinate, yet must, to keep pace with social changes, have recourse to fictions;

1 Owen Barfield, 'Poetic Diction and Legal Fiction', in C. S. Lewis (ed.), *Essays Presented to Charles Williams* (OUP, 1947).
2 Ibid., p. 121.

so language is fixed and determinate, to satisfy needs of logic, yet must, to keep pace with changes in thought and life, evolve new meanings by way of metaphor.

Mr Barfield finds a neat example in Bacon (*Novum Organum*, iii, 2), where the writer seeks to define the notion now familiar as the dead metaphor, the 'laws of nature'; Bacon tries by simile to appropriate to this signification the word *forma*, the Platonic 'form', and it is only in a casual metaphor that he produces the word *lex*. But the casual metaphor was adopted. It is a dead metaphor now; yet it can come to embarrassing and dangerous life. For that reason we have to be aware, or be made aware, of the force still latent in metaphors that sham dead.

Most interesting in the present connection is an observation which Mr Barfield does not care to develop. After dealing with figurative language, he remarks:

> I do not say that these particular methods of expression are an absolute *sine qua non* of poetic diction. They are not. Poetry may also take the form of simple and literal statement. But figurative expression is found everywhere; its roots descend very deep, as we shall see, into the nature, not only of poetry, but of language itself. If you take away from the stream of European poetry every passage of a metaphorical nature, you would reduce it to a very thin trickle indeed, pure though the remainder beverage might be to the taste. Perhaps our English poetry would suffer the heaviest damage of all.[1]

Is this the purity of which we speak when we talk of 'a pure diction'? It may be, since many critics were seen to agree in making economy in metaphor a feature of pure diction. But, as Mr Barfield points out, almost all language is metaphorical at bottom. It would be hard, perhaps impossible, to find a poem in English where the literal statement is completely unmetaphorical. And so, when we say of a pure diction that it has few passages of a metaphorical nature, we must be supposed to speak only of metaphors which are *overt*. It would, therefore, be almost true to

1 Ibid., p. 107.

say that the poet who employs a diction chooses to include only metaphors that are dead. This would seem to condemn such poetry, but it need not do so. For such poetry, by exploiting 'rhythm, sound, music' (elements which Mr Barfield deliberately excludes from his study), may revivify metaphors gone dead. It could be agreed, for instance, that the personifications of Pope are newly minted and live metaphors; and if it could be proved that Johnson limited himself for the most part to the personifications of Pope (metaphors gone dead in the hands of Pope's imitators), it could be argued that Johnson, by his different use, brought these metaphors to life again. If so, this would be the poetry which attempts, in Mr Eliot's phrase, to 'purify the language of the tribe'. For if the poet who coins new metaphors *enlarges* the language, the poet who enlivens dead metaphors can be said to *purify* the language.

As Mr Barfield says, this kind of poetry is rare in English; and we must beware of thinking we find it when we do not. Crabbe describes Chaucer as one of 'those who address their productions to the plain sense and sober judgement of their readers, rather than to their fancy and imagination'; and we certainly do not think of Chaucer as a highly metaphorical poet. But of course Chaucer's poems are not examples of chaste diction. Chaucer is, more than Pope, an original, revolutionary poet, expanding the language, creating metaphors, and creating, through them, new areas of meaning. We should look for a poet who stands, in relation to Chaucer, much as Johnson stands to Pope; and it is in Gower that we find a chaste diction.[1]

If the function of pure diction in poetry is to purify the language by revivifying dead metaphor, we shall look for purity of diction in writing at the end of a strong tradition. This explains why we have recourse to the term in respect of Johnson, Goldsmith, Collins and Cowper, poets writing more or less completely in the Augustan tradition, and late in that tradition.

1 Cf. C. S. Lewis, *The Allegory of Love* (OUP, 1936), p. 201.

But not only the language of previous poetry can provide dead metaphors; they appear no less in conversation and in prose. Hence pure diction can be found where a poet has tried to revivify the dead metaphors of studied conversation or artless prose. Indeed, who that has read the letters of Mrs Boscawen or Mrs Thrale could affirm that Johnson's personifications, or Cowper's, do not derive from letters or conversation rather than the *Essay on Man* or Shaftesbury's *Characteristics*? Because eighteenth-century prose was conversational, it is idle to debate whether the diction of a poem of that period is conversational or prosaic.[1] So, in the case of a modern 'prosaic' poem like Karl Shapiro's 'Essay on Rime', the poet's intention can be defined as 'an advance of one degree in shapeliness of statement';[2] but one cannot say whether it is an advance on conversation or on prose.

In any case what is important is the source of that impulse towards shapeliness, in Gower and Johnson and Shapiro alike. This tug away from 'common use' can come only from art, from the usages of previous literature. Thus it appears that a pure diction is governed by two sorts of precedent, on the one hand the usages of previous poets, on the other hand the usages of polite conversation. These were just the standards to which, in the beginning of this discussion, we saw Johnson appealing, when he criticized a locution of Gray. In the case of Johnson himself, the literary precedent was usually Dryden, and through him the poets of Rome; and the conversational precedent was Mrs Thrale's drawing-room. The dead metaphors of poetry are brought to life by the tang of common usage; and vice versa.

1 C. S. Lewis, however, can not only define the diction of Gower as conversational rather than prosaic, but can specify the *sort* of conversation, common to what classes and in what conditions.

2 I am indebted for this accurate formulation to my friend Douglas Brown.

(ii) *Enlivened Metaphors*

On Owen Barfield's showing, metaphor is an extension of areas of meaning; and poets who use a diction engage themselves not to extend meaning, but to work over areas already explored. Their principal object is the re-creation of metaphors which have ossified into meanings, rubbed smooth by too much handling.

The crassest example of this is the Latinate pun, as found in three examples which Mr John Arthos takes from Dryden: 'the morning dew prevents the sun'; 'horrid with fern'; 'with steel invades his brother's life'.[1] If we are to use the language with circumspection, it is good for us to be reminded of the metaphor embalmed in the word 'horrid', the image of hair standing up on the observer's head. Even in Dryden's time, however, this diction must have been unchaste, for these expressions are too far from conversational usage. In other words the metaphor is not really re-created at all. There is too wide a gap between the 'horrid' of common use and the 'horrid' of scholarly use for the metaphorical spark to leap across. And this is true of most, not all, of such puns.

A different but still crude example comes from *The Deserted Village*:

> O luxury! thou cursed by heaven's decree,
> How ill exchanged are things like these for thee!
> How do thy potions, with insidious joy,
> Diffuse their pleasures only to destroy!
> Kingdoms by thee, to sickly greatness grown,
> Boast of a florid vigour not their own:
> At every draught more large and large they grow,
> A bloated mass of rank unwieldy woe;
> Till sapp'd their strength, and every part unsound,
> Down, down they sink, and spread a ruin round.

1 John Arthos, *The Language of Natural Description in Eighteenth Century Poetry* (University of Michigan Press, 1949).

This is an attempt to revivify the dead metaphor of 'the body politic', the metaphor which Burke spent his time bringing to life; and it is most nearly successful with the prosaic epithet 'florid'.

More subtle and remarkable are Shenstone's beautiful lines:

> So first when Phoebus met the Cyprian queen,
> And favour'd Rhodes beheld their passion crown'd,
> Unusual flowers enrich'd the painted green,
> And swift spontaneous roses blush'd around.

The image comes out of common poetic stock;[1] Shenstone refreshes it. It is just as logical to describe the flowers as unusual, swift and spontaneous as it is to describe their flowering in those terms. But because we had thought of these as features of the event, not of its effects, Shenstone presses upon our notice the logic of his transference of these terms to the roses. The logic of the usage being thus impressed upon us, these words strike us as dry and prosaic; and they have the effect of a taunting gravity and sobriety which chastens the reader as it pleases him.

Moreover, by taking adverbs and turning them into other parts of speech, the poet leaves the verb singularly naked and powerful. Probably there was something in the metrical exigencies of the couplet which demanded that the verb should beat so sharply into the line, pinning it and making it quiver. At any rate it is true that the best eighteenth-century verse strikes us as active and weighty, governed by the forceful verb. We do not remember this when we censure this verse for luxuriance of

1 Cf., for instance, Sir John Suckling, 'Upon my Lady Carlisle's walking in Hampton Court Gardens':

> Didst thou not find the place inspired,
> And flowers as if they had desired
> No other sun, start from their beds,
> And for a sight steal out their heads?

epithets. The poets themselves censured it on the same grounds; and of course it is true that this luxuriance is the bane of the poor poetry of the period. But where it appears in the good poets, it is often the condition of an unusual metaphorical force residing in the verb. This can be seen, to begin with, simply in accurate register of appearances, as in this extract from Langhorne:

> Urging at noon the slow boat in the reeds
> That wav'd their green uncertainty of shade.

Here 'urging', naked and conspicuous because 'slow' has been removed (at no expense to logic) to qualify 'boat', comes over with all the force of muscular exertion. 'Wav'd', too, profits from being left alone; and 'uncertainty' is dry, prosaic and chastening. So again, Goldsmith:

> No more thy glassy brook reflects the day,
> But choked with sedges works its weedy way

– where 'works' takes all the thrust of the meaning and bears along the clutter of epithets. The same thing occurs when the theme is more abstract:

> The bold Bavarian, in a luckless hour,
> Tries the dread summits of Caesarian pow'r,
> With unexpected legions bursts away,
> And sees defenceless realms receive his sway;

The metaphor submerged in the expression 'rebellion broke out' comes, in Johnson's hands, to violent life. 'Breaks' becomes 'bursts', and strikes out, naked and powerful, because the unexpectedness of the outbreak has been transferred to the instrument, the legions. 'Unexpected', as applied to the legions, seems prosaic and grave, yet taunting in its moderation – 'There's no need to get so excited'.

Once the trick has been noticed, one finds it everywhere. It can even work through and over a whole poem. This is the case, for instance, with Gray's 'Impromptu', where the stock image (corrupt politicians = foxes) comes to shocking life[1] in the last line:

> Owls would have hooted in St Peter's choir
> And foxes stunk and littered in St Paul's.

The metaphor comes to life because the force of it has shifted on to the verbs, those magnificently 'foxy' verbs 'stunk' and 'littered', both coming straight out of speech.

This is a poetry of energy, of force and momentum. This is especially true of Johnson, much truer of him, I think, than of Charles Churchill, who is frequently singled out of his period for his 'energy'. Johnson's verse trembles over our heads, like a thin ceiling shaken by a heavy tread: 'For such the steady Romans shook the world.' Sound echoes sense, and the verse *is* what it says. Dr Leavis shows how dead metaphors are brought to life when he remarks finely (*Revaluation*, p. 118), 'That "steady" turns the vague cliché , "shook the world" into the felt percussion of tramping legions'. It is the tread that is steady, but we are shaken by it only when the steadiness is transferred to the Romans.[2]

1 This poem seems to me, together with the fragmentary 'Education and Government' and (in the main) the *Elegy*, the only work of Gray in which the diction is chaste in Johnson's sense or any other. The effect of Gray's example (e.g. in his Odes) was decadent and disruptive; and I can find little of value in his other poems.

2 I have been puzzled by Dr Leavis' description of Johnson as 'weighty'. Not that I would disagree; but I cannot decide whether the critic is aware of his own puns. For instance, he quotes:

> For why did Wolsey near the steeps of fate,
> On weak foundations raise th' enormous weight?

And I find something comical in the comment: 'The effect of that is massive; the images are both generalized, and unevadably concrete'. Must I think that Dr Leavis is being impish?

(iii) *Personification*

This habit of throwing metaphorical force from noun to verb produces personification. For it must seem that an abstraction is personified to some extent as soon as it can govern an active verb:

> When fainting nature call'd for aid,
> And hovering death prepar'd the blow,
> His vigorous remedy display'd
> The power of art without the show.

Here, surely, 'nature', 'death' and 'remedy' are all, somehow, personified. But 'remedy' is less abstract than 'nature' or 'death'; and 'calling' and 'preparing' are associated, more often than 'displaying', with a personal agent. Hence we have to say that 'remedy' is personified hardly at all; just as in Cowper's line – 'Obscurest night involv'd the sky' – the verb 'involv'd' is so remote from human action that 'night' can hardly be said to be personified. This may seem to be a quibble, but without it we are at a loss to detect personification except by a capital letter.

What matters is the extent to which personification can be truly metaphorical; and on this showing the extent to which it can be metaphorical depends upon the verb it governs:

> Then with no fiery, throbbing pain,
> No cold gradations of decay,
> Death broke at once the vital chain,
> And freed his soul the nearest way.

The verb 'broke', reaping the cumulative interest and movement of the first two lines, enlivens alike the personification which governs it and the dead metaphor ('the vital chain') which follows. And the effect is reinforced by the conversational looseness of the final line.

The true personification, the one with the force of metaphor, is often left, in this way, until the last lines. This is the case, for instance, with that paraphrase of Proverbs, which Wordsworth thought beneath contempt:

> Till Want now following, fraudulent and slow,
> Shall spring to seize thee, like an ambush'd foe.

The process of beggary is gradual, yet indigence comes on a sudden. Johnson's 'spring' is faithful to this painful paradox, as true to his Scripture as to the human experience of the Bankruptcy Court. And the method is the one we have analysed, stripping the action of adverbs ('deceitfully', 'slowly') and transferring the sense of them to the personified agent, making them prosaic and logical, with a sobering ring, like the fine 'fraudulent'.[1]

(iv) *Generalization*

ANOTHER sort of personification in these poets comes with the habit of generalizing. This habit has been accounted for in three ways. In the first place we are invited to consider an analogy with the visual arts, and remember how Reynolds, for instance, insisted that beauty resided only in the general and typical. Then there are critics (usually adverse) who remind us of the obtrusive moral concern of these poets, their didacticism which made them push on to draw their moral without waiting to see things 'in themselves'. And finally we are asked to notice (and to deplore)

1 This seems to me the most important sort of personification, the most capable of exerting metaphorical force. There is another sort, which will be recalled more readily. This is the allegorical set piece:

> O vale of bliss! O softly swelling hills!
> On which the power of cultivation lies,
> And joys to see the wonders of his toil.

Goldsmith comments on these lines: 'We cannot conceive a more beautiful image than that of the Genius of Agriculture, distinguished by the implements of his art, imbrowned with labour, glowing with health, crowned with a garland of foliage, flowers, and fruit, lying stretched at his ease on the brow

how these poets confounded their function with that of the scientists,[1] looking always for the laws governing experience, and (again) careless of the thing in itself.

All three of these explanations are true, yet none is wholly true in itself. For instance, it is easy to point out, when we rise from reading Reynolds, how Johnson's elegy on Robert Levett is also 'the character of a good physician', so that we mourn in the poem not the death of a man but the mortality of a profession; or how Goldsmith's elegy on Thomas Parnell is, in the same way, the character of a good poet. But Pope, too, through the eyes of a moralist, thought man should be classified under types. And when he wrote that 'the proper study of mankind is man', he seems to have meant that men were objects of study as flowers were for botanists – his own theory of the ruling passions is a pseudo-scientific classification of human behaviour.

---

of a gently swelling hill, and contemplating with pleasure the happy effects of his own industry.' We cannot deny that there is beauty in the picture visualized by Goldsmith, and though he contributes much that is unsaid by Thomson, he probably contributes nothing that was not in Thomson's intention. For Thomson could count on finding in his readers a ready allegorical imagination, such as seems lost to us today. The loss is certainly ours. A symptom and, it may be, a cause of this allegorical sense was the popularity of the allegorical history-painting in the style of Thornhill. We probably mistake the joke in chapter xvi of *The Vicar of Wakefield* if we find it ridiculous that Mrs Primrose should wish to be painted as Venus. The absurdity lies rather in the refusal of the rest of the group to be painted in roles in keeping with hers. On the other hand this was the practice which led Goldsmith to suppose that all imagery was pictorial (a supposition elevated into absurd principle by Erasmus Darwin later). And in any case this sort of personification has little or nothing to do with language, and is found most often in the dissident or decadent poets of the period, poets whose diction was, for better or worse, impure.

1 Johnson's comment on lines from Dryden's *Annus Mirabilis* – 'It had better become Dryden's learning and genius to have laboured science into poetry, and have shewn, by explaining longitude, that verse did not refuse the ideas of philosophy'. The science of marine navigation was laboured into poetry, soon after Johnson wrote, by Falconer in 'The Shipwreck'.

Again, all Christians in the eighteenth century were natural theologians. It was not only deists who thought the nature of God could be seen in His Creation; everybody thought so, and nearly everybody thought that He could be deduced by tracing laws and classes, not perceived in a leap of insight. The poets were anxious to prove this in their verses. It is impossible, therefore, to decide whether the poets, in generalizing, were governed by aesthetic or moral or scientific principle. Probably it would not have occurred to them to make these distinctions. Moralist and poet and scientist and painter thought confidently that they were moving to the same point from different directions. Reynolds and Pope and Newton are at one.

The workings of the scientific principle are especially interesting:

> It may very well be that many poets accepted the idea of a conventional language for poetry because they considered the interests of poetry and natural philosophy to be the same in many important respects. Scientific writing required a set vocabulary according to set principles, and it must therefore follow that poetry's needs were similar. This is the extreme conclusion. It is, of course, truer of some poets than of others. But its general validity seems proved by the fact that so many of the same terms are found in scientific prose and in the poetry of the eighteenth century.[1]

When Wordsworth asserted that there is no essential difference between the language of prose and that of poetry, he seemed to think that his principle was revolutionary. And we have taken him at his own valuation ever since. But John Arthos establishes that, for instance, the adjectives formed by the *-y* suffix ('beamy', 'moony', 'sluicy'), words we have thought eminently false-poetical, are to be found frequently in scientific writing of the seventeenth and eighteenth centuries. It seems, then, that the language of eighteenth-century poetry is close to prose even

1 Arthos, op. cit., p. 88.

when it seems most remote. Wordsworth's contention therefore was not revolutionary at all.[1]

Of course all this is historical explanation. It explains why poets adopted such language as they did; it does not justify their doing so. We justify them when we can show how, in the best of them, this language became poetic; and for the moment we can continue to suppose language poetic when it is deeply and seriously metaphorical. I propose to show how the generalizing habit can produce poignant and memorable metaphor.

This habit can be seen at work on all the parts of speech. The most obvious sort of generalized noun, for instance, is 'grove', as used by eighteenth-century poets to denote all assemblies of trees, or 'gale' as used to denote all movements of air. Often these usages offend the modern reader. He is aware of niceties of discrimination represented by 'thicket', 'wood', 'forest', 'copse', 'clump', 'brushwood', 'spinney'; or by 'squall', 'breeze', 'hurricane', 'whirlwind', 'gust', 'breath', 'wind'. And the eighteenth-century poets, by ignoring these words, seem culpably to miss so many chances of seeing the world more nearly. But a grove is planted, and to see all groups of trees as groves is to see them all in the park of a creator-god. Hence this generalization implies a view of the natural creation as a divinely ordered hierarchy. In the same way, to see a breeze and a hurricane alike as 'gales' is to come so much nearer seeing all movements of air as breathing from the mouth of God. In modern critical parlance, to describe an image as 'specific' is to approve it; but it is important to remember that an image can be more specific, and in one sense less exact.

Another sort of generalized name, just the same in principle, is used by these poets to describe the phenomena of human behaviour and feeling. These again are personifications, personi-

1 Of course the language of eighteenth-century natural philosophy was not, like scientific language today, dry and colourless; it was figurative and excited. We can note how Berkeley's prose becomes most metaphorical and 'poetic' when most scientific, in 'Siris'. See my 'Berkeley's Style in "Siris"', *Cambridge Journal,* vol. iv, no. 7.

fied passions such as Scorn, Anger, Envy, Sloth, and personified moral principles, Honour, Charity, Virtue, Tolerance. These words cause the modern reader the same discomfort as words like 'grove'. For he is conditioned by his reading of the European novel, reading which has instructed him how many different histories and processes, what different sorts of attitude and outlook, are herded under the one blanketing term, 'Envy', or 'Shame', or 'Anger'; and, again, what different sorts of behaviour must, at a push, be approved alike as 'virtue' or condemned alike as 'vice'.[1] But Johnson or Goldsmith was not concerned with those features which make a man unique, but with those which he has in common with his fellows. The two sorts of concern are different though not incompatible; but there are no a priori grounds for thinking one less interesting or less moral than the other.

The sort of interest one can expect from the generalizing habit, when it works in this way, can be seen in Johnson's 'Prologue to *A Word to the Wise*':[2]

> This night presents a play which public rage,
> Or right, or wrong, once hooted from the stage.
> From zeal or malice, now no more we dread,
> For English vengeance wars not with the dead.
> A generous foe regards with pitying eye
> The man whom fate has laid where all must lie.
> To wit reviving from its author's dust,
> Be kind, ye judges, or at least be just,
> For no renew'd hostilities invade

1 The way the novel gets between us and eighteenth-century poetry is exemplified by John Crowe Ransom (*Kenyon Review*, XII, 3, p. 504). Speaking of the good prose which Wordsworth liked, he says, 'It would not be the merely utilitarian prose, but the prose to be found in sermons, in literary essays, above all in our time in prose fiction, and wherever else the style develops the concretions of nature rather than the lean "concretions of discourse"'. This was not the prose our poets esteemed, and their achievement is in concretions of discourse, like personifications.

2 I should like to acknowledge that I was first directed to this admirable poem by Mr Yvor Winters.

The oblivious grave's inviolable shade.
Let one great payment every claim appease;
And him, who cannot hurt, allow to please;
To please by scenes unconscious of offence,
By harmless merriment or useful sense.
Where aught of bright, or fair, the piece displays,
Approve it only – 'tis too late to praise.
If want of skill, or want of care appear,
Forbear to hiss – the poet cannot hear.
By all, like him, must praise and blame be found;
At best a fleeting gleam, or empty sound.
Yet then shall calm reflection bless the night,
When liberal pity dignify'd delight;
When pleasure fired her torch at Virtue's flame,
And Mirth was Bounty with an humbler name.

The sudden cluster of capital letters in the last two lines of this poem is no accident. The words thus dignified – Virtue, Mirth, Bounty – are personified moral principles of the sort to which we have objected on the score that they ignore the many and baffling ways in which they exert and display themselves in the world. But it is plain that this aspect of their activity is not disregarded by Johnson. They come at the end of the poem because they have been worked for in the rest. They struggle into the light, under pressure from the poet, through the brakes and tangles of human behaviour. Johnson brings home to the audience of a second-rate play by a dead author the truth that their reception of the play involves a moral decision on their part and lays them open to moral judgement by others. A response which appears in the first lines as 'no more than common decency' ('For English vengeance wars not with the dead') has become, by the end, a moral judgement appealing to moral absolutes. And the judgement shrugged aside at first, in respect of the first performance – 'or right, or wrong' – is inflexibly applied to the play's revival. If the reader looks back, from the vantage point of the last couplet, he sees how earlier lines which pretend to finality of judgement (by their epigrammatic balance) are in fact only partial resolutions and intermediate stages. Thus:

> To wit reviving from its author's dust,
> Be kind, ye judges, or at least be just . . .

The pronouncement has a memorable neatness. But by the end of the poem Johnson has shown that to be kind is the only way of being just, in the given set of circumstances. Personifications and generalizations are justifiable according as they are 'worked for'.[1] If Johnson had concluded his poem with 'Be kind, ye judges, or at least be just', or with 'By harmless merriment or useful sense', the poem would have been trivial. And for merriment or sense to take capital letters would have been more than the poem could bear. As it is, a dead metaphor comes to life. Bounty is plenitude and *bonté* (goodness); Mirth is thankful enjoyment of the plenitude of creative providence. It is a compelling and dignified idea.

The case of the epithet is more complicated. It is the function of an epithet to define more nearly the thing to which it refers. One can hardly speak, therefore, of *generalizing* epithets. Yet the characteristic epithets of eighteenth-century poetry have a generalizing effect, for they specify only to the extent that they place a thing in its appropriate class, or assign it its appropriate function. Mr Arthos makes an interesting suggestion to this effect,[2] when he compares the habitual coupling of one epithet with one noun with the Linnaean system of classification in botany. Probably the epithets in *-y* ('beamy', 'moony' and the rest) were adopted from science for the same purpose of classification. These are not really adjectival in their form or their effect, but nouns only disguised by the termination. Other epithets, as we saw with

1 Cf. 'custom' and 'ceremony' at the end of Yeats's 'A Prayer for my Daughter'. They have been worked for like Johnson's 'Mirth' and 'Bounty', and could sustain capital letters no less imperturbably.

2 Arthos, op. cit., p. 41.

Shenstone's 'swift spontaneous roses', are really disguised adverbs. And others again are verbs in their participial form – 'the pleasing strain', 'the smiling land'.

Of course if we say that the epithets of this verse describe a thing only by giving it its place in a system or its function in a scheme, we speak only of their original purpose in the hands of the best poets. Bryant, for instance, addresses the waterfowl:

> Seek'st thou the plashy brink
> Of weedy lake or marge of river wide,
> Or where the rocking billows rise and sink
> On the chaf'd ocean-side?

Bryant here is moralizing the instance, and arguing from the waterfowl to God, quite in the way of Johnson or Cowper. But he came into contact with that English tradition largely through his reading of Blair and Kirke White, poets in whom the characteristic diction had become corrupt. This corruption usually took a Miltonic or a Spenserian form. This is the impurity in 'plashy'. 'Weedy', however, is strong and chaste; for bulrushes are weeds, and to call them so shuts out Sabrina and Midas and their whispering, placing them firmly in the vegetable kingdom where, for this poet as for the botanist, they belong. In using the word, Bryant has already taken one step away from the specific instance towards the divine law which governs it.

What is common to all these epithets is the way they turn their back upon sense-experience and appeal beyond it, logically, to known truths deduced from it.[1] It is always possible, by a

1 There is an interesting example of the dry and abstract prosaic epithet in Wordsworth's 'The Brothers':

> and, when the regular wind
> Between the tropics filled the steady sail.

But Wordsworth does not know what to do with this felicity, and blunts it by repeating himself:

discreet extravagance, to widen this gap between the evidence of the senses and the evidence deduced from them, until the image seems absurd while we know it to be true. This is one of the sources of the mock-heroic, which is therefore a possibility inherent in this sort of diction. One obvious way of widening the gap is to invade the world of the microscope:

> Fair insect! that, with threadlike legs spread out
> And blood-extracting bill and filmy wing,
> Dost murmur, as thou slowly sail'st about,
> In pitiless ears full many a plaintive thing,
> And tell how little our large veins should bleed
> Would we but yield them to thy bitter need; –

The 'threadlike legs' of the mosquito, his 'blood-extracting bill' and 'filmy wing', are known facts deduced from experience. But they cannot be said to agree with experience. For the mosquito, thus described, appears grotesque and comical,[1] because, in our experience, the smallness of the insect prevents us from noting these features.

This union of the comical and the grotesque can be made horrific:

> And blew with the same breath through days and weeks,
> Lengthening invisibly its weary line
> Along the cloudless main . . .

This is redundant and prolix.

1 Bryant's verse is not wholly successful. Comical and grotesque it is, but I think he meant it to be pathetic too. This union of the comic, the grotesque and the pathetic is achieved by Parnell:

> Where stands a slender Fern's aspiring Shade,
> Whose answ'ring Branches regularly lay'd
> Put forth their answ'ring Boughs, and proudly rise
> Three stories upward, in the nether skies.

It belies the evidence of the senses to call the stalk and stems of a fern 'branches' and 'boughs', which we think of as massive. Yet, logically, that is what they are. The pathos comes in with the Latinate pun on 'aspire'.

Th' insulted sea with humbler thoughts he gains,
A single skiff to speed his flight remains;
Th' incumber'd oar scarce leaves the dreaded coast
Through purple billows and a floating host.

However many men have bled into the sea, we know that they never made it look purple; and yet we know that a single drop of blood must purple the sea to some tiny extent. Again, however many men fall dead into the sea, we know that they can never look like a floating host, although we know that that is what they are. Johnson, going behind the sense-impression to what he deduces from it, produces an effect which is farcical, grotesque and horrific all at once. It seems to me comparable with what Mr Wilson Knight calls the 'tragedy of the grotesque' in *King Lear* ('Horns whelked and waved like the enridged sea'), or what Mr Eliot found in Marlowe's *Jew of Malta* and *Dido Queen of Carthage*:

At last, the soldiers pull'd her by the heels,
And swung her howling in the empty air . . .

Mr Eliot calls this 'intense and serious and indubitably great poetry, which, like some great painting and sculpture, attains its effects by something not unlike caricature'. Johnson's lines, though they use a different method, seem to me to answer to the same description. They enliven a metaphor gone dead.

In the same way, though to different effect, Goldsmith enlivens the metaphor gone dead in the locution 'smiling land':

As some fair female, unadorn'd and plain,
Secure to please while youth confirms her reign,
Slights every borrow'd charm that dress supplies,
Nor shares with art the triumph of her eyes;
But when those charms are pass'd, for charms are frail,
When time advances, and when lovers fail,
She then shines forth, solicitous to bless,
In all the glaring impotence of dress:

Thus fares the land, by luxury betray'd,
In nature's simplest charms at first array'd:
But verging to decline, its splendours rise,
Its vistas strike, its palaces surprise;
While, scourged by famine, from the smiling land
The mournful peasant leads his humble band;
And while he sinks, without one arm to save,
The country blooms – a garden and a grave.

I do not pretend to explain the triumphant felicity of 'the glaring impotence of dress'. But one cannot miss the startling force given to 'smiling land', when it is seen to smile with heartless indifference on the ruined peasant. The smiling is far more powerful than the more specific 'blooms'. And it is more powerful because we know that in Goldsmith's verse it would have smiled though no peasant had been ruined, whereas Thomas Hardy would not have made it smile unless there were the peasant to be smiled on.

In this passage Goldsmith renovates, too, his conventional verbs. All vistas are striking; but Goldsmith's vistas strike like impotence, and like a plague. As we noted earlier, in this verse the vehicle of metaphor is often the verb. And verbs, like the other parts of speech, are often generalized:

Here where no springs in murmurs break away,
Or moss-crowned fountains mitigate the day.

Collins's verb is entirely abstract. It does the verb's proper work, describing not appearance but function, and, by implication, function in a divine scheme. Verbs, like epithets, can be made deliberately at odds with the appearance of the actions they denote:

Who dash'd the plum-trees from the blossomy ridge?
From bank to bank who threw the baby bridge . . .?[1]

1 This example is from 'The Splendid Village'. Elliott, alas, is still embalmed in the histories as 'The Corn Law Rhymer'. But the loose couplets in his early work are far superior to what appears in the anthologies.

The vandal and the jerry-builder do not work so fast. In our day the image of the hairy arm, in one hard movement upsetting an orchard, is almost true to reality. Yet even those who have seen a bulldozer at work must admit that the word 'dashed' is something of an exaggeration. In Ebenezer Elliott's day, this word, like 'threw', belied more blatantly the evidence of the senses. Yet Elliott had his authorities, and could appeal to literary precedent for the one usage and to the language of architects and engineers for the other. Moreover, the word 'dashed', although it belies the appearance, corresponds to the truth of vandalism. Still more to the purpose is 'threw', which has the same connotations of rude violence. It is, as we have said, prosaic or conversational, and, after the literary 'dash'd', it roots the language in sober reality. Finally it has, in conjunction with 'baby bridge', a valuable effect of scornful comedy, as if the gimcrack toy in the villa's garden could indeed be tossed into place by the improver's arm.

At its most powerful this sort of usage can express by metaphor a whole view of human life and destiny. This happens in Cowper's 'The Castaway':

> At length, his transient respite past,
> His comrades, who before
> Had heard his voice in every blast,
> Could catch the sound no more.
> For then, by toil subdued, he drank
> The stifling wave, and then he sank.

'Stifling' is a characteristic use of the participial adjective. It generalizes the fact of drowning, because 'stifling' is equally applicable to all the ways of dying; and so it affects us as dry, chastening and logical. More powerful still, in the same way, is 'drank'; for drinking we think of as a wilful imbibing for pleasure, whereas Cowper generalizes it to mean all drawings in of liquid to the throat. This is horrible, and strikes to the heart of Cowper's view of human life. For Cowper the Calvinist maintained that, even in a world of rigid predestination, the salvation or damnation of the soul was still the responsibility of the individual. He had cried out, in 'Truth':

> Charge not, with light sufficient and left free,
> Your wilful suicide on God's decree.

By presenting the rush of water into the drowning throat as a voluntary act of 'drinking', Cowper brings this idea to appalling life. The death of the castaway is 'wilful suicide'. And the one word 'drank', in this place, takes up all the Calvinist arguments of free will and fate. The generalizing word re-creates the metaphor.

(v) *Circumlocution*

THE generalizing habit, the habit of personifying, and the habit of talking round – these are the features we are often asked to see as the vices of much eighteenth-century writing in verse. I have tried to show that personifications and generalizations are often the sources of the most poetic effects in this writing, and also that they are often the way in which the poet purifies the spoken language. The same is true, I believe, of the habit of talking round.

In this verse talking round takes two distinct forms, a distinction which we roughly retain when we speak of periphrasis in some cases and circumlocution in others. Periphrastic writing can be dealt with fairly shortly, on the lines of an argument broached already. We can take, for a ludicrous instance, the schoolroom example 'denizen of the deep' as a periphrasis for 'fish'. Needless to say, if we hunted up a case in which this periphrasis was used, we should probably find the use made of it was ludicrous and vicious. For the moment I am concerned only to show how it need not be vicious, by supposing a case in which it was used with effect. It was observed that conventional epithets were sometimes justifiable, as classificatory rather than specific or particular. In the same way it is not hard to think of a case in which the poet, ranging over the natural creation, to draw out of it the divine scheme of plenitude, should wish to present fish as creatures of the sea, birds as creatures of air, beasts as creatures of earth. If the poet's intention was not to see fish in and for themselves, but as one class of the natural hierarchy, it would be proper for him to present them as 'denizens of the deep'. If he added 'finny' – 'finny denizens' – he might still be right, if he wanted to present the scheme in some minuteness and distinguish sea-creatures with fins from those without fins.

Of course this is special pleading. But we can see how the principle could be applied in practice, if we consider three typical periphrases:

> A Tyger roaming for his prey,
> Sprung on a Trav'ler in the way;
> The prostrate game a Lion spies,
> And on the greedy tyrant flies:
> With mingled roar resounds the wood,
> Their teeth, their claws distil with blood;
> Till vanquish'd by the Lion's strength,
> The spotted foe extends his length.
> The man besought the shaggy lord,
> And on his knees for life implor'd.

'The prostrate game' is correct and dryly pleasant, for we look on the man through the eyes of the lion, and this is how he appears to the beast. But Gay writes here as a fabulist, that is, as a moralist peculiarly interested in the animal creation as a hierarchy of signs acknowledging the creative wisdom. And from this point of view, as the lion is king of beasts, it is correct and exact to denote him by 'the shaggy lord'. But even if a tiger were spotted, it would be trivial and annoying to describe him as 'the spotted foe'. This does not put him in his place in the hierarchy, and, although 'foe' defines his relationship to the lion, it is a definition we could have done without. The locution for the tiger is vicious, as the locutions for the man and the lion are not.

Circumlocution is another matter. The trouble with this diction, we hear it said, is its limitation. For all assemblies of trees there is the convenient generality 'grove', for all movements of air the convenient 'gale'. But what is to be done when it is necessary to write of sofas, cucumbers and billiard-balls? We are led to think that for the eighteenth-century poet such things were merely unpoetic, and that he evaded, when possible, treatment of them. When evasion was impossible (so the argument runs) he talked round them. Now it is true to say that these poets talked round these things; but it is not true that they evaded them. On the contrary, some of the poets welcomed them. When Cowper began, 'I sing the sofa', he wrote *The Task*, a serious discursive poem, not a comical *tour de force*. The task that he set himself was not arbitrary or fanciful; in a sense it was the task of all his sort of poetry, the task of seeing the minutiae of social life in the light of moral truths. And the poem really is about sofas. It does not depart from the sofa, never to return. It circles back on the sofa time and again, and on kindred objects like reading-lamps and cards and newspapers. The theme is always the sofa, for the theme is the justification of secluded domestic life, that life of which the sofa is the emblem.

In fact the whole poem is one vast circumlocution, and it is built out of repeated circumlocutions on a smaller scale. Here, for instance, Cowper talks round the cucumber:

> To raise the prickly and green-coated gourd
> So grateful to the palate, and when rare
> So coveted, else base and disesteemed, –
> Food for the vulgar merely, – is an art
> That toiling ages have but just matured,
> And at this moment unessayed in song.

> Yet gnats have had, and frogs and mice long since
> Their eulogy; those sang the Mantuan bard,
> And these the Grecian in ennobling strains;
> And in thy numbers, Phillips, shines for aye
> The solitary shilling. Pardon then,
> Ye sage dispensers of poetic fame,
> The ambition of one meaner far, whose powers
> Presuming an attempt not less sublime,
> Pant for the praise of dressing to the taste
> Of critic appetite, no sordid fare,
> A cucumber, while costly yet and scarce.

The circumlocution, we observe, is not adopted to avoid mentioning a supposedly vulgar object, but to prepare and apologize for its introduction. The poet gradually lets down the tone until the cucumber can be introduced. This gradual introduction makes a case which will bear scrutiny for seeing the cucumber in generalized terms, in terms of those selected generalities within which the whole poem is working. Thus the phrase 'when rare So coveted, else base and disesteemed' chooses just that aspect of the fruit which is relevant to Cowper's theme. He is concerned with the corruption of fashionable life, the metropolitan corruption to which this account of his gardening is to be a contrast.

The tone of course is humorous, but humorous in a special way. Humour, when allied to circumlocution, is suspect; it is the vice of the schoolboy's magazine and of some tiresome writing by Charles Lamb. But this is the humour of the mock-heroic, not of the whimsy; it is comical in parts, but serious in sum. Cowper's humour plays round the ideas of modesty and ambition. His modesty is serious when he compares his poetic activity with that of gardeners who work, through generations, to acclimatize a fruit. His ambition is serious when he claims to write and to esteem only verse which is morally instructive. His modesty is ironical when he agrees that he can praise the cucumber only while it is scarce. And his ambition is ironical when he thinks to rival Virgil by recommending the cucumber to the palates of Georgian London. By comparison with this, Wordsworth in 'Simon Lee' seems singularly inflexible. Wordsworth sees no reason why swollen ankles should be vulgar or comical, and he is determined to write as if they are not. Cowper may think that the idea of the cucumber as vulgar is part of our unredeemed frivolity; but he does not blink the fact that vulgar and comical they are or seem. By irony and exaggeration he destroys these false barriers even as he acknowledges them.

This is the place to take up some suggestions I have thrown out already, about diversity of tone in this poetry, and in all poetry which employs chaste diction. It may be agreed that Cowper's circumlocution is better than Wordsworth's bathos. Yet, it may be objected, both poets go wrong in pitching their styles, from the start, in too high a key. If Cowper had not adopted a lofty tone, he would not have needed to let it down to accommodate the cucumber. It may even be felt that the bane of eighteenth-century verse is the lofty tone it seems forced to adopt on all occasions. This may be partly what Mr Eliot meant when he called the bad verse of the period 'intolerably poetical'. Where the good poets are concerned, one retorts in one way by pointing to *John Gilpin* or Goldsmith's *Haunch of Venison*, poems where the tone is not lofty. It may be replied that these, pleasant though they are, are trivial at best. But surely that is the point: these poets took a serious view of their profession, and where the business in hand was of such moment as instruction in moral conduct, they can hardly be blamed for being lofty about it. Even Puttenham allowed that, while the speech of peasants would usually demand the base style, yet, when they treated of weighty matters of 'civil regiment', the style should be lofty. It could be said of Johnson, Goldsmith and Cowper that their concern in their serious verse was always 'civil regiment'. Certainly this is the theme of *The Task*; and Cowper was right, therefore, to maintain an elevated tone.

It may be thought, incidentally, that by admitting Cowper's predilection for the lofty tone I come near to denying that I find in him that tie with conversational usage which I have put forward as one of the two conditions of chastity in diction. But this is not so. For Puttenham the three styles of verse (the lofty, the mean, the base) are equally closely in touch with spoken usage. The lofty style uses the speech of the court; the mean style, the speech of merchants and yeomanry; the base style, the speech of menial trades and the peasantry. However much the social structure may have changed since Puttenham's day, there is no excuse for supposing (as we often do) that the loftier the verse, the less conversational. An example of modern verse at once lofty and conversational I take to be Yeats's 'In Memory of Major Robert Gregory'.[1]

Circumlocution is vicious when it is merely prolix. Cowper's procedure can be as inflexible as Wordsworth's:

> Nor envies he aught more their idle sport
> Who pant with application misapplied
> To trivial toys, and pushing ivory balls
> Across the velvet level, feel a joy
> Akin to rapture, when the bauble finds
> Its destined goal of difficult access.

We can echo Mr Eliot and say of this that what the poet has to say appears surprised at the way in which he chooses to say it. The tone is not humorous at all; compare, for instance, the different force of 'pant' in this passage and in the lines on the cucumber. The substance of what the poet has to say is said already in the one phrase 'misapplied to . . . toys'. The rest is verbose, repeating that idea in less powerful ways. This passage comes from Book VI of *The Task*, where Cowper, preparing for a peroration, becomes more and more Miltonic. Cowper's blank

1 The point is neatly made by C. S. Lewis, describing the lofty and chaste diction of Gower (*Allegory of Love*, p. 201).

verse is not substantially Miltonic.[1] But it is true that, when he approaches the mock-heroic effect, Cowper draws upon Milton, where Johnson draws upon Dryden. At such moments Cowper uses the Miltonic magniloquence for his own purposes, and with success. Undoubtedly, though, some of Cowper's blank verse is Miltonic in the bad sense that it challenges comparison with Milton and is damned by the comparison. In view of Cowper's repudiation of the Miltonic model it is fair to suppose that, where the magniloquence asserts itself to no mock-heroic effect, it is a sign of flagging invention. And this is surely what happens here. 'Its destined goal of difficult access' has a Miltonic grandeur. In other words its grandeur is merely verbal and sonorous, reaping the easy reward of culminating rhythms. That was why, perhaps, the paragraph had to run to length through an agglomeration of subordinate phrases. Nothing in the simple idea justifies this length or this complication. In the 'grandeur' of the last line, 'destined' only repeats the notion of 'application', and it cheapens shockingly the idea of destiny. Only the billiard-player has destined the ball for a pocket, but in the scheme of the Miltonic grandeur the word trumpets like Jehovah's predestination of Adam. This is adulteration of the spoken tongue.

Thus circumlocution is neither good nor bad in itself. When it is good, it ensures a consistent tone of discourse. And if, as I. A. Richards maintained, tone is an aspect of meaning, then to preserve a consistent tone is one way of defining meanings and purifying the language. After all, what is 'The Castaway' but a circumlocutory account of Cowper's damnation?

1 Cf. Cowper in a letter (quoted by Gilbert Thomas, *William Cowper and the Eighteenth Century*, Allen & Unwin, 1949, p. 217): 'Milton's manner was peculiar. So is Thomson's. He that should write like either of them, would, in my judgement, deserve the name of a copyist, but not of a poet. A judicious and sensible reader therefore . . . will not say that my manner is not good, because it does not resemble theirs, but will rather consider what it is in itself.'

IV

Poetic Diction and Prosaic Strength

A PURE poetic diction can purify the national language by enlivening metaphors gone dead. But, since nearly all meanings are metaphorical by origin, we have to say that poetry re-creates a metaphor whenever it makes us aware, with new or renewed nicety, of the meaning of almost any word. To say this is to use 'metaphor' in a specially extended sense. And in general there is something ludicrous about the way modern criticism circles round and round 'metaphor', explaining poetry more and more in terms of 'images'; this is sufficient reason for not extending the use of the word even further, and, if 'metaphor' is taken in a more usual and restricted sense, one of the conclusions to be derived from the present study is that poetry can be written in unmetaphorical language. This is no new discovery – we have seen it affirmed, in different ways, by both Goldsmith and Wordsworth – but it is an aspect of poetry little considered today. In the 'Prologue to *A Word to the Wise*', Johnson renovates the word 'Bounty' and makes us more conscious of its meaning. In a sense he does so by re-creating a metaphor gone dead in the word, but to say so is to use 'metaphor' in a specially extended sense; and it is better, when dealing with this sort of achievement, to forget about metaphor and, following Johnson, to call it 'strength'.

Johnson used 'strength', and defined it, sufficiently for his purpose, in 'The Life of Denham': 'The "strength of Denham", which Pope so emphatically mentions, is to be found in many lines and couplets, which convey much meaning in few words, and exhibit the sentiment with more weight than bulk.' The term 'strength' was much used by critics in the seventeenth century, and Johnson agrees, in substance though not in sentiment, with Hobbes: 'To this palpable darkness I may also add the ambitious obscurity of expressing more than is perfectly conceived, or perfect conception in fewer words than it requires, which expressions, though they have had the honour to be called strong lines, are indeed no better than riddles . . .'[1] By Hobbes's time 'strength' was identified with Clevelandism, that is, with a decadent and frivolous form of 'conceited' and hyperbolical writing; and this explains Hobbes' dislike of compression and concentration when pursued as ends in themselves, under pressure of no informing purpose or feeling. Throughout the seventeenth century 'strong' or 'masculine' writing is associated with what modern critics have called 'the line of Wit', and others, the 'marinist' or 'metaphysical' strain. But Pope and Johnson were right, I think, when they judged that Denham had saved the essential 'strength' – the concentration – while disengaging it from the hyperbolical conceit.

This view is confirmed by the three examples from Denham which Johnson considered. Because Denham is unjustly neglected today, I make no excuse for quoting these pieces again.[2] The first is a passage on the Thames, from *Cooper's Hill*:

> Though with those streams he no resemblance hold,
> Whose foam is amber, and their gravel gold;
> His genuine and less guilty wealth t'explore,
> Search not his bottom, but survey his shore.

This is still a conceit, though muted and less hyperbolical than those we remember from Marvell or Donne. Its distinction cannot be better phrased than by Johnson: it 'exhibits the sentiment with more weight than bulk'. The same is true of

1 Hobbes, essay on 'Gondibert' (1651). See Appendix B for a sketch of the history of 'strength' as a term of criticism in the seventeenth century.

2 For the literary historians, Denham and Waller make up one set of twins, as Shenstone and Akenside sometimes make up another. The coupling is unjust to Denham, as it is to Shenstone.

Johnson's second example, the lines on Strafford:

> His wisdom such, at once it did appear
> Three Kingdoms' wonder, and three Kingdoms' fear;
> While single he stood forth, and seem'd, although
> Each had an army, as an equal foe.
> Such was his force of eloquence, to make
> The hearers more concern'd than he that spake;
> Each seem'd to act that part he came to see,
> And none was more a looker-on than he;
> So did he move our passions, some were known
> To wish, for the defence, the crime their own.
> Now private pity strove with publick hate,
> Reason with rage, and eloquence with fate.

The hyperbole here is as delightfully arrogant as the hyperboles of Marvell; but it is achieved not at all in Marvell's way. The ghost of a 'conceited' image hovers over the third and fourth lines, but thereafter the hyperbole, and the concentration which goes with it, is carried through in conversational and unmetaphorical language, chiefly by apt handling of syntax. And the reader has to define anew each of the words clustered and opposed in the last couplet – 'private' and 'publick', 'reason' and 'rage', 'eloquence' and 'fate'. Each word, arranged thus artfully with and against the others, and taking up the exposition which went before, takes on new life, defined freshly and closely. This is to purify the language. It occurs more clearly still in a passage on Cowley:

> To him no author was unknown,
> Yet what he wrote was all his own;
> Horace's wit and Virgil's state,
> He did not steal, but emulate!
> And when he would like them appear,
> Their garb, but not their cloaths, did wear.

It had not occurred to the reader that the distinction between 'garb' and 'clothes' was so fine yet so definite. It is forced on his attention in a way that is salutary, pleasing, and relevant to the poet's theme.

Of another excerpt Johnson says:

so much meaning is comprised in so few words; the particulars of resemblance are so perspicaciously collected, and every mode of excellence separated from its adjacent fault by so nice a line of limitation; the different parts of the sentence are so accurately adjusted; and the flow of the last couplet is so smooth and sweet; that the passage, however celebrated, has not been praised above its merit.

I know no better account of the effect of prosaic 'strength' and pure diction in poetry. These are Johnson's comments on 'The four verses, which, since Dryden has commended them, almost every writer for a century past has imitated'.[1] They appear in *Cooper's Hill*:

> O could I flow like thee, and make thy stream
> My great example, as it is my theme!
> Though deep, yet clear, though gentle, yet not dull;
> Strong without rage, without o'erflowing full.

This is what it describes, a prosaic strength, concentrated and discriminating, which purifies the language as it uses it. It possesses a distinction which has nothing to do with metaphor; and Johnson indeed affirms that it would be better without those metaphors it has: 'The lines are in themselves not perfect; for most of the words, thus artfully opposed, are to be understood simply on one side of the comparison, and metaphorically on the other; and if there be any language which does not express intellectual operations by material images, into that

1 And the poets continued to imitate; cf. Cowper's wretched attempt, in 'Conversation':

> A veteran warrior in the Christian field,
> Who never saw the sword he could not wield;
> Grave without dullness, learned without pride,
> Exact, yet not precise, though meek, keen-eyed.

language they cannot be translated.' Is a poem the better the more it is translatable? We may wonder.[1] But in any case Johnson's objection emphasizes that this sort of achievement is the greater according as the language is less figurative.

It seems to me that this distinction has just reappeared in English poetry, after too long an absence, as in this extract from 'Little Gidding':

> If I think, again, of this place,
> And of people, not wholly commendable,
> Of no immediate kin or kindness,
> But some of peculiar genius,
> All touched by a common genius,
> United in the strife which divided them . . .

If I want to find the ancestry, in English verse, of this nicety of statement, I have to go, if not with Johnson to Denham, then to Ben Jonson or Greville or Dryden:

> . . . To like what you lik'd, and at Masques or Playes
> Commend the self-same Actors, the same wayes;
> Ask how you did? and often with intent
> Of being officious, grow impertinent . . .[2]

> Is it the mark or majesty of Power
> To make offences that it may forgive?[3]

> Reveal'd Religion first informed thy sight,
> And Reason saw not till Faith sprung the Light.
> Hence all thy Natural Worship takes the source:
> 'Tis Revelation what thou think'st Discourse.[4]

1 T. S. Eliot comes near to saying that translatability is a test of one sort of poetic excellence. According to him it is a sign of the excellence of some of Dante.

2 'Officious' (in its Latinate sense, as in Johnson's 'On the Death of Dr Robert Levet') defines and is defined by 'impertinent'. The passage is from Jonson, *Underwoods*, xxxix.

3 The question is rhetorical and has the effect of nice and momentous statement.

4 'Discourse' is redefined by striking off from 'Revelation'.

Or I can find it in Johnson and in Thomas Parnell.[1] In other poets it occurs only with a difference. In Shakespeare the prosaic statement is only a momentary shaft of light through the foliage of metaphor. In Pope it is superbly clear and taut, but always pointed, limited in tone. In Wordsworth what seems to be statement is really rumination.[2] Where this strength occurs in poetry, that poetry must be said to have the virtues of good prose.

This strength of statement is found most often in a chaste or pure diction, because it goes together with economy in metaphor; and such economy is a feature of such a diction. It is achieved by judgement and taste, and it preserves the tone of the centre, a sort of urbanity. It purifies the spoken tongue, for it makes the reader alive to nice meanings. The poet who tries for such chastity and strength will never have his reader's love, but he may have his esteem. As C. S. Lewis says of John Gower: 'He can be dull: he can never be affected, strident, or ridiculous.' And as T. S. Eliot says of a greater master:

> The language of each great English poet is his own language; the language of Dante is the perfection of a common language. In a sense, it is more pedestrian than that of Dryden or Pope. If you follow Dante without talent, you will at worst be pedestrian and flat; if you follow Shakespeare or Pope without talent, you will make an utter fool of yourself.

It seems to follow that if we want to find in English 'the perfection of a common language' (and that is a good definition of pure diction) we should look not among our great poets, but among our good ones. Gower and Greville and Denham, Parnell and Goldsmith, Johnson and Cowper, seem to me good poets of this sort.

Mr Eliot has proved as good as his word. In the *Four Quartets* his verse has the virtues of good prose:

1 See Appendix A for an appreciation of the diction of Parnell.

2 Cf. Leavis, *Revaluation*, p. 162.

And every phrase,
And sentence that is right (where every word is at home,
Taking its place to support the others,
The word neither diffident nor ostentatious,
An easy commerce of the old and the new,
The common word exact without vulgarity,
The formal word precise but not pedantic,
The complete consort dancing together)
Every phrase and every sentence is an end and a beginning,
Every poem an epitaph.

Of these lines we must say, as of Denham's lines, that they are what they describe. These should engage the twentieth century as those did the eighteenth.

V

The Classicism of Charles Wesley

IN so-called lyrical poetry we may expect to find less of those felicities which I have here connected with the idea of a chaste diction. Certainly this will be so, so long as we consider 'lyrical' and 'didactic' poetry as poles apart. They are often so considered, and therefore many readers will applaud the late-Augustan poets as masters of didactic verse, for what that is worth (and the usual implication is that it is worth very little), at the same time as they regret the scarcity in the period of notable lyrical verse. On the other hand, though in much the same way, I have heard it asserted that the eighteenth century is poor in religious poetry, because (so we assume) religious poetry is not didactic either. This attitude is, of course, a legacy from the long period when religious experience was considered almost exclusively a matter of fervent feeling, and dogma was disreputable. The point to be made for the present purpose is that between these two preconceptions, about 'lyrical' poetry on the one hand and 'religious' poetry on the other, a large body of the best verse of this period goes unregarded altogether. I mean the hymns of Cowper and Charles Wesley and John Newton, not to mention the rather earlier achievements of Doddridge and Watts. 'Lyrical' or not, 'religious' or not (and to my mind it is as absurd to deny them the one status as the other), these poems manifest the same virtues as the secular poetry of the period; and to prove that they do so is to show that such qualities as prosaic strength, exactness and urbanity are not to be looked for only in poetry of a special and very limited kind, but can flourish and give pleasure in kinds of poetry which seem very different from *The Vanity of Human Wishes* or even *The Deserted Village*.

It must be admitted from the start that there is something reasonable in a reluctance to consider hymns as merely one genre of poetic writing. As Bernard Manning remarks; 'A hymn like "Jesu, Lover of my soul" may be poor religious poetry: but, in face of its place in English religion, only imbecility will declare it a poor hymn.'[1] That is a comment from the point of view of the hymnologist. As readers of poetry, our difficulties are, first, the need to disentangle, in the effect made upon us by a hymn, the appeal which is literary from others which derive from our own religious persuasions, our memory of musical melodies, or even such less tangible attractions as childhood associations; and, secondly, I think, our sense of an unfair advantage enjoyed by the hymn-writer over other poets. The themes of the hymn-writer are, to use a favourite late-Augustan expression, so important, that our sense of their urgency can excuse or even conceal in our minds the poverty of their expression. We feel that the hymn-writer, unlike the secular poet, has only to avoid certain fairly obvious pitfalls in order that his message may carry him through. In the poet, mere competence is not enough; in the writer of hymns, we feel it is. And it is probably taken for granted, among those who have never exerted themselves to see Wesley's hymns as literature, that his acknowledged pre-eminence is a matter of metrical facility, resourcefulness in rhyme, and a dead level of honest and sober language.

As a matter of fact, this is true of a good deal of Wesley's writing. Inevitably, writing so much, he composed many good hymns which are undistinguished or indifferent poems. But it requires, after all, no great exertion to appreciate other pieces as good poems in their own right. In particular, it is not true that his language is all on one level. If it were so he would be incapable of the poignant simplicity which is one of his best effects; for that effect, as in *King Lear* ('Pray you, undo this

1 Bernard L. Manning, *The Hymns of Wesley and Watts* (Epworth Press 1948), p. 109.

button') is brought about by sudden and calculated descent from a relatively elaborate level of language:

> Sinners, believe the gospel word,
>   Jesus is come your souls to save!
> Jesus is come, your common Lord;
>   Pardon ye all through Him may have,
> May now be saved, whoever will;
> This Man receiveth sinners still.[1]

The piercing directness of that last line is an achievement of literary form. As Ezra Pound says:

> Neither prose nor drama can attain poetic intensity save by construction, almost by scenario; by so arranging the circumstance that some perfectly simple speech, perception, dogmatic statement appears in abnormal vigour. Thus when Frédéric in *L'Éducation* observes Mme Arnoux's shoelaces as she is descending the stair; or in Turgenev the quotation of a Russian proverb about the 'heart of another', or 'Nothing but death is irrevocable' towards the end of *Nichée de Gentilshommes*.[2]

The construction of Wesley's hymn is an example of 'scenario' in this sense, and his last line reaps the reward in 'abnormal vigour'. It is one of Wesley's most common devices.[3] His is a sophisticated art.

It is not different in kind from that of his contemporaries, the secular poets. For instance, John Wesley was right when he claimed for his brother's verse that it was 'Scriptural', in the sense that almost every metaphor or striking turn of phrase can be traced to a biblical original. But this does not mean that Wesley was restricted and hampered in his composition; still less that he was condemned to a sectarian jargon, like Zeal-of-the-Land Busy. On the contrary it means that Wesley enjoyed, as

1 *The Methodist Hymn-book* (1904), no. 283 [not in *Hymns and Psalms*, 1983].
2 Ezra Pound, *Make it New: Essays* (Faber, 1934), p. 289.
3 Cf. *Hymn-book*, nos. 192 [not in *Hymns and Psalms*], 594 [788].

Pope did or Johnson, a sort of extra poetic dimension. He could expect his congregations to know Scripture as Johnson and Pope could expect their readers to know Virgil and Horace. All of them, therefore, had given to them a sort of literary resource which Mr Eliot, for instance, has had to re-create for himself. Johnson could refer to Horace, and Wesley to Isaiah, subtly and discreetly; whereas Mr Eliot, when he wants to refer to Dante, Baudelaire or Webster, has, in *The Waste Land*, to quote at length and draw the reader's attention in a note. A critic has well described this Augustan myth as 'a field of force' lying behind the most apparently guileless of eighteenth-century poems; Wesley's poetry can draw upon a field no less powerful. The modern reader will miss all but the most obvious of the Scriptural references, just as he will miss all but the loudest classical echoes in Pope. A crude example is no. 256 in the *Hymn-book* [469 in *Hymns and Psalms*]

> Expand Thy wings, celestial Dove,
> Brood o'er our nature's night;
> On our disordered spirits move,
> And let there now be light.

The activity of the Holy Spirit in the human soul is described in terms which recall the Creative Spirit in Genesis; and as a result the word 'disordered' is set against the vast image of primeval chaos. It is the exact word; but by its very exactness, like the epithets of Johnson, it gives a dry effect of understatement, which creates the urbane tone.

Occasionally, Wesley refers to other than revealed writings. Bernard Manning gives an example:[1]

> Lord, we Thy will obey,
> And in Thy pleasure rest;
> We, only we, can say,
> 'Whatever is, is best.'

1 Manning, op. cit. pp. 73, 74.

Faith, mighty faith, the promise sees,
And looks to that alone;
Laughs at impossibilities,
And cries, 'It shall be done!'

The reference in line 4 is to Pope's 'Whatever is, is right'. Similar are the lines in 'Christ the Lord is risen to-day':

Lives again our glorious King!
Where, O death, is now thy sting?
Once He died our souls to save:
Where's thy victory, boasting grave?[1]

Or, again, any number of references to 'the undistinguished grave' come to life with the twist:

Love, like death, hath all destroyed,
Rendered all distinctions void . . .

This habit of inconspicuous reference to previous literature and especially to a hallowed canon, classical or Scriptural, is obviously related to what I have argued is the distinguishing excellence of a pure diction, the practice of refurbishing old metaphors gone dead, rather than the hunting out of new ones. Because Wesley aimed to be Scriptural, he coined even fewer novel metaphors than his secular contemporaries did. When he does take the liberty, he is capable, as Cowper is,[2] of a seventeenth-century wit:

1 The same famous Popian tag is treated in the same way in no. 474 [not in *Hymns and Psalms*]:

O death! where is thy sting? Where now
Thy boasted victory, O grave?
Who shall contend with God? or who
Can hurt whom God delights to save?

2 Cf. the gypsies in *The Task*:

The sportive wind blows wide
Their fluttering rags, and shows a tawny skin,
The vellum of the pedigree they claim.

Love's redeeming work is done;
Fought the fight, the battle won:
Lo! the sun's eclipse is o'er;
Lo! he sets in blood no more.[1]

And sometimes the whole conceit is carried in one word:

Captain of our salvation, take
  The souls we here present to Thee,
And fit for Thy great service make
  These heirs of immortality;
And let them in Thine image rise,
And then transplant to paradise.[2]

But more typically he takes a dead metaphor and enlivens it:

Strike with the hammer of Thy word,
  And break these hearts of stone.[3]

Or again:

Impoverish, Lord, and then relieve
  And then enrich the poor;
The knowledge of our sickness give,
  The knowledge of our cure.

That blèssed sense of guilt impart,
  And then remove the load;
Trouble, and wash the troubled heart
  In the atoning blood.[4]

And this is only the simplest version of this rejuvenation. As with the secular poets, so with Wesley, the enlivening of dead metaphors is in the end indistinguishable from all those arrange-

1 *Hymn-book*, no. 170 [193 in *Hymns and Psalms*, but, in the rearranged text, lines 3 and 4 of this verse no longer appear].
2 Ibid., no. 894 [not in *Hymns and Psalms*].
3 Ibid., no. 305 [418].
4 Ibid.

ments of words which, by contrast, antithesis, juxtaposition, force us to redefine meanings and pick our words with nicety:

> His adorable will
> Let us gladly fulfil,
> And our talents improve,
> By the patience of hope and the labour of love.[1]

Whatever the effect of this on the congregations of Wesley's time, for us both 'adorable' and 'labour of love' are shockingly cheapened expressions which, once we have read Wesley's verse, become once again taut and definite. In Wesley, as in Johnson, the blunted meaning or the buried metaphor comes sharp and live again in a sort of Latinate pun:

> This instant now I may receive
> The answer of His powerful prayer;
> This instant now by Him I live,
> His prevalence with God declare.[2]

And sometimes too, as in the 'Prologue to *A Word to the Wise*', pairs of abstractions are generalized in parallel, with an effect of mounting tension:

> The atonement of Thy blood apply,
> Till faith to sight improve,
> Till hope in full fruition die,
> And all my soul be love.[3]

– where 'faith' opposed to 'sight', is generalized to 'hope', as 'sight' is to 'love'.

The use of language is always responsible. There is a Johnsonian weighing of epithets – 'as pure, as even and as strong', 'obscurely safe', 'spotless and peaceable and kind'. A word such as 'seer', in no. 196 of the *Hymn-book* [not in *Hymns and Psalms*],

1 Ibid., no. 930 [354].
2 Ibid., no. 192 [not in *Hymns and Psalms*].
3 Ibid., no. 532 [not in *Hymns and Psalms*].

is not employed for its affecting connotations, but exactly, with the etymologist's exactness; and in the same hymn, for instance, as much can be said of 'signify', 'cancelled', 'meritorious', each offering a different temptation to looseness yet always used strictly for the sense.

It is only from this point of view that one sees the true force of Wesley's Latinisms. They are not threaded on the staple Anglo-Saxon of his diction in order merely to give a pleasing variety in sound and pace (though they do that incidentally), but so that Saxon and classical elements can criss-cross and light up each the other's meaning. Occasionally there occur bad pseudo-Miltonic Latinisms ('Implunged in the crystal abyss', '... through life's disparted wave ...') but in general the Latinisms are Johnsonian:

> Author of faith, appear!
> Be Thou its finisher.[1]

– where the ungainly 'finisher' is there to remind us that 'Author' means 'originator'. And the ungainliness disappears when the same wordplay is handled again:

> Author of faith, eternal Word,
> Whose Spirit breathes the active flame;
> Faith, like its Finisher and Lord,
> To-day as yesterday the same.[2]

Sometimes the Anglo-Saxon word, when it comes, seems to take us by the throat:

> The millennial year
> Rushes on to our view, and eternity's here.[3]

At its best, the Latinism can be, in Bernard Manning's phrase, the 'classic summary' of a whole doctrine:

1 *Hymn-book*, no. 630 [not in *Hymns and Psalms*].
2 Ibid., no. 345 [662].
3 Ibid., no. 930 [354].

Adam, descended from above!
  Federal Head of all mankind.

And in the process it purifies the language of the tribe. As the same critic remarks of another such, 'congregations bred on such stuff should not suffer from flabbiness of thought'.[1]

It is obvious that Wesley's verse exhibits these virtues because it is throughout doctrinal, that is, didactic. His hymns are not, like most later hymns, so many geysers of warm 'feeling'. And yet, heaven knows, the 'feeling' is there. We respect its integrity and we take its force just because it is not offered in isolation but together with its occasion, an occasion grasped and presented with keen and sinewy intelligence. Intelligence comes into the poetry of this period not as contraband, smuggled into a conceit as 'ingenuity', or intangibly as ironical tone, but straightforward and didactic. And the intellectual strength does not desiccate the emotions but gives to them validity and force.

Wesley's themes, then, are the central paradoxes of the Christian faith. His favourite figure is oxymoron: 'Impassive, He suffers; immortal, He dies.' This is the figure in which Wesley employs his Latinate puns, his 'curial' language, with most force. And sometimes, out of an original oxymoron, flowers a whole growth of crucial paradox:

Victim divine, Thy grace we claim,
  While thus Thy precious death we show:
Once offered up, a spotless Lamb,
  In Thy great temple here below,
Thou didst for all mankind atone,
And standest now before the throne.

Thou standest in the holy place,
  As now for guilty sinners slain:
The blood of sprinkling speaks, and prays,
  All prevalent for helpless man;
Thy blood is still our ransom found,
And speaks salvation all around.

1 Manning, op. cit., p. 107.

We need not now go up to heaven,
To bring the long-sought Saviour down;
Thou art to all already given,
Thou dost even now Thy banquet crown:
To every faithful soul appear,
And show Thy real presence here.[1]

Because the original paradox ('Victim divine') is developed, we realize that it is not an accidental fuzziness like Tennyson's 'divine despair'. Because Christ was both sacrifice and priest, and because the smoke of that atonement both cast a veil and rent it too, we are made conscious that 'invisible' means 'unshowable', what cannot be shown and yet was shown. A common word takes on unusual clarity and force.

In the Methodist chapel, as in the drawing-room, the poet used the language spoken by his hearers. He did not try to heighten, to disrupt, or even, in the first place, to enrich that language, but to sharpen it, to make it more exact and pure, and thereby (paradoxically) more flexible. He seldom used shock tactics. His concern was not to create a distinctive style, but to contribute to a common stock, to safeguard a heritage and to keep it as bright as new. Ezra Pound remarks:

Anatole France is said to have spent a great deal of time searching for the *least possible* variant that would turn the most worn-out and commonest phrases of journalism into something distinguished.

Such research is sometimes termed 'classicism'.

This is the greatest possible remove from the usual English stylist's trend or urge towards a style different from everyone else's.[2]

From this point of view Charles Wesley is a classical poet, as Dr Johnson is.

1 *Hymn-book*, no. 727 [629].
2 *A B C of Reading* (Routledge, 1934), p. 54.

VI

The Vanity of Human Wishes *and* De Vulgari Eloquentia

THE connection proposed in the title of this essay is, at first sight, a queer one. The association of Johnson's respectable poem with Dante's treatise on poetic diction must seem bizarre and more than a little gauche. In recent years Johnson's poem has risen greatly in critical esteem and has attracted the more or less admiring attention of Ezra Pound, T. S. Eliot and F. R. Leavis, to name no more. But there would be a sort of pathetic insularity about any pretence that it is one of the great achievements of European culture, or that Dr Johnson as poet can, as a result, stand comparison with a figure such as Dante. And Pound, at any rate, will clearly deny to it anything of the sort.[1]

Nevertheless, for the intelligent English reader, to whom a poem in his own tongue must always be more immediate than a poem, however illustrious, in another – for such a reader the connection exists. Mr Eliot, for instance, can use Johnson's poem and Dante's poetry to much the same end – to the one end of insisting that language is not more poetic the further it is removed from the language of prose. It is because, in their view, the poetry of Milton has lent support to this fallacy that the three critics cited were at one in their depreciation of Milton as in their appreciation of Johnson. And Johnson himself was of their opinion:

Gray thought his language more poetical as it was more remote from common use: finding in Dryden *honey redolent of Spring*, an expression

1 *Guide to Kulchur* (Faber, 1938), pp. 179–81, 183–4, 193.

that reaches the utmost limits of our language, Gray drove it a little more beyond apprehension by making *gales* to be *redolent of joy and youth*.

In this comment Johnson, by adopting the twin criteria of literary precedent (Dryden) and 'common use', is on the same ground as Ezra Pound when the latter asserts: 'The borderline between "gee whizz" and Milton's tumified dialect must exist'.[1] And Pound goes on to say that 'Dante, in *De Volgari Eloquio* seems to have thought of a good many particulars of the problem'. There is some reason, then, for supposing that in Dante's treatise we find a more comprehensive exposition of certain principles of poetic diction implicit in Johnson's poetry and criticism, and, when found there, embraced by contemporary critics and practising poets as peculiarly relevant to the writing of poetry today. In this essay I propose to establish this relevance, and I am concerned with Johnson's poem only by the way, as exhibiting in English and in a small way the principle which Dante promotes. The principle in question is that of purity in poetic diction, and it appears to have been lost to English poetry and criticism between Dr Johnson and Mr Pound. After so long an absence from the English scene, it was not to be re-established in a hurry. And because, even after Mr Eliot's writing and Mr Pound's, it is still hardly acknowledged, there is some point in revealing it again in its classical expression by Dante. I am concerned, then, with the treatise only as it has interest for the English poet and the reader of English poets, not as it takes its place in the canon of Dante's works or in the history of Italian literature.

From this point of view, of the two books which exist, the most interesting portions are chapters xvi, xvii and xviii of Book I, and chapters ii and iv of Book II.

In his first fifteen chapters Dante has insisted first on the

1 D. D. Paige (ed.) *The Letters of Ezra Pound 1907–1941* (Faber, 1951), p. 349.

unprecedented nature of the speculation he proposes. He distinguishes between the Vulgar Tongue (the vernacular) and 'Grammar', that is, Latin; and decides that the first is 'the nobler as being natural to us'. Speech, he points out, is a specifically human endowment, for angels know each other immediately and have no need of speech; human communication, therefore, is neither instinctive, like that of the brutes, nor spiritual, as with angels, but partakes of both qualities, being 'rational and sensible'. That is, it appeals to the reason but also to the senses.

After so much by way of introduction, Dante devotes four chapters to telling of the first universal language and how it was broken up as a penalty for human presumption in attempting the tower of Babel. The field narrows to Europe, wherein, Dante states, there were once three languages: the Northern or Teutonic, the Greek or Eurasian, and the language then common to 'Spaniards' (i.e. the men of Provence), Frenchmen and Italians. Each of these is now divided further, the last of them into the language of 'oc' (Provençal), the language of 'oil' (French) and the language of 'si' (Italian). After giving examples of the essential identity of French, Provençal and Italian, Dante explains that it is human instability which has produced this progressive disintegration, and that it continues to have this effect, setting up provincial dialects inside the languages; hence the need for the artificial stability of Latin. After a digression on the peculiar virtues of French (best, says Dante, for prose), of Provençal (as having the longest established poetic tradition) and of Italian (as the tongue of Cino da Pistoia and Dante himself), the critic surveys the dialects of Italy, and the claims of each of these to be the most 'illustrious'.

All of this seems sufficiently remote from anything of interest to the modern reader. It ceases to be so when Dante remarks that no one of the dialects can be considered the most illustrious, since the best poets have always departed from their own dialect for the purposes of their poetry. This leads him in chapter xvi to the conclusion:

Having, then, found what we were looking for, we declare that the Illustrious, Cardinal, Courtly, and Curial Vulgar Tongue in Italy is that which belongs to all the towns in Italy, but does not appear to belong to any one of them; and is that by which all the local dialects of the Italians are measured, weighed, and compared.[1]

That is, Dante esteems, as T. S. Eliot does, a poetic diction which is not personal and distinctive but 'the perfection of a common language'. From George Puttenham we learn that in Elizabeth's England, as in Dante's Italy, the poet, in forming his diction, had still to consider different sorts of English spoken in different parts of the country. The modern English poet has to con over dialects in just the same way, but the dialects are no longer regional ones. Instead there are class dialects, period dialects, the jargons of schools, cliques, generations, political or religious parties; and the pure diction of the modern poet, like the 'illustrious tongue' of Dante, will be intelligible to all of these elements, but peculiar to none of them.

In chapter xvii Dante explains what he means by calling this language 'illustrious'. That is illustrious 'which shines forth illuminating and illuminated'; and this lustre belongs to things which are exalted either by authority or by training and discipline, and which reflect this lustre on those who follow and honour them. Dante says of the common language of Italian poetry:

Now, it appears to have been exalted by training, inasmuch as we see it (purified) from so many rude Italian words, involved constructions, faulty expressions, and rustic accents, and brought to such a degree of excellence, clearness, completeness, and polish, as is displayed by Cino of Pistoja and his friend in their *Canzoni*.[2]

This corresponds to what we have said of a pure diction as 'choice', and this choiceness appears, we have said (and Dante

1 *De Vulgari Eloquentia* (tr. A. G. Ferrers Howell, 1890), p. 38.

2 Ibid., pp. 39, 40.

implies as much), as 'a sense as of words and expressions thrusting at the poem and being fended off from it'.

In the next chapter, which is of crucial importance, Dante explains his other three epithets. First, why does he call the poetic language 'cardinal'?

> ... because, as the whole door follows its hinge, and whither the hinge turns the door also turns, whether it be moved inwards or outwards; so the whole herd of local dialects turns and returns, moves and pauses, according as this [Illustrious language does], which really seems to be the father of a family. Does it not daily root out the thorny bushes from the Italian wood? Does it not daily insert cuttings or plant young trees? What else have its foresters to do but to bring in and take away as has been said? Wherefore it surely deserves to be adorned with so great a name as this.[1]

Herein is implied all that Mr Eliot has said about the poet's duty 'to purify the language of the tribe', and it supports us in our argument that this purification can only come about through purity, or chastity, of diction.

Then, what does Dante mean by 'courtly'?

> ... if we Italians had a Court it would be an Imperial one; and if a Court is a common home of all the realm, and an august ruler of all parts of the realm, it would be fitting that whatever is of such a character as to be common to all [parts] without being peculiar to any should frequent this Court and dwell there; nor is there any other abode worthy of so great an inmate. Such, in fact, seems to be that Vulgar Tongue of which we are speaking; and hence it is that those who frequent all the royal palaces always speak the Illustrious Vulgar Tongue. Hence, also, it happens that our Illustrious Language wanders about like a wayfarer and is welcomed in humble shelters, seeing we have no Court.[2]

This may serve as our justification in linking with the idea of a pure diction all the Arnoldian doctrine, as to Attic prose, that it

1 Ibid., pp. 40, 41.
2 Ibid., p. 41.

embodies 'the tone and spirit of the centre', as opposed to the provincial. Dante's 'courtliness' is our 'urbanity'. And from the last sentence quoted we see that for Dante too the question was of a spiritual quality, 'urbanity' as opposed to 'provincialism', not of any actual metropolis or any actual provinces, in the sense of the geographer.

Finally, why is the pure diction 'curial'?

> . . . because Curiality is nothing else but the justly balanced rule of things which have to be done; and, because the scales required for this kind of balancing are only wont to be found in the most excellent Courts of Justice, it follows that whatever is well balanced in our actions is called Curial. Wherefore, since this Illustrious language has been weighed in the balances of the most excellent Court of Justice of the Italians, it deserves to be called Curial. But it seems mere trifling to say that it has been weighed in the balances of the most excellent Court of Justice of the Italians, because we have no [Imperial] Court of Justice. To this the answer is easy. For, though we have no Court of Justice in Italy in the sense of the one [Supreme] Court of the King of Germany, still the members of such a Court are not wanting. And just as the members of the German Court are united under one Prince, so the members of ours have been united by the gracious light of Reason. Wherefore, it would be false to assert that the Italians have no such Court of Justice, though we have no Prince, because we have a Court, though, as a body, it is scattered.[1]

This takes us beyond our brief. 'Curial' seems to mean 'judicious', and the passage seems to be Dante's way of insisting that to attain this pure diction is a moral achievement, a product of integrity and equilibrium in the poet, in some sense, perhaps, a manifestation of the Aristotelian mean.

Book II is of less interest, chiefly because we feel here the lack of the Book III and Book IV which were planned but never written. This is especially true of chapters ii and iv, in which Dante begins to sketch a structure of distinction by genres:

1 *De Vulgari Eloquentia*, pp. 41, 42.

Next, we ought to possess a sound judgement as to those things which suggest themselves to us as fit to be uttered, so as to decide whether they ought to be sung in the way of Tragedy, Comedy, or Elegy. By Tragedy we understand the Higher Style, by Comedy, the Intermediate Style, by Elegy we understand the Lower Style. If our subject appears fit to be sung in the Tragic Style we must then assume the Illustrious Vulgar Tongue, and consequently we must write a properly constructed *Canzone*. If it appears fit to be sung in the Comic Style, sometimes the Illustrious and sometimes the Lower Vulgar Tongue should be used, and the judgement to be exercised in this case we reserve for treatment in the Fourth book. If our subject appears fit to be sung in the Elegiac Style we must adopt the Lower Vulgar Tongue alone.[1]

This, which explains, of course, what Dante meant by the title *The Divine Comedy*, is plainly his version of the distinction made by Puttenham and other Elizabethans between the high or lofty, the mean, and the base styles. That distinction strikes us now as mere pedantry and there is some reason for arguing that it was made only to be blurred almost at once, by Donne. And yet it dies hard. The three styles, lofty, mean and base, or sublime, familiar and pathetic, are still, I would guess, a governing factor in the activity of the practising poet. It is notable, for instance, that J. M. Synge, when he had to write of poetic diction, was forced into a distinction very like that between the sublime and the pathetic; and Miss Rosemond Tuve claims to find the distinction maintained in practice by W. B. Yeats. All the same, it is perhaps as well that we are in no danger of finding these difficult questions of tone reduced once more to a hard and fast system. But what emerges from this examination is a substantial identity of outlook, as to poetic diction, in Dante and Dr Johnson and certain modern poets. One may go further indeed, and speak of a consistent doctrine in this matter shared by all these writers. I suggest that the term is correctly used only when it is used as Dante and Dr Johnson used it. In other words the

1 Ibid., pp. 55, 56

most important question to be asked of any poetic diction concerns its purity or impurity. And that is a question which is never or very seldom asked by modern critics.

VII

'To speak but what we understood'

WHEN Mr Eliot asserted that 'to have the virtues of good prose is the first and minimum requirement of great poetry', he was echoing Ezra Pound, who was in turn repeating what he had learnt from Ford Madox Ford. If we read the poetry of these three writers we can see them trying to practise what they preach; in some sense, therefore, their poetry exhibits a renewed drawing together of prosaic and poetic language. And yet we cannot deny that in some other respects their poetry exhibits language removed further than ever before from prosaic discipline. When all is said and done 'Little Gidding' is less prosaic than *The Vanity of Human Wishes*. Mr Eliot, therefore, does not mean all that he seems to say.

In what sense, then, are we to understand him? To put it another way, what is the gulf that remains to be bridged, after all the compliments to *The Vanity of Human Wishes*, between Augustan and contemporary verse?

Historically, of course, the gulf that yawns is the tradition of Romantic poetry. Both T. S. Eliot and Ezra Pound have freely acknowledged their debts to this tradition, especially in its final phase as 'Symbolism'; and it is there that we must seek for whatever it is that draws their poetry away from prose, while their other allegiances draw these together.

To explain this we must return to an earlier stage of our argument (p.24, n.2), where we considered Dr Leavis's objection that the poetry of 'Ash Wednesday' has not, after all, 'the virtues of good prose'. In a line such as 'The infirm glory of the positive hour', one sees, it is true, the lexicographer's weighing of the epithet, the prosaic exactness which Mr Eliot has admired in Johnson. But, as Dr Leavis points out, such prosaic features are only incidental to a poem which, in its total structure, is as far as possible from the procedure of prose.

At that earlier point we were able to turn the force of this criticism by pointing to a passage from 'Little Gidding' in which syntax, no less than vocabulary, was employed with more rigour and subtlety than is usual in all but the best prose. But this stratagem, which sufficed us then, can do so no longer. For five minutes spent on 'Little Gidding' will show that this, no less than 'Ash Wednesday', is a poem in the symbolist tradition, a poem which works by the arrangement of images, letting the meaning flower unstated, as it were, from the space between them. It follows, I think, that dislocation of syntax is essential to all poems written in this tradition. And this is less apparent in 'Little Gidding' only because, in respect of that poem, the word 'image' must be given the very widest meaning, so as to comprehend whole substantial blocks of verse. The whole of the passage we quoted ('There are three conditions which often look alike') is, from this point of view, a single 'image', and in the massive scheme of 'Little Gidding' as a whole, or the *Four Quartets* as a whole, it stands to other such images in a relation which is musical, not prosaic. The difference between 'Ash Wednesday' and 'Little Gidding' is only a difference of scale; in the later poem the poet works with extensive blocks of material, where before he dealt only in snatches of verse. But the relationship between the blocks is the same as that between the snatches: it is symbolist, not syntactical.

So far as I know, Mr Eliot as critic has never committed himself on this matter of syntax. As usual we can go to Pound to find a principle common to both poets pushed explicitly to its logical conclusion:

A people that grows accustomed to sloppy writing is a people in process of losing grip on its empire and on itself. And this looseness and blowsiness is not anything as simple and scandalous as abrupt and disordered syntax.

It concerns the relation of expression to meaning. Abrupt and disordered syntax can be at times very honest, and an elaborately constructed sentence can be at times merely an elaborate camouflage.[1]

With this no one can quarrel. But the observation occurs so often in Pound's writing that we have to suspect he means more than he says. We are told so often that we can do without syntax that we begin to think we can do better without it. And there is no doubt that this is what the writer means. It is on this count, for instance, that he prefers Confucius to Aristotle:

As working hypothesis say that Kung is superior to Aristotle by totalitarian instinct. His thought is never something scaled off the surface of facts. It is root volition branching out, the ethical weight is present in every phrase.

The chief justice had to think more soberly than the tutor and lecturer.

Give the Greek points on explanatory elaborations. The explicitness, that is literally the unfoldedness, may be registered better in the Greek syntax, but the loss must be counted.[2]

It is clear that, in Pound's view, when the loss is counted, it will more than counterbalance the gain in 'unfoldedness'. In military language, syntax is 'expendable'. So far as this writer can see, it is more of a hindrance than a help; and this explains his affection for the Chinese ideogram. Only an Orientalist can decide whether Fenollosa and Pound are right about the nature of the Chinese written character. But one sees plainly enough, from Pound's own observations and examples, the connection which existed for him between the ideogram and the symbolist aesthetic. The ideogram, as he saw it, was made up out of several radical signs, each standing for a concrete particular. The sign for 'tree', the

1 *A B C of Reading*, p. 86.
2 *Guide to Kulchur*, p. 279.

sign for 'grass', the sign for 'man', the sign for 'sea' are arranged, it seems, in such a way as to make a wall round a mental space wherein is the meaning of the whole. An arrangement of signs makes the meaning of an ideogram as an arrangement of symbols makes the meaning of a symbolist poem. The *Guide to Kulchur* attempts to use the ideogram in prose as the *Cantos* do in verse. To Ezra Pound questions of language were central to all human experience; and so this train of thought about syntax finds its counterpart in his ethics. It goes very deep indeed. But it is enough for the moment to point out that when Pound tells the poet he must compete with Flaubert, he is far from thinking in the first place about Flaubert's syntax. Indeed he is thinking of just that element in prose fiction (when he speaks of prose he means nearly always novelists' prose) which in the end led him to abandon syntax altogether; he is thinking of the great novelist's terseness and precision in rendering a feature of experience in all its concreteness. He is thinking, in fact, of the novelist's achievement in rendering the image with clean edges and hard colours, all that he himself had striven for in his Imagist phase; he is not thinking at all of the novelist's practice of relating those features by way of syntax.

Pound, then, while he exhorts the poet to learn from the prose writer, exhorts him no less to avoid prose syntax. On the other hand there are poets who argue that poetry is vastly different from prose at the same time as they take it for granted that poetry and prose use the same syntax:

Both employ the same words, *the same syntax*,[1] the same sounds and tones – though differently arranged and differently stimulated. What separates prose from poetry is the difference of those associated relationships which are for ever coming into being and passing away within our psychological and nervous constitution – even though the *elements* which compose the raw material of these activities may be identical. That is why we must be careful never to apply to poetry the same kind

1 My italics.

of reasoning that we apply to prose. What may be true of one may, quite easily, be utterly without meaning when sought in the other.[1]

This seems, at first blush, to contradict all that has been said about the need for the poet to learn from prose usage. But it need not do so, and there is nothing in this passage to which Mr Eliot, at least, could not subscribe. Nothing, indeed, could be better, as defining the relationship to prose of certain parts of 'Little Gidding', than to say, as Valéry does, that they exhibit 'the same syntax . . . though differently arranged'.

And yet the passage is ambiguous. When Valéry asserts that the 'raw material' of prose and of poetry is one and the same, he may be agreeing with all that Dr Johnson thought about the necessity of prosaic discipline in poetry; or he may agree with none of it. For what are the 'elements' of language? Where do they end, and where does 'arrangement' begin? It is plain that 'syntax' is not an element of language in the sense in which 'sounds and tones' are elements. And after all what is syntax but arrangement? The sense of the passage is not far to seek. It is to be found of course in Valéry's practice as a poet. And on that showing there is nothing to disprove the contention that dislocation of syntax is the essential secret of symbolist technique. For even where the forms of prose syntax are retained, it does not follow that the syntax is prose syntax; for concepts may be related in formally correct syntax when the relationship between them is not really syntactical at all, but musical, when words and phrases are notes in a melody, not terms in an ordered statement.

I would guess that English poets are led to acknowledge their duty to purify the language, where French poets are not, because in France the prose writer does this job where the English prose writer notoriously scamps it. Because in England the prose stylist is usually 'poetical', the poet has to become 'prosaic'. However this may be, it seems plain that the contemporary poet

1 Paul Valéry, 'Poetry and Abstract Thought', tr. Gerard Hopkins, in J. L. Hevesi (ed.), *Essays on Language and Literature* (Wingate, 1948), p. 97.

cannot, after all, agree with the late-Augustan poet about the relation of prose to poetry. It may be already too late for poetry to revert to the pre-symbolist attitude to syntax. For there are undoubtedly compensations to be derived from the dislocation of syntax, though they may not be those which, according to Mr Pound, overweighed the absence of the Aristotelian 'unfoldedness'. To dislocate syntax in the symbolist manner undoubtedly makes possible an unprecedented concentration of one kind of poetic pleasure. Less certainly it may, as certain of its adherents claim, provide for the communication of experiences too tenuous, fugitive or rarefied to be expressed in any of the older ways. On the other hand it may be doubted whether, unless syntax reappears in our poetry, we can say of it, as Bernard Manning says of Wesley's hymns, that 'congregations bred on such stuff should not suffer from flabbiness of thought'. For 'congregations' read 'publics'; and it will be doubtful whether, after all, Mr Eliot has purified the language as Dr Johnson did, or whether any poet in the symbolist tradition can do so. Finally, of course, one cannot avoid the fact that the poet's churches are empty, and the strong suspicion that dislocation of syntax has much to do with it. After all, there is no denying that modern poetry is obscure and that it would be less so if the poets adhered to the syntax of prose.

Changes in linguistic habit are related to changes in man's outlook and hence, eventually, to changes in human conduct. Language does not merely reflect such changes; a change in language may precede the other changes, and even help to bring them about. To abandon syntax in poetry is not to start or indulge a literary fashion; it is to throw away a tradition central to human thought and conduct, as to human speech. Pound, at least, knew this and realized what he was doing. He discusses Erigena's remark that 'Authority is the possession of right reason':

You may assert in vindication of values registered in idiom itself that the man who 'isn't all there' has only a partial existence. But we are by that time playing with language? as valuable as playing tennis to keep oneself limber.

Even Erigena's dictum can be examined. Authority can in material or savage world come from accumulated prestige based on intuition. We have trust in a man because we have come to regard him (in his entirety) as sapient and well-balanced. We play his hunch. We make an act of faith. But this is not what Erigena meant, and in any case it does not act in contradiction to his statement, but only as an extension of it.

Shakespeare gets TO the far orientals because he does not shut his meaning into egg-shells. Or at least . . . picked up I can't remember where . . . the memory of an oriental viva voce defending Shakespeare's formlessness on the ground that he reached out and merged into nature.

One is here on very dangerous ground. The ideogram is in some way so much more definite, despite its root filaments, than a shell-case definition.[1]

One has to quote at some length, in order to consider more than one component of the 'prose ideogram'. The components here are, on the one hand, certain observations about language, on the other, observations about political conduct. It may be, as Pound says, that the relationship between these components can be truthfully expressed only as he has expressed it, 'in ideogram', but at least we can see that, in grasping what is common to them, we go to the heart of Pound's dilemma. By hunting his own sort of 'definiteness' (truth only in the particular) he is led to put his trust not in human institutions but in individuals. Similarly he pins his faith on individual words, grunts, broken phrases, half-uttered exclamations (as we find them in the *Cantos*), on speech atomized, all syllogistic and syntactical forms broken down. Hence his own esteem of the definite lands him at last in yawning vagueness, the 'intuitive' welcome to Mussolini (he 'plays his hunch'), or, elsewhere in *Guide to Kulchur*, the 'intuitive' perception of form as something over and above pigment, stone, chords, and notes, phrases and words.

It would be too much to say that this is the logical end of

1 *Guide to Kulchur*, pp. 165, 166.

abandoning prose syntax. But at least the development from imagism in poetry to fascism in politics is clear and unbroken. From a similar conviction about language and poetry Eliot has developed, not quite so obviously, to Royalism and Anglo-Catholicism. And yet it is impossible not to trace a connection between the laws of syntax and the laws of society, between bodies of usage in speech and in social life, between tearing a word from its context and choosing a leader out of the ruck. One could almost say, on this showing, that to dislocate syntax in poetry is to threaten the rule of law in the civilized community.

Once one has seen this connection between law in language and law in conduct, observations about the nature of language take on an awful importance, and one comes to see potential dangers in attitudes which seemed innocuous. Paul Valéry, for instance, seems almost excessively aware of his responsibilities towards language when he begins a discussion by 'cleansing the verbal situation'. And there is truth in the analogy he draws between choosing a form of words to express a personal insight and casting a vote in party politics:

> None of the available programmes ever fits precisely the needs of our temperament or the nature of our interests. By the mere fact of choosing one of them we gradually become the kind of man who fits the one particular set of proposals and the one particular party.[1]

But since he himself invites the political parallel, we have a right to ask him to pursue it. What, in these circumstances, is the rational course to take? Should one stand as an Independent? Should one refuse to use one's vote at all? Should one pin one's faith on an individual, a leader, and 'play his hunch'? Or should one merely choose as best one can, and not cast one's vote carelessly? In terms of language should one construct a private language? Should one trust the word and distrust the syntax, as

1 Valéry, *op. cit.*, p. 72.

Pound does? Or should one scrutinize accepted meanings and choose among them with all possible nicety?

Valéry does not answer these questions, but gives another metaphor instead. He remarks that a word such as 'Time', when 'used in the ordinary course of communication', is for the most part manageable; but can 'become almost magically embarrassing' when withdrawn from circulation and considered by itself. Language, then, he says, is like a plank across a crevasse, which will bear a man provided he does not loiter, or else like an issue of banknotes:

> Those pieces of paper have passed through many hands . . . But words, too, have passed through many mouths, have formed part of many phrases, have been so used and abused that only the most meticulous precautions will save us from falling into mental confusion, caught between what we think, or try to think, and what the dictionary, the tribe of authors, and, in general, the rest of mankind, have been striving, ever since the dawn of language, to make us think.[1]

This again is true, but perverse; for it seeks the more recondite difficulties and ignores those which are obvious. For if it is true that a word is a plank on which we must not loiter, may we assume that across a given crevasse there is nothing to choose between one plank or another? Or, if words are dirty notes, should it not be the first of our 'meticulous precautions' to see if the note is for ten shillings or a pound? To Valéry, we observe, the lexicographer is the enemy of the poet, whereas to Pound or Eliot, when they talk of Johnson, he is the natural ally. So he was in the seventeenth century:

> Since then, he made our language pure and good,
> And us to speak but what we understood,
> We owe this praise to him, that should we join
> To pay him, he were paid but with the coin
> Himself hath minted, which we know by this,

1 Ibid., p. 75.

That no words pass for current now but his.
And though he in a blinder age could change
Faults to perfections, yet 'twas far more strange
To see (however times, and fashions frame)
His wit and language still remain the same
In all men's mouths; grave preachers did it use
As golden pills, by which they might infuse
Their heavenly physic; ministers of state
Their grave dispatches in his language wrate;
Ladies made curt'sies in them, courtiers legs,
Physicians bills; – perhaps, some pedant begs
He may not use it, for he hears 'tis such,
As in few words a man may utter much.[1]
Could I have spoken in his language too,
I had not said so much, as now I do,
To whose clear memory I this tribute send,
Who dead's my Wonder, living was my Friend.[2]

It is true that ideas of lexicography have changed, and the dictionary is now expected to record usage, not to establish a standard of propriety. But there is no room for any sort of dictionary in the poet's library so long as we believe, with Valéry, that, since words are planks on which we must not loiter, 'we understand others . . . we understand *ourselves*, by not *dwelling on our words*'. From this point of view, for 'us to speak but what we understood', we ought to have given no thought to what we were saying.

This is, perhaps, to bear too hard on what is no more than a graceful paradox. There is a notable absence, in Valéry's writing as in Eliot's, of that 'ethical weight' which Pound esteemed in others, and which we may notice in him. But for all these important differences of tone, the three poets drive to the same conclusion. For Valéry's solution to the difficulties of communica-

1 An interesting example of the intimate connection between a pure diction and the 'strength' which is concentration and economy. See *ante*, pp. 54–60.

2 Sir John Beaumont, 'To the memory of him who can never be forgotten, Master Benjamin Jonson'.

tion is to draw a distinction 'when dealing with intellectual problems, between those that I have constructed for myself, those that express some genuine need felt by my mind, and those that are really only the problems of other people'.[1] This is the same distinction as that made by Pound when he says 'The chief justice had to think more soberly than the tutor or lecturer', and so goes on to dismiss the Greek syntax as a world well lost. Valéry, like Pound, judges an argument not by its coherence but by the weight of personal experience behind it; and to him, no doubt, as to Pound, syntax is a concession to coherence and a betrayal of the 'unsophisticated impulses and images which make up the raw material of my personal needs, my personal experience'.

He looks at poems in the same way:

> I am inclined, personally, to pay much more attention to the formulation and composition of a work of art than to the work itself, and it is my habit, which amounts almost to a mania, to appreciate such works only in terms of the activity that produces them.[2]

For a poet to make such an astonishing admission may be regarded as a *trahison des clercs* on the grand scale. Yet it is not without parallel; Pasternak, for instance, has declared that 'every poem describes its own birth'. This attitude produces works of which one can say, as I have said of *The Prelude*, that at no point do we move out of the poet's mind into the poem. And Mark van Doren is probably right when he maintains that *The Prelude* is the first of such poems. Pound's *Cantos* are of this kind. This poem is at once licentiously formless and austerely formal; for, as Yeats noted of the early Cantos, they go towards a poem which shall stand or fall as a whole, from which no part can be extracted, quoted, and argued over in itself. In that sense Pound's poem constitutes the most elaborately 'made thing' that modern

1 Valéry, op. cit., p. 75.
2 Ibid., p. 93.

poetry has yet seen. And yet this made thing, this artefact, is not the poem, the made thing that Sidney conceived of; not a poem as even *The Vanity of Human Wishes* is, something standing apart from and independent of its maker. For it invites, as *The Prelude* does, the admiring reflection, 'What an interesting mind he has'; not that older reaction, 'What an interesting thing to say'.[1]

It seems rather ludicrous to consider a collection of poems as if it were a substitute for Fowler's *Modern English Usage*. And yet it was not ludicrous to Sir John Beaumont. But of course no one will argue that the poem's existence in this capacity is in any way so important as in its other capacities, as communiqué and creation, as thing said and thing made. But the three functions hang together. As the language of poetry becomes more private and distinctive, the poem becomes less and less a manual of correct usage; but at the same time it becomes less and less a thing said and a thing made.

1 An interesting situation arises when we find, or think we find, a pre-Wordsworthian poet who meets our post-Wordsworthian expectations. This is the case of John Donne.

Conclusion to Part I

THIS book is an attempt to arrive at the principles underlying purity of poetic diction in English. It is not a historical survey of all English poetry that achieves or attempts such purity. I have taken most of my examples from the most obvious field, where such purity was most to be expected, in certain poetry of the eighteenth century. Though I have found examples in other periods, I am in no position to establish a standard for them as I have tried to do for part of the eighteenth century. And I might have to modify my account even of the principles if I had looked, from this point of view, at the difficult case of Milton, for example. Still, I am fairly confident that the principles governing this sort of writing are such as I have described.

At many stages in this enquiry I have been glad of the guidance of Mr T. S. Eliot, whether as critic or poet. It is part of his achievement, I think, that he has renovated in practice some of the principles I have grouped together under the heading of 'pure diction'. On the other hand, as I have tried to show in the last chapter, he has adopted only some of those principles, not all of them. It may be that he has done all that was practicable and renovated only so much as is appropriate to the present day. At any rate there are many other sides to what he has done, and indeed the other sides have been acknowledged more widely. Just for that reason, and because Mr Eliot's criticism has always been occasional, not systematic, many critics have invoked his authority for views of poetry which are as different as possible from mine. For that matter, I put forward no personal systematic view of poetry as a whole, but only of one kind of poetry which seems to me to have been neglected. There can be no question of my attacking the systems of others in order to erect my own. I can think of influential critics who have neglected what I will call for the moment my kind of poetry, but who would have no difficulty in fitting it into the systems they have erected or the views they hold. The case is rather different, however, with critics who go out of their way to deny it any status as poetry at all. And it is especially confusing when for their views they invoke the authority of Mr Eliot no less than I have done for mine.

This is the case, for instance, with Mr Cleanth Brooks:

T. S. Eliot has commented upon 'that perpetual slight alteration of language, words perpetually juxtaposed in new and sudden combinations', which occurs in poetry. It *is* perpetual; it cannot be kept out of the poem; it can only be directed and controlled. The tendency of science is necessarily to stabilize terms, to freeze them into strict denotations; the poet's tendency is by contrast disruptive. The terms are continually modifying each other, and thus violating their dictionary meanings. To take a very simple example, consider the adjectives in the first lines of Wordsworth's evening sonnet: *beauteous*, *calm*, *free*, *holy*, *quiet*, *breathless*. The juxtapositions are hardly startling; and yet notice this: the evening is like a nun breathless with adoration. The adjective 'breathless' suggests tremendous excitement; and yet the evening is not only quiet but calm. There is no final contradiction, to be sure; it is *that* kind of calm and *that* kind of excitement, and the two states may well occur together. But the poet has no one term. Even if he had a polysyllabic technical term, the term would not provide the solution for his problem. He must work by contradiction and qualification.[1]

There is no getting round this. Mr Brooks says as plainly as possible that the poet must never use one word where two will do. And so there can be no room in his view of poetry for the exactness, the economy and the concentration which go with the 'strength' of a pure diction. Where there is such head-on collision

1 *The Well Wrought Urn* (Dobson, 1949), pp. 8 and 9.

as this, there is not much point in arguing the matter. I think Mr Brooks is wrong, and that his view of poetry pushes to the extreme some quite common ideas which will drive the poet further than ever into a private wilderness and alienate more and more potential readers.

For it is, after all, to the would-be poet of today that I should like to address myself. I hope that no one who reads this book will see in it only a Quixotic preference for the pedestrian and the prosaic in English poetry. I readily admit the existence of some English poetry which is prosaic in this bad sense; many poems by John Byrom are of this sort. And on the other hand such a high-flown poem as Yeats's 'Ribh at the Tomb of Baile and Aillinn' is prosaic in the sense that it has 'the virtues of good prose'.

It is now several years since the most eminent of living English poets looked forward to a recrudescence of poetic diction in contemporary writing. I should like to think that this study might help some practising poet to a poetry of urbane and momentous statement.

PART II

I

Diction and Invention: A View of Wordsworth

WORDSWORTH was his own worst critic. Coleridge was right. The Preface to *Lyrical Ballads* is great literature; but it is great as a personal testament, not as criticism, or if as criticism then criticism at its most theoretical. It is not theoretical in the sense that Wordsworth did not know from personal experience what he was talking about. He did, of course; that is what is meant by calling it a testament. It is theoretical in the sense that it is wise about the nature and the function of poetry and poetic pleasure, and foolish about poetic techniques.

To be particular, Wordsworth invites us to approach his poems by considering their diction; whereas most of those poems bypass questions of diction altogether. For the question of diction only arises when a poem begs it. It is never perhaps indifferent, but it is often of little importance. In the eighteenth century this was generally acknowledged; Goldsmith, for instance, says that a chaste diction is less important in the sublime poem than in the pathetic. And it is notable that modern poets when they have approached the question have been forced to the same distinction.[1] We may well be reluctant to reopen an old controversy which proved so often sterile; but we need 'sublime', or something like it, to classify the many poems which merely avoid questions of diction altogether.

We can do so sufficiently for the present purpose by exhuming another critical term which has fallen into disuse. I mean the notion of 'invention', or finding. There are poems which are poetic by virtue of the finding and conduct of a fable, over and

1 J. M. Synge, Preface to *Poems and Translation* (1909).

above the poetry of their language. I am well aware of the dangers of this contention. It is always dangerous to divorce poetry from words and locate it in some air-drawn 'form'. Nevertheless, T. Sturge Moore is an example of the poet whose language is undistinguished, but whose powers of invention, at least in his longer works, are strikingly poetic. We can call a poem 'sublime' when it displays powers of invention so conspicuously that considerations of diction, while never indifferent, are of only minor moment.

Now Wordsworth is a conspicuous example of a poet in whom invention is so powerful that diction hardly ever matters. De Quincey said as much in a fine passage[1] when he hailed Wordsworth as above all a discoverer of new or forgotten truths. And of no part of Wordsworth's work is this so true as of *Lyrical Ballads*. Wordsworth was technically incompetent at least until 1801, when he seems to have put himself to school with Chaucer, Shakespeare and Milton. By luck or genius (they amount to the same thing) he had before that hit upon some primitive forms which could just sustain what he had to say; and what he had found to say before that was so novel and surprising that it could carry the day. Even 'The Brothers' and 'Michael' are great in spite of, not because of, their language. And even so, luck failed him on occasions; for instance 'The Two Thieves' of 1800 displays a nobly poetical conception (similar to 'The Old Cumberland Beggar') thrown away in an inappropriate form. The early poems, when they succeed, do so by virtue of invention; the language is as nearly irrelevant as it can be in poetry.

After the turn of the century Wordsworth emerges, through some uncomfortable experiments, as a highly accomplished poet. He creates not one style, but many, according to what he needs to do. There is the style of the political sonnets; the style of *The Prelude*; and the style of the Immortality Ode. There are others,

1 *De Quincey's Literary Criticism* (ed. Darbishire, 1909), p. 234. Quoted *post*, p. 166.

but these are the most important. And each of these styles can be called a 'diction', in the sense of a private language, a distinctive vocabulary and turn of phrase. Wordsworth's own criticism had paved the way for this loose usage. And the shift in meaning is further obscured for us by the circumstance that some later poets, such as Arnold, made use of one or other of the Wordsworthian styles; so that we detect 'Wordsworth diction' in other poets.

But this use of diction, to mean a private language, is the very opposite of the older one, by which it was 'the perfection of a common language'. It is only the latter of which one can say that it is pure or impure. And this is a diction which hardly ever appears in Wordsworth's work. The question of purity does not arise. Almost to the end what matters in Wordsworth is his invention, his astonishing discoveries about human sentiments. As he pieced his discoveries together into systems, he had to learn his trade and master techniques more elaborate and sophisticated than those which had served him in *Lyrical Ballads*. But at no time does the question of pure or impure diction enter into the matter.

After all, how could it? A pure diction embodies urbanity; a vicious diction offers to do that, and fails. But Wordsworth was not interested in urbanity, and had no faith in it; he pledged himself to its opposite, a determined provincialism. He spoke as a solitary, not as a spokesman; urbanity was none of his business, nor diction either. It is one way of explaining what went wrong with Wordsworth's poetry, in his later life, to say that as recognition came to him, he saw himself more and more as, after all, a spokesman of national sentiment.[1] No poet was less fitted, by training and temperament, for such a role; and no poet's art was so unsuitable for carrying it.

1 Quite early in Wordsworth's career he began to produce patriotic sonnets on the Miltonic model, in which he aimed to express national sentiment. Some of these are widely admired; but it is an enthusiasm which I cannot share.

There are two or three exceptions. The most important is *The White Doe of Rylstone.* It is a poem which will never be popular, because it does without so many attractions incidental and usual in poetry. Alone of all Wordsworth's poems, it requires of the reader that he come to terms with the famous contention that 'There neither is, nor can be, any essential difference between the language of prose and of metrical composition'. In the Preface to *Lyrical Ballads*, Wordsworth's views on diction are so ill-considered that, to the reader baffled by *The White Doe of Rylstone*, they can still give little assistance. But they are far more pertinent to that poem than to any of the ballads.

The verse form of *The White Doe* has been variously defined as derived from Scott and from Virgil. More probably, I think, the model was Samuel Daniel. A prefatory note to 'Yarrow Visited' implies that Wordsworth read Daniel about the time he was reading Chaucer, soon after the turn of the century. Now Daniel was the poet selected by Coleridge, when he discussed Wordsworth's style, to exemplify the genuinely and culpably prosaic in verse:

> Ten Kings had from the Norman Conqu'ror reign'd
> With intermix'd and variable fate,
> When England to her greatest height attain'd
> Of power, dominion, glory, wealth, and state;
> After it had with much ado sustain'd
> The violence of princes, with debate
> For titles and the often mutinies
> Of nobles for their ancient liberties.
>
> For first, the Norman, conqu'ring all by might,
> By might was forced to keep what he had got;
> Mixing our customs and the form of right
> With foreign constitutions, he had brought;
> Mast'ring the mighty, humbling the poorer wight,
> By all severest means that could be wrought;
> And, making the succession doubtful, rent
> His new-got state, and left it turbulent.

These are two of the stanzas quoted from Daniel by Coleridge; and it would be hard to find in English poetry another passage so similar as this from *The White Doe*:

> It was the time when England's Queen
> Twelve years had reigned, a Sovereign dread;
> Nor yet the restless crown had been
> Disturbed upon her virgin head;
> But now the inly-working North
> Was ripe to send its thousands forth,
> A potent vassalage, to fight
> In Percy's and in Neville's right,
> Two Earls fast leagued in discontent,
> Who gave their wishes open vent;
> And boldly urged a general plea,
> The rites of ancient piety
> To be triumphantly restored,
> By the stern justice of the sword!
> And that same Banner on whose breast
> The blameless Lady had exprest
> Memorials chosen to give life
> And sunshine to a dangerous strife;
> That Banner, waiting for the Call,
> Stood quietly in Rylstone-hall.

It seems likely that those who dislike *The White Doe* as prosaic can call upon the authority of Coleridge.

And yet the comparison is unjust. For if Wordsworth's verse has 'the virtues of good prose' (as Daniel's has), it has also a felicitous concentration that can only be called poetic. That Wordsworth's account of the reasons for the Rising of the North should tally with the findings of modern historians is interesting, but not so important as the consistency and conciseness of his treatment. A modern editor[1] has drawn attention to the propriety of 'inly-working', pithily characterizing the compli-

1 Alice Pattee Comparetti, *The White Doe of Rylstone* (Cornell, 1940), p. xxix

cated discontents which were at work. Dynastic and personal quarrels lay behind the insurrection and were the cause of it at least as much as the stubborn adherence to the Old Faith. Wordsworth's acknowledgement of this colours his whole treatment, and gives an ironic aptness, for instance, to his account of the banner. Embroidered with the Cross and the wounds of Christ, it was to give 'life and sunshine to a dangerous strife'; 'sunshine' is played off against the 'inly-working', expressing the symbolic with the actual function of the flag, and throwing on the whole enterprise the shadow of divided loyalties and coming doom. More, the theme of the whole poem, the hard-won serenity of the abandoned lady, symbolized in her creature, the doe, is an example of just such 'inly-working'.

In the verse of *The White Doe of Rylstone*, Wordsworth achieved, as nowhere else in a poem of any length, a pure diction, a speech of civilized urbanity which can 'purify the language of the tribe'. Of course the poem exhibits only one mode of such a diction, the mode proper to the peculiar purpose of historical narrative, and to the correspondent tone, neither elevated nor intimate, of the so-called 'mean style'. This is a staple verse and does not lend itself to purple passages, though Coleridge, who thought Wordsworth a poet of purple passages, claimed to find one. Throughout, the verse maintains one level of subdued excellence. There are impurities,[1] but they are few. The verse of *The White Doe*, a poem which Wordsworth believed to be 'in conception, the highest work he had ever produced', answers to the programme announced in the Preface to *Lyrical Ballads*; but not to the programme which Coleridge would have substituted. It is notable, for instance, that the poem avoids

1 An example of such 'impurity' may help – lines 720–21:

> Like those eight Sons – who, in a ring,
> (Ripe men, or blooming in life's spring)

– where the second line is too 'literary'. Wordsworth tried to change it in 1827, but returned to this version in the 1837 text.

personification and generalization, those components of the diction which Wordsworth rejected. Miss Comparetti has shown that *The White Doe* depends upon an abstraction, upon the 'melancholy' not of Shakespeare and Robert Burton, nor of Matthew Arnold, but of Thomson and Gray, the Miltonic 'melancholy' which is strong and composed. The poem depends on that notion; but, true to his principles, Wordsworth eschews all reference to it as a personified abstraction, and embodies it instead in the symbolic or emblematic figure of 'the doe'. By so doing he reaped just the benefits which he had promised himself. For Melancholy had been handled so often by the decadent poets of the sensibility-cult that in its form as a personified abstraction it was unmanageable to any serious ends; Wordsworth, adopting a diction which did not permit him to personify, was able to make the Miltonic melancholy once again a respectable topic and a moral force.

I have called the doe 'a symbolic or emblematic figure'. One hesitates to find in the doe the force of a symbol; and yet it is hard to say that it is anything else. Wordsworth was right when he compared it with the 'milk-white lamb' in *The Faerie Queene*. *The White Doe* is a thoroughly Spenserian poem. For all the great difference between Spenser's opulent rhetoric and the sobriety of Wordsworth's language, although the structure has none of Spenser's complexity, although Wordsworth does not think in Spenser's terms, we infer a marked similarity between the ways of thought and feeling which produced the two poems. Wordsworth speaks of Una's lamb as 'that emblem'; and there is no need to quarrel about terms. If the doe is symbolic, it is so as Una's lamb is, or Dryden's hind, or the statue of Hermione in *The Winter's Tale*. These figures seem to arise from conceptions dwelt upon so intently that they assume at last a wraithlike substance and life. They are quite different from such recognized 'symbols' as Perdita–Marina, the girl lost and found, or Blake's Little Boy Lost, or Wordsworth's own man upon the moor who stands or strides or sits, wreathed in mist, through poem after poem. These others are the images which walk about the poet's mind, asking to be explained. The poetry which uses them is a poetry of wise passiveness; the poetry which uses symbols of the other kind is a work of will, of contrivance and persistence, not a finding but a making.

The poem cannot be appreciated until we realize this effort of will behind it, and the internal tension which that produces. On a first reading it appears innocent of compression, concentration, contrast or irony. There seems to be no tension, whether in the eddying narrative or the fluent language. This impression must persist until the reader can cultivate an ear or a palate for diction, for a central purity; then the tension appears, in our awareness of the words that have been left out. Because the tone is less elevated, it is easy to miss the point that the poem is written in a choice language, as *The Deserted Village* is, or *The Task*. Once we appreciate that, the poem takes its place in the line of activity inaugurated by the 'Ode to Duty' or, even earlier, in 'Resolution and Independence'. In these poems Wordsworth acknowledges that the first springs of his creativeness have dried up, and that what comes after can be no longer buoyant with invention, with new discoveries given, but must be worked for, with self-discipline. At least this is the implication for his art of the changes Wordsworth announces in his morality. Will and duty are to take the place of idleness and spontaneity. Perhaps Wordsworth misjudged the situation or his own temperament; at any rate the new programme was much poorer than the old one, from the point of view of the poems it produced. And one is inclined to agree with Dr Leavis that 'the Wordsworth who in the "Ode to Duty" spoke of the "genial sense of youth" as something he happily surrendered had seen the hiding-places of his power close'.[1] But *The White Doe of Rylstone* seems to me one poem in which the new programme justified itself. The heroine is herself the embodiment of resolution, endurance, and the will

1 *Revaluation*, p. 183.

kept at a stretch: for all her exclusively passive role (here is the paradox, the pathos, and most of the interest), the lady, by embracing that role as a duty, makes of it something active, resolute and noble. This is Wordsworth's original and compelling variation on the theme of Miltonic melancholy. And apart from this, regarded from the poet's point of view, *The White Doe* itself is similarly an achievement of resolution, effort and self-denying endurance. It is the most absolutely 'made' thing that Wordsworth ever produced. It is free-standing, in its own right; not, like *The Prelude* or, to a lesser degree, *The Excursion*, taking half of its strength along the cord which still connects the poem to its parent. *The White Doe* is impersonal and self-contained, thrown free of its creator with an energy he never compassed again. He tried again, but with little success, in 'Laodamia'.

II

Coleridge and Improvised Diction

> Your poem must eternal be,
> Dear Sir! it cannot fail!
> For 'tis incomprehensible,
> And without head or tail.

THUS Coleridge, 'To the author of "The Ancient Mariner"'. It is a silly rhyme, for 'The Ancient Mariner' has both head and tail, and in fact is one of the best constructed poems of the Romantic Revival. The architectural analogy is out of fashion; and 'construction' and 'form' have been suspect in criticism since 1928: 'Construction, Design, Form, Rhythm, Expression ... are more often than not mere *vacua* in discourse, for which a theory of criticism should provide explainable substitutes.'[1] I am not aware that the substitutes have appeared. A poem exists in printed space and reading time, and with some poems we feel that the space and time they occupy are not chosen at random, but are exactly or nearly right, or too little, or too much. We may feel further that the several components of a poem are given too much or too little room, as when we say that the stanza chosen is too short, or that the exposition takes up too much time, or that a theme would be better in another place. 'The Ancient Mariner' begs such questions as these, and so one can say that it is well or ill formed, well or badly constructed.

There are other poems by Coleridge which challenge the same kind of judgement, notably the little haunting allegories such as 'Time, Real and Imaginary' and a beautiful love-poem, 'The

1 I. A. Richards, *Principles of Literary Criticism*, p. 20. (Routledge, 1926)

Happy Husband'; but most of his better known poems evade such questions. They are truly formless, precisely amorphous. And if this amorphousness was deliberate (as I think it was), the poet's intention explains much that is peculiar in his diction.

That the diction is peculiar will hardly be denied:

> Her front sublime and broad,
> Her flexible eyebrows wildly haired and low,
> And her full eye, now bright, now unillumed,
> Spake more than Woman's thought . . .

These lines are from 'The Destiny of Nations', written in 1796, the year before 'The Ancient Mariner' and two years after 'Lewti'. It is certainly a poor poem, but not so poor that we can dismiss the vicious diction as the bungling of one who knew no better. In its very excess it seems wilful. That, at any rate, was the opinion of C. H. Herford, writing of the 'Religious Musings': 'And though the manner swells too loftily, partly under the infection of Schiller's *Robbers*, and the style bristles with daring neologisms, marks of the literary rebel, yet the poetic material chaotically strewn on the page is very rich . . .'[1] The impurity of diction is thrust before our eyes in such words (from 'Religious Musings') as 'contemplant', 'operant', 'unsensualized', 'imbreathe', 'twy-streaming', 'rapture-trembling', 'toy-bewitched', 'sure-refuged'. And Coleridge later apologized for his 'profusion of double epithets', 'general turgidness', 'the swell and glitter both of thought and diction'[2] and 'a too ornate, and elaborately poetic diction'.[3] But the real perversity of the language is only to be seen in the dislocation of normal syntax and word order, in a style as eccentric as Milton's but less consistent. And it occurs in such a way as to seem (precisely) a perversity, a wilful ugliness, not the simple result of knowing no better.

1 C. H. Herford, *The Age of Wordsworth 1798–1832* (1897), p. 172.

2 See Coleridge's Preface to the *Collected Poems*, 1st and 2nd editions.

3 *Literary Life*, i, 51, quoted as footnote to the Preface.

According to Herford the piece is not only unchaste but chaotic. And Coleridge admits as much in his title. What is one to make of a poem with a plural title? Is it one thing or several, a cycle or a series? The difficulty is ever present as one reads Coleridge. 'Kubla Khan' is a fragment; *Christabel* a torso; others are better described as 'pieces of poetry' than as 'poems'. Coleridge talks, to himself or to others, and we 'listen in'. In all these cases, I think, we tacitly agree that we are listening to Coleridge talking, not to a poetic statement, but to a section cut from a stream of talk. Coleridge again admitted as much when he called 'The Nightingale' a 'conversation poem'. And in 'The Improvisatore' we see the poem actually emerging out of conversation.

In this curious piece, subtitled 'John Anderson, my Jo, John', and in some editions called 'New Thoughts on Old Subjects', the Friend is engaged in conversation by two young women and, when fully launched on his stream of discourse, he modulates out of prose into verse. The improviser was a heroic figure of the Romantic movement through Europe. He provides the title for an early novel by Hans Andersen. Mickiewicz was a famous improviser and uses the figure in *Forefathers' Eve*. Pushkin used him elaborately in 'Egyptian Nights'. He belongs with the Aeolian Harp and the Upas Tree, amid the characteristic furniture of the Romantic Age. He could be used in many ways. He embodied the spontaneity of poetic creation. He strained himself, in inventing against the clock, and so embodied the view of poetry as a sort of painful possession. He was a professional entertainer, and so he could be used, as by Pushkin, to lay bare the relationship between the Romantic poet and his society. In the present connection what matters most about the cult of the improviser is the most obvious thing about him: he makes it up as he goes along, and 'it', therefore, the thing he makes, is not a poem, a statement, having shape and finality, but a piece of poetry, the record of a visitation, the section of a flow of talk, a spasm or a series of spasms. The poetry which tries to seem improvised will be spasmodic; a consistent tone of discourse will not be wanted in such poetry, any more than the consistent development of a single theme. It follows that, in such poetry, a pure diction will not be merely irrelevant, but positively unwanted.

This is one of the most momentous changes in the history of poetry. It marks the disappearance of the Renaissance conviction about the poem as a made thing, thrown free of its maker, something added to creation and free-standing in its own right. The poet hereafter is legislator, seer, scapegoat and reporter; he is no longer an artificer. And from this time forward 'artificial' is a term of dispraise whereas to Sidney and Puttenham and Gabriel Harvey it had been the highest praise. Now 'artificial' is opposed to 'natural' where before it had belonged with it:

Verum id est maxime naturale, quod fieri natura optime patitur.[1]

This glorification of the natural, and its equation with the spontaneous, the amorphous, the artless and the personal, is still a potent force in the writing and reading of poetry; so much so that it is still impossible to see this revolution in perspective. Plainly much was lost and something was gained; it is still impossible to balance the profit and loss. Meanwhile, though some poems appeared which were still consummately 'made', the Romantic age is inevitably rich in fragments, pieces of poetry rather than poems, and preludes to poems that were never written. The schoolboy says that the Romantics rebelled against form. He is often corrected – the Romantics, we say, rebelled against certain existent forms, and substituted others of their own. And of course so they did. But the schoolboy is right, all the same; at times the Romantics rebelled not only against the forms they inherited, but against all forms, form as such.

Between amorphous poems and impure diction the connection is obvious. It is one function of a pure diction to maintain a

1 'In truth that is most natural which Nature permits best to realize itself.'

consistent tone of discourse throughout a poem. Where a poem in that sense is not wanted, but only a passage of poetic thought, the diction is wilfully dislocated to mark the spasmodic nature of the whole. We need a complete poem to see how the two work together:

TO A FRIEND, WHO HAD DECLARED HIS INTENTION OF WRITING NO MORE POETRY

Dear Charles! whilst yet thou wert a babe, I ween
That Genius plung'd thee in that wizard fount
Hight Castalie: and (sureties of thy faith)
That Pity and Simplicity stood by,
And promis'd for thee, that thou shouldst renounce
The world's low cares and lying vanities,
Steadfast and rooted in the heavenly Muse,
And wash'd and sanctified to Poesy.
Yes – thou wert plung'd, but with forgetful hand
Held, as by Thetis erst her warrior son:
And with those recreant unbaptizéd heels
Thou'rt flying from thy bounden minist'ries –
So sore it seems and burthensome a task
To weave unwithering flowers! But take thou heed:
For thou art vulnerable, wild-eyed boy,
And I have arrows mystically dipped,
Such as may stop thy speed. Is thy Burns dead?
And shall he die unwept, and sink to earth
'Without the meed of one melodious tear'?
Thy Burns, and Nature's own belovéd bard,
Who to the 'Illustrious of his native Land
So properly did look for patronage.'
Ghost of Maecenas! hide thy blushing face!
They snatch'd him from the sickle and the plough –
To gauge ale-firkins.
Oh! for shame return!
On a bleak rock midway the Aonian mount
There stands a lone and melancholy tree,
Whose agéd branches to the midnight blast

> Make solemn music: pluck its darkest bough,
> Ere yet the unwholesome night-dew be exhaled,
> And weeping wreath it round thy Poet's tomb.
> Then in the outskirts, where pollutions grow,
> Pick the rank henbane and the dusky flowers
> Of night-shade, or its red and tempting fruit,
> These with stopped nostril and glove-guarded hand
> Knit in nice intertexture, so to twine,
> The illustrious brow of Scotch Nobility!

The poem is certainly wayward. Considered as a poem about Burns, it occupies itself for half its length on an introduction to the theme which is no introduction at all since, even after so much, the transition to the name of Burns is very abrupt. Even within that section there is no connection between the embarrassed Spenserian diction of the opening and the fantastic conceit of the heels by which Charles was dipped in Castaly, as Achilles in another fount by Thetis, and with which he now flies from his duty. But when we reach the end of the paragraph, and the withering contempt in the drop from elevated diction to 'ale-firkins', we realize that the abrupt transitions and the spasmodic development are part and parcel with the veering, swerving tone, and the condition of the poet's achieving the contempt he wants. The same deliberate bathos is contrived to the same effect at the end of the second paragraph. And one is left with the solitary criticism that the convention is not sufficiently established from the first. In other words, the Spenserian diction of the first lines should be even more grotesque than it is.

In the eighteenth century poets had known how to exploit bathos, but never to this effect. Coleridge's bathos has nothing to do with the mock-heroic. He achieves a contempt as withering as Pope's, but by quite different means. And I think it is even more caustic. For Sporus was immortalized; the gentry of the Caledonian Hunt are dismissed to limbo. Coleridge in fact – it is a commonplace – had to express experiences, thoughts and feelings for which he could find no room in existent poetic forms. It may be doubted, though, whether some of them could be expressed in poetic form at all, at least if we give any weight to 'form'.

'Dejection' is one of the great poems in the language. It is a true poem, not a piece of poetry; a made thing, not a snatch of talk. And it is no accident that Coleridge in his title should seek the sanction of a traditional form, the Horatian ode. The poem seeks that sanction and obtains it. It came, as we now know, from a harrowing personal predicament; yet the voice which speaks it is impersonal and timeless, the voice of a language, the voice of Man, of no one and everyone. It goes without saying, after this, that the diction is pure. It has none of the characteristic devices, personification and the rest. But the diction is pure as Johnson's is, because it mediates between conversation and rhetoric, and because it embodies an urbanity. The point is made already when we call it impersonal, the voice of a language:

> Well! If the Bard was weather-wise, who made
> The grand old ballad of Sir Patrick Spence,
> This night, so tranquil now, will not go hence
> Unroused by winds, that ply a busier trade
> Than those which mould yon cloud in lazy flakes,
> Or the dull sobbing draft, that moans and rakes
> Upon the strings of this Aeolian lute,
> Which better far were mute.

This extraordinary sentence achieves in little all that the poem does. It is largely a matter of syntax. The sentence, coiling through eight lines, brings together moods and ideas which would seem incompatible did we not see them living together easily in one logical structure. The first two lines are positively jaunty, with a cracked gaiety which only betrays itself five lines later when it breaks into the depression which underlies it. At the same time the external wind and the inward rush of thought come together, not by metaphor nor in the conventional 'Aeolian' (for by that time the fusion has happened) but again by syntax. In the same way, and as part of the same process, the near-colloquialism of the first lines moves, not veering abruptly but as if inevitably, into the elevated rhetoric of 'the dull sobbing draft, that moans and rakes/Upon the strings'. The two poles of the diction are thus established, and the poem slides eloquently between them into the key which is to govern the whole. The struggle with the medium issues in a moral conquest. For the purity thus established is a sign of good breeding, and this is essential to a poem which is to deal in intimate matters, taboo in normal discourse, where the speaker continually skirts self-pity. The diction is sustained and he never steps over. It is permissible to call this a profound urbanity.

'Dejection', then, is a poem consummately 'made', and far from improvisation. Yet one may think that it owes something to the deliberately improvised pieces that stand near to it in the history of Coleridge's verse. The first personal version, printed by Professor de Selincourt, is interesting in this connection, quite apart from its poignancy as a human document. To go no further than the lines quoted, the swiftness of startling transition at the very start of the poem almost certainly owes something to such experiments in abrupt changes of mood and in harsh changes of wilfully eccentric diction. And a conservative can make the point that Coleridge proved himself in the wrong. At least once he found elastic enough those traditional laws of form and diction, and accommodated in them the new experiences which had seemed to demand new forms and new diction, or even the disappearance of form and diction altogether.

Coleridge's experiments in amorphous poetry and dislocated diction can be compared to some purpose with the *tour de force* of Romantic improvisation, *Don Juan*. Byron too is the improvisatore and with him, too, the experiment takes the same form, a deliberate courting of impurities in diction:

> He that reserves his laurels for posterity
> (Who does not often claim the bright reversion)

> Has generally no great crop to spare it, he
> Being only injured by his own assertion;
> And although here and there some glorious rarity
> Arise like Titan from the sea's immersion,
> The major part of such appellants go
> To – God knows where – for no one else can know.

'Is there no bright reversion in the sky . . .?' Fragments from Pope gleam, like spars from a shipwrecked world, all about the tumultuous sea of Byron's verse, a criterion acknowledged but no longer to the point, thrown with a sort of desperate jocularity into this poem which veers crazily in rhyme and diction and movement about the poet's inexhaustible mind. For here the poem as artefact has utterly disappeared. However long we read we are never into the poem and out of the poet's mind. The two have become one, as in *The Prelude*.

Byron, of course, 'caught on', as Coleridge never did. And ever since 'urbanity' has meant the manner of Don Juan, an assurance never occupied but only acknowledged as the poet veers past it, a sort of raffish insouciance, above all a pervasive irony. After this a poet can write about nothing, and defend himself with irony. A poet has only one subject – himself. And so long as he quizzes himself, we cannot complain. For this is civilization, maturity, urbanity – the quizzical stance.

Of course this is unfair. It is not so easy to write a poem like *Don Juan*. No one has done it since Byron, or not on such a scale. But it is true that the amorphous poem, the improvisation, is drastically limited in tone after *Don Juan*. The sublime poems continue. But in poems about human affairs the Byronic irony is hard to avoid, even today. In Coleridge's hands the amorphous poem had a far wider range of mood, but it is a range which we have lost. We can only choose between traditional forms (the diction goes with them) and, on the other hand, a deprecating wit.

III

Shelley's Urbanity

(i) *The Shelleyan Sublime*

HOWEVER we look at it, Shelley affects the sublime. We may not know what the sublime is, and yet know that, to be acceptable, it must include *The Triumph of Life* and *Prometheus Unbound.* Whatever we think of these poems (and the latter at any rate makes dull reading in my experience), there can be no doubt how high the poet aims in them, what large pretensions he makes. In short, whatever his performance, Shelley promises in these poems to move on a level where (for instance) 'urbanity' cannot count.

But this is what makes criticism of Shelley so difficult; he evades so many standards. In this he is peculiar even among the poets of the sublime. His sublimity is peculiarly indefinite and impalpable. From one point of view his poetry is certainly sensuous; but the sensuousness is not of a sort to bring into poetry the reek and grit of common experience. For Shelley goes as far as poetry can go, while it uses intelligible language, in cutting the hawsers which tie his fancies to the ground. His metaphors are tied so tenuously to any common ground in experience that it is peculiarly hard to arrive at their mooring in common logic or association. It was this, for instance, which gave Mr Eliot so much trouble with an image in 'To a Skylark':

> Keen as are the arrows
>   Of that silver sphere,
> Whose intense lamp narrows
>   In the white dawn clear
> Until we hardly see – we feel that it is there.

It is typical of Shelley's obscurity that, as it happens, I find no difficulty here, but only the accurate register of a sense-perception[1] – the fading of the morning star. For Shelley evades as many standards as he can and when he cannot evade them, makes their application as difficult as he can; or so it must seem to the harrassed critic. And as a result we can expect to find the critics even further than usual from agreement about the nature of his achievement. All one can say is that the period of uncritical adulation is past, and that we have learnt, since Dr Leavis's damaging scrutiny,[2] to be on our guard when Shelley is most sublime.

At any rate, if Shelley is great, in *Prometheus Unbound*, in *The Triumph of Life*, even in such shorter poems as 'The Cloud', he is so by virtue of *invention*, the characteristic virtue of the sublime. And the eighteenth-century critics would agree that in poems of this sort the poet has considerable licence. We can expect (and it is only right) that the diction of an epic or a hymn will be less chaste than the diction of a familiar epistle. And we can go so far as to say that in the case of such poems the question of diction should not be introduced at all. But this is not quite true. There are always limits. As Keats remarked, 'English must be kept up' – even in the epic. And Shelley, as usual, goes to the limit, or over it.

'The Cloud' is a good example:

> Sublime on the towers of my skiey bowers,
>   Lightning my pilot sits;
> In a cavern under is fettered the thunder,
>   It struggles and howls at fits;

1 Cf. from 'Ode to Naples':

> The isle-sustaining ocean-flood,
> A plane of light between two heavens of azure.

2 *Revaluation*, pp. 203–40.

> Over earth and ocean, with gentle motion,
> This pilot is guiding me,
> Lured by the love of the genii that move
> In the depths of the purple sea;
> Over the rills, and the crags, and the hills,
> Over the lakes and the plains,
> Wherever he dream, under mountain or stream,
> The Spirit he loves remains;
> And I all the while bask in Heaven's blue smile,
> Whilst he is dissolving in rains.

The image is audacious to begin with. There is no reason in natural philosophy to give a basis in logic to the notion that a cloud is directed by electric charges. The image depends entirely on association, and the leap of association is something of a strain. However, it is made easier by the elaboration which makes the thunder a prisoner in the dungeons of the cloud. Natural philosophy lends its aid to the logical association of a cloud with the genii of the sea; and the lightning is supposed amorous of the sea – a link sanctioned by neither logic nor association (however 'free'), but carried as it were on the cloud's back. The real difficulty comes with the 'he', appearing three times in the last six lines. Is this 'he' the lightning, the actual cloud, or the idea of the cloud which is always present even in a cloudless sky? We are given no indication that this 'he' is any other than 'the pilot', i.e. the lightning. And yet this is surely impossible in the last two lines:

> And I all the while bask in Heaven's blue smile,
> Whilst he is dissolving in rains.

Shelley means to say, I think, that the ideal cloud continues to bask while the actual cloud, dissolves in rains; but in fact he says that the cloud, ideal or actual, rides high, while the lightning dissolves. And this is lunacy.

The fault here lies in the conduct and development of a metaphor, not, in the first place, in choice of language. And yet the two cannot be distinguished since the metaphor only comes to grief on the loose use of a personal pronoun. This looseness occurs time and again:

> The stars peep behind her and peer;
> And I laugh to see them whirl and flee,
> Like a swarm of golden bees,
> When I widen the rent in my wind-built tent,
> Till the calm rivers, lakes, and seas,
> Like strips of the sky fallen through me on high,
> Are each paved with the moon and these.

The grotesque 'and these' is an affront to all prosaic discipline. So again:

> I am the daughter of Earth and Water,
> And the nursling of the Sky;
> I pass through the pores of the ocean and shores;
> I change but I cannot die.

– where 'ocean and shores' is unthinkable in speech or prose. And finally:

> From cape to cape, with a bridge-like shape,
> Over a torrent sea,
> Sunbeam-proof, I hang like a roof, –
> The mountains its columns be.

Here the language is quite indiscriminate; the adjectival 'torrent' is a Latinate urbanity, 'sunbeam-proof' is an audacious coining, and 'The mountains . . . be' is a *naïveté*.

Obviously the conduct of the metaphor in the second stanza is a more serious flaw than any of these later examples. And obviously too, Shelley pitches his poem in a high key, to advise us not to expect nicety of discrimination and prosaic sense. The poem offers compensations. But all the same, when the barbarities are so brutal and the carelessness so consistent, it may be doubted whether we can let them pass on any understanding. In poems of this sort the weight to be given to diction and invention respectively is something that must be left to the taste of the reader. But this may serve as an example of how, even in sublime poems, the poet may take such liberties with his diction as to estrange his reader's sympathies. For one reader, at any rate, 'The Cloud' remains a poem splendid in conception but ruined by licentious phrasing.

(ii) *Shelley and the Familiar Style*

THIS does not dispose of Shelley's pretensions to sublimity. They confuse at almost every point the issue of his diction. In reading Wordsworth it is comparatively easy to distinguish the 'sublime' poems from the others, and to say that this poem begs the question of diction, this other does not. In the case of Shelley this is not so easily done. And yet there are poems by Shelley which plainly make no sublime pretensions. It was Ernest de Selincourt, I think, who proposed Shelley as one of the masters of the familiar style. The term, like all those which we find we need, is out of fashion; but plainly it refers to a quality of tone, of unflurried ease between poet and reader, in short to urbanity, the distinctive virtue of a pure diction.

It is worth remarking how unlikely this was in the period when Shelley wrote. Plainly urbanity will come most easily to a poet who is sure of his audience, sure that he and his reader share a broad basis of conviction and assumption. The whole pressure of Shelley's age was against anything of the kind. Urbanity, except in the raffish version of Byron and Praed, was out of fashion among critics and readers; but that was the least of the difficulties. In the Elizabethan, the Caroline and the Augustan ages, the poet moved in a society more or less stable and more or less in agreement about social propriety. Most poets moved in circles where manners were ceremonious. The courteous usages were mostly hypocritical, but at least they were consistent; and they furnished the poet with a model urbanity which he could preserve in the tone of his writing. This was as true of the ponderous decorum of Mrs Thrale's drawing-room as of the elaborate frivolity of the court of Charles II. Presumably the violent dislocation of English society at the end of the eighteenth century (the Industrial Revolution) had destroyed the established codes of social behaviour. At any rate, in the Godwin household, in the family of Leigh Hunt, in the extraordinary domestic arrangements of Lord Byron, personal suffering and passion broke through into conversation and social demeanour. These were people who lived on their nerves, whom an established code of behaviour no longer protected. Therefore we cannot expect to find in the poetry of 1820 the exquisite assurance, the confident communication between poet and reader, which dignifies the slightest pieces of Thomas Carew or Thomas Parnell. We cannot expect it; but we find it. It is only natural that Spenser and Dryden, Carew and Parnell, enjoy this assurance. It is anything but natural – it seems almost impossible – that Shelley should do so.

The familiar style in this sense derives from the mean style of the Elizabethans, distinguished by them from the high style, proper to the heroic poem and the hymn, and from the base style of satire and pastoral. It is related, too, to what Coleridge, in *Biographia Literaria*, called the 'neutral' style. It is distinguished from the other styles, in the nineteenth century as in the sixteenth, by being comparatively prosaic. Now, according to Johnson, a diction was pure when it was sanctioned by speech usage on the one hand, and by literary precedent (classic and neo-classic) on the other. The poet's needs tugged him now one way, now the other; to tread a middle course, in touch with both sorts of usage, was to write a pure diction. But as the literary models varied (Juvenal for satire, Virgil for epic), so did the spoken models. The speech of a cobbler was not the model for epic, nor the speech of bishops for satire. There survived, in fact, though mostly unacknowledged, Puttenham's rule that the model for the high style was the speech of courtiers and governors; for the mean style, the speech of merchants and yeomen; for the base style, the speech of peasants and menial trades. In theory Wordsworth ignored the other criterion, literary precedent, and, as Coleridge confusedly saw, came near to asserting that the only permissible style was the mean. In any of the styles, to maintain a pure diction was to preserve 'the tone of the centre' which Arnold was to esteem in Attic prose. It is one way of explaining 'the sublime' to say that, as England in the eighteenth century became a bourgeois state, the spoken model for the high style disappeared, and in poetry which 'affected the sublime' (the Augustan version of the high style) the question whether the diction was pure became meaningless. We are usually asked to acknowledge that Shelley's greatest poetry was of this sort. But there are other poems which are in the base and the mean styles; and it is among these that we have to look for Shelley the master of the familiar style.

The clearest example of Shelley's base style is the 'Letter to Maria Gisborne'. If we continue to talk in terms of Elizabethan decorum, this corresponds to *The Shepheardes Calender*, as 'Julian and Maddalo', in the mean style, to *Colin Clouts Come Home Again*, as 'The Cloud', in the high style, to *Fowre Hymnes*. Shelley himself invites the Spenserian parallel:

> Near those a most inexplicable thing,
> With lead in the middle – I'm conjecturing
> How to make Henry understand; but no –
> I'll leave, as Spenser says, with many mo,
> This secret in the pregnant womb of time,
> Too vast a matter for so weak a rhyme.[1]

The archaism, like others ('I wist', 'they swink') is used partly as Spenser used it in *The Shepheardes Calender* or *Mother Hubberds Tale*, partly as Byron used it in *Don Juan*, to draw attention to its

1 Or, as Sidney says (*Astrophel and Stella*):

> Too high a theme for my low style to show.

ungainly self. But the 'Letter to Maria Gisborne' is neither Spenserian nor Byronic. It belongs to the tradition of Donne and Browning, who use the base style to unusual ends. There is no gainsaying that Shelley's verse resembles Browning's more than Donne's; it is an exercise in agility, not energy. Still, it is heartening, not hearty; and affectionate without being mawkish. It is too exuberant to be called urbane in the usual sense. But it is so, in the sense that the poet is sure of his relationship with the person he addresses, that he knows what is due to her and to himself, that he maintains a consistent tone towards her. She is not a peg to hang a poem on, nor a bosom for him to weep on, but a person who shares with him certain interests and certain friends and a certain sense of humour.

This poem is prosaic only in the relatively unimportant sense that it introduces things like hackney coaches, Baron de Tott's Memoirs, 'self-impelling steam-wheels', and 'a queer broken glass/With ink in it'. But like Donne's verse or Browning's, Shelley's is far more figurative than normal prose. For truly lean and bare prosaic language, we turn to 'Julian and Maddalo':

> I rode one evening with Count Maddalo
> Upon the bank of land which breaks the flow
> Of Adria towards Venice; a bare strand
> Of hillocks, heaped from ever-shifting sand,
> Matted with thistles and amphibious weeds,
> Such as from earth's embrace the salt ooze breeds
> Is this; an uninhabited sea-side,
> Which the lone fisher, when his nets are dried,
> Abandons; and no other object breaks
> The waste, but one dwarf tree and some few stakes
> Broken and unrepaired, and the tide makes
> A narrow space of level sand thereon,
> Where 'twas our wont to ride while day went down.

This of course represents a specifically Romantic purity – the adoption, from prose or careful conversation, of a vocabulary of natural description. At their best, the eighteenth-century poets had good reason for believing that features of natural appearance had to be dignified by figures, if they were to be pleasing and instructive; but more often their fussing with metaphors and personifications represented an impurity even by their own standards, for there can be little doubt that their practice in this particular was very far from any spoken usage. Shelley's assumption that accuracy confers its own dignity produced a much purer diction; and there are satisfying examples of this elsewhere in 'Julian and Maddalo', as elsewhere in his work.[1]

But what the Romantics gained with one hand they lost from the other. For if Johnson, for example, was 'intolerably poetical' when he essayed natural description, he had an enviable prosaic assurance in his dealings with the abstractions of moral philosophy. And it is in this province that Shelley's diction is woefully impure. He expressed, in *The Defence of Poetry*, his concern for these large abstractions, and his Platonic intention to make them apprehensible and 'living' in themselves. In 'The Witch of Atlas' he came near to effecting this; but more often this programme only means that an abstraction such as Reason or Justice must always be tugged about in figurative language. The moment they appear in Shelley's verse (and they always come in droves) the tone becomes hectic, the syntax and punctuation disintegrate. In 'Julian and Maddalo', by inventing the figure and the predicament of the maniac, Shelley excuses this incoherency and presents it (plausibly enough) as a verbatim report of the lunatic's ravings, and in this way he preserves the decorum of the conversation piece (the poem is subtitled 'A Conversation'). As a result, this passage, tiresome and unpoetic as it is, impairs but does not ruin the whole. The urbanity is resumed in the close:

> If I had been an unconnected man
> I, from this moment, should have formed some plan
> Never to leave sweet Venice, – for to me

1 Notably in 'Lines' (1815), 'The Sunset' (1816), 'Summer and Winter' (1820) and 'Evening: Ponte al Mare, Pisa' (1821).

It was delight to ride by the lone sea;
And then, the town is silent – one may write
Or read in gondolas by day or night,
Having the little brazen lamp alight,
Unseen, uninterrupted; books are there,
Pictures, and casts from all those statues fair
Which were twin-born with poetry, and all
We seek in towns, with little to recall
Regrets for the green country. I might sit
In Maddalo's great palace, and his wit
And subtle talk would cheer the winter night
And make me know myself, and the firelight
Would flash upon our faces, till the day
Might dawn and make me wonder at my stay.

The conversation we have attended to in the poem is just as civilized as the intercourse of Maddalo and Julian here described. It is in keeping that Julian should know little of Maddalo and not approve of all that he knows, but should be prepared to take him, with personal reservations, on his own terms. It is the habit of gentlemen; and the poet inculcates it in the reader simply by taking it for granted in his manner of address. The poem civilizes the reader; that is its virtue and its value.

'To Jane: The Invitation' and 'To Jane: The Recollection' were originally two halves of one poem called 'The Pine Forest of the Cascine near Pisa'. In the second working over, 'The Invitation' gained enormously, 'The Recollection' hardly at all. The evolution of the latter poem illustrates very forcibly the process (analysed by Dr Leavis) by which the characteristically Shelleyan attitude emerges from a Wordsworthian base. The original version is strikingly Wordsworthian in metre and diction:

A spirit interfused around,
A thinking, silent life;
To momentary peace it bound
Our mortal nature's strife; –

And still, it seemed, the centre of
    The magic circle there,
Was one whose being filled with love
    The breathless atmosphere.

This becomes:

A spirit interfused around,
    A thrilling, silent life, –
To momentary peace it bound
    Our mortal nature's strife;
And still I felt the centre of
    The magic circle there
Was one fair form that filled with love
    The lifeless atmosphere.

As Dr Leavis notes, the changes ('thrilling' for 'thinking', 'being' to 'fair form', and 'lifeless' for 'breathless') are all in the direction of eroticism. It is more pertinent to the present enquiry to notice that they all remove the discourse further from prosaic sense. One could write, in sober prose, of a '*breathless*' atmosphere; one could never describe it as '*lifeless*'. And by the same token a prose writer can make us conceive how a person can seem to imbue a locality or a moment with a peculiar spiritual flavour; but that the emanation should be physical, an attribute of 'form' rather than 'being', is something far more difficult. It is, of course, part of the poetic function to persuade us of realities outside the range of prosaic sense. But this can hardly be done by the familiar tone; and certainly Shelley does not do it here. He does not persuade us of the novelty, he only tricks us into it. His verse neither appeals to an old experience nor creates a new one. These passages are a serious flaw in such a short poem.

The other piece, 'The Invitation', is a nonpareil, and one of Shelley's greatest achievements. It maintains the familiar tone, though in highly figured language, and contrives to be urbane about feelings which are novel and remote. This poem presents the experience which 'The Recollection' tries to define and rationalize; and the definition is there, already, in the expression. Jane's influence upon the scene where she moved is here entirely credible; what Shelley afterwards tried to express, first in Wordsworthian and then in erotic terms, here persuades us from the start with no fuss or embarrassment. It is the lack of fuss, the ease and assurance, which persuades us throughout. In other words the poem is first and foremost a triumph of tone. We can accept Jane as 'Radiant Sister of the Day', largely because the lyrical feeling has already accommodated such seemingly unmanageable things as unpaid bills and unaccustomed visitors. It is an achievement of urbanity to move with such ease from financial and social entanglements to elated sympathy with a natural process; just as it is a mark of civilization to be able to hold these things together in one unflurried attitude.

(iii) *'The Sensitive Plant' and 'The Witch of Atlas'*

It is important that we should understand the reservations we have to make about 'The Recollection'. We dislike Shelley's eroticism, in the end, because it seems a vicious attitude, morally reprehensible; but we dislike it in the first place only because it produces a vicious diction, a jargon. In the end every true literary judgement is a moral judgement. But many critics go wrong, and many readers misunderstand them, because they pass too rapidly into the role of moralist. Even so, those critics are doing their duty better than others who think that moral judgement is no part of their business. I think we should value the significant ambiguity in such phrases as '*chaste* diction', '*pure* diction', '*vicious* style', 'the *conduct* of a fable'. But I am willing to let the ambiguity tell its own tale and to stop short, in this argument, before the point at which literary criticism moves over and becomes philosophical. It is best to think, therefore, that we condemn Shelley's eroticism (as we do) because it produces a jargon, and not because we dislike it 'in itself'.

For the Elizabethan, the lovesong (the 'praise' or the 'complaint') demanded the mean style, unless it used the pastoral convention. And the best of Shelley's love songs (not those, like 'Love's Philosophy', which figure in the anthologies) are distinguished, like the best Caroline lyrics, by urbanity. As early as 1814, the 'Stanza, written at Bracknell' can control self-pity by controlled and judicious phrasing:

> Thy dewy looks sink in my breast;
>   Thy gentle words stir poison there;
> Thou hast disturbed the only rest
>   That was the portion of despair!
> Subdued to Duty's hard control,
>   I could have borne my wayward lot:
> The chains that bind this ruined soul
>   Had cankered then – but crushed it not.

It is not serious, of course, only album verse, as is some of Carew. It all depends on how good the album is; in other words, on the degree of civilization in the society which calls for such trifles. And of course there is no question of comparison with Carew. But the Caroline neatness in the third and fourth lines, and the Augustan echo in the fifth, represent an urbane control which Shelley later threw away. More urbane still are the stanzas, 'To Harriet', written in the same year:

> Thy look of love has power to calm
>   The stormiest passion of my soul;
> Thy gentle words are drops of balm
>   In life's too bitter bowl;
> No grief is mine, but that alone
> These choicest blessings I have known.
>
> Harriet! if all who long to live
>   In the warm sunshine of thine eye,
> That price beyond all pain must give, –

Beneath thy scorn to die;
Then hear thy chosen own too late
His heart most worthy of thy hate.

Be thou, then, one among mankind
Whose heart is harder not for state,
Thou only virtuous, gentle, kind,
Amid a world of hate;
And by a slight endurance seal
A fellow-being's lasting weal.

For pale with anguish is his cheek.
His breath comes fast, his eyes are dim,
Thy name is struggling ere he speak.
Weak is each trembling limb;
In mercy let him not endure
The misery of a fatal cure.

Oh trust for once no erring guide!
Bid the remorseless feeling flee;
'Tis malice, 'tis revenge, 'tis pride
'Tis anything but thee;
Oh, deign a nobler pride to prove,
And pity if thou canst not love.

Of course we cheapen the idea of urbanity by applying it to such polished nothings as these. But in their brittle elegance they represent a tradition which could have made Shelley's later love verse a source of delight instead of embarrassment. The consciously elegant wording in places suggests another poet and even another period. Indeed there is more than a hint of pastiche; but that very period flavour represents a discipline which Shelley threw away.

He can be seen doing so in the 'Bridal Song' of 1821, which is admirable in its first version. In this first:

O joy! O fear! what will be done
In the absence of the sun!

– is as manly and wholesome as Suckling's 'Ballad upon a Wedding'. In the last version:

> O joy! O fear! there is not one
> Of us can guess what may be done
> In the absence of the sun . . .

– is just not true. And the familiar tone of 'Come along!' which securely anchors the first version, is merely silly in the others.

As Dr Leavis points out, it appears from parts of *Peter Bell the Third* that Shelley quite deliberately worked erotic elements into the Wordsworthian base of many of his poems. He seems to have mistaken for prudery the master's natural frigidity. No doubt, too, the erotic jargon was bound up with his dedicated flouting of all the sexual morality of his society. For whatever reason Shelley in his love lyrics adopted a hectic and strident tone, and the urbanity of his early pieces never bore fruit. At the same time he threw into lyrical form more and more of his poetry. The lyric became confused with the hymn and so moved into the orbit of the sublime.

But the jargon came to be habitual with him, whatever sort of poem he wrote, until it taints them nearly all, sublime or not. One of the least tainted is 'The Sensitive Plant', which I find one of his greatest achievements, and of great interest from the point of view of diction. In this poem and 'The Witch of Atlas', Shelley is as daring as ever in invention, making his fable as wayward and arbitrary as possible. In both poems the sensuousness is of his peculiar sort which makes the familiar remote. (He takes a common object such as a rose or a boat, and the more he describes it, the less we remember what it is.) In short, the vision in both these poems has all the difficulties of the Shelleyan sublime, impalpable and ethereal. What distinguishes these poems, however, from such a similar (and maddening) piece as *Alastor* is the presence, at the end of each of them, of a tough hawser of sober sense which at once pulls the preceding poem into shape and (what amounts to the same thing) gives it as much prose meaning as it will bear.

'The Sensitive Plant' is in three parts, with a conclusion. The first part presents in ecstatic detail the garden in summer, and dwells with particular weight upon one plant in the garden, which appears endowed with almost human intelligence in so far as it seeks to express the love it feels and the beauty it aspires to. Devoid of bloom and scent, it is unable to do so. But this predicament is subordinate to the poet's more general purpose, which is, in Part I, to make the garden seem like a dream. He does so with persuasive ease, partly by metrical resourcefulness (the metres induce a dream, not a pre-Raphaelite swoon), partly by deliberate confusion between the five senses, and partly by exploiting the vaporous, atmospheric and luminous features in the scene which he describes. Part II is short and concerned with the presiding human deity of the garden, a woman who is a sort of human counterpart of the Sensitive Plant. Part III begins with the death of the lady and describes how the garden, through autumn and winter into the next spring, falls into unweeded ruin.

In the scheme of this fable there is plainly room for an erotic element. The garden, for all its dreamlike quality, pulses with germinating energy; and this 'love' is what the sensitive plant seeks to express:

> But none ever trembled and panted with bliss
> In the garden, the field, or the wilderness,
> Like a doe in the noontide with love's sweet want,
> As the companionless Sensitive Plant.

We know Shelley's eroticism is vicious only by the vicious diction it produces. Therefore we can have no complaints about the third line of this stanza, at the same time as we condemn the first. There the trembling and the panting and the bliss, coming thus together, are Shelleyan jargon, reach-me-down words which obviate the need for thinking and feeling precisely. The vice in question is not lasciviousness but, more generally, self-indulgence which betrays itself in lax phrasing as in lax conduct. Once we have read a certain amount of Shelley's verse, we recognize and dislike words from the private jargon, even when they are used with propriety:

> And the hyacinth purple, and white, and blue,
> Which flung from its bells a sweet peal anew
> Of music so delicate, soft, and intense,
> It was felt like an odour within the sense.

This is deliberate confusion between the senses, not used as later poets used it for definition of a compound sense-experience, nor only for intensification, but to throw over waking experience the illusion of a dream. Unfortunately 'intense' is a word we learn to suspect in Shelley, and it irritates. So again:

> The plumèd insects swift and free,
> Like golden boats on a sunny sea,
> Laden with light and odour, which pass
> Over the gleam of the living grass;
>
> The unseen clouds of the dew, which lie
> Like fire in the flowers till the sun rides high,
> Then wander like spirits among the spheres,
> Each cloud faint with the fragrance it bears;
>
> The quivering vapours of dim noontide,
> Which like a sea o'er the warm earth glide,
> In which every sound, and odour, and beam,
> Move as reeds in a single stream.

Here the confusion between the senses is particularly persuasive, for it appeals to known facts about atmospheric conditions, or else to the evidence of the senses in such conditions. Unfortunately 'faint' and 'dim' are words from the jargon, and this perturbs the reader, even though both are plausible in this context.

Occasionally, too, there are flagrant violations of prosaic discipline:

> But the Sensitive Plant which could give small fruit
> Of the love which it felt from the leaf to the root,
> Received more than all, it loved more than ever,
> Where none wanted but it, could belong to the giver . . .

and:

> The snowdrop, and then the violet,
> Arose from the ground with warm rain wet,
> And their breath was mixed with fresh odour, sent
> From the turf like the voice and the instrument

– which is culpably ambiguous like Byron's lines which appalled Wordsworth:

> I stood in Venice on the Bridge of Sighs
> A palace and a prison on each hand.

And yet at the very crux of the argument lies the beautiful stanza:

> And the beasts, and the birds, and the insects were drowned
> In an ocean of dreams without a sound;
> Whose waves never mark, though they ever impress
> The light sand which paves it, consciousness.

This is memorably poetic, and yet, in the distinction between 'mark' and 'impress', and in the logical tautness of the whole image, it is 'strong' with the prosaic strength which Dr Johnson found in Denham.

The object of these many examples is not to pick holes in a masterpiece, still less to reduce judgement to some ridiculous balancing of good stanzas against bad. They are meant to illustrate what is after all the capital difficulty in reading Shelley: his unevenness. He has hardly left one perfect poem, however short. In reading him one takes the good with the bad, or one does without it altogether. The business of private judgement on his poems is not a weighing of pros and cons but a decision whether the laxity, which is always there, lies at the centre of the poem (as it often does) or in the margin. I have no doubt that the faults of 'The Sensitive Plant' are marginal, and that at the centre it is sound and strong.

In any case, the second and third parts of the poem are an improvement on Part I. Part III, in particular, presents a rank and desolate scene as in 'Julian and Maddalo', but in greater detail. It is done more poetically than by Crabbe, but no less honestly.

The six stanzas of the Conclusion are of a quite different kind. They ask to be judged on the score of diction, and they triumphantly pass the test they ask for:

> Whether the Sensitive Plant, or that
> Which within its boughs like a Spirit sat,
> Ere its outward form had known decay,
> Now felt this change, I cannot say.
>
> Whether that Lady's gentle mind,
> No longer with the form combined
> Which scattered love, as stars do light,
> Found sadness, where it left delight,
>
> I dare not guess; but in this life
> Of error, ignorance, and strife,
> Where nothing is, but all things seem,
> And we the shadows of the dream,
>
> It is a modest creed, and yet
> Pleasant if one considers it,
> To own that death itself must be,
> Like all the rest, a mockery.
>
> That garden sweet, that lady fair,
> And all sweet shapes and odours there,

In truth have never passed away:
'Tis we, 'tis ours are changed; not they.

For love, and beauty, and delight,
There is no death nor change: their might
Exceeds our organs, which endure
No light, being themselves obscure.

There is not a phrase here which would be out of place in unaffected prose. If that is strange praise for a piece of poetry, it is what one can rarely say of the poetry of Shelley's period. If these stanzas stood by themselves, they might seem tame and flat. In their place in the longer poem they are just what is needed to vouch for the more florid language of what has gone before.

The only comparable achievement among Shelley's poem is 'The Witch of Atlas'. In most editions this poem is introduced by some loose-jointed jaunty stanzas in which Shelley replies to the objection that his poem is lacking in human interest. He compares it with *Peter Bell*:

Wordsworth informs us he was nineteen years
  Considering and re-touching Peter Bell;
Watering his laurels with the killing tears
  Of slow, dull care, so that their roots to Hell
Might pierce, and their wide branches blot the spheres
  Of Heaven, with dewy leaves and flowers; this well
May be, for Heaven and Earth conspire to foil
The over-busy gardener's blundering toil.

My Witch indeed is not so sweet a creature
  As Ruth or Lucy, whom his graceful praise
Clothes for our grandsons – but she matches Peter,
  Though he took nineteen years, and she three days,
In dressing. Light the vest of flowing metre
  She wears; he, proud as dandy with his stays,
Has hung upon his wiry limbs a dress
Like King Lear's 'looped and windowed raggedness'.

If you strip Peter, you will see a fellow
  Scorched by Hell's hyperequatorial climate
Into a kind of a sulphureous yellow:
  A lean mark, hardly fit to fling a rhyme at;
In shape a Scaramouch, in hue Othello.
  If you unveil my Witch, no priest nor primate
Can shrive you of that sin, – if sin there be
In love, when it becomes idolatry.

The point of the comparison with *Peter Bell* is not very clear. The implication is that both poems are free fantasies, and that Wordsworth spoiled his by labouring it, whereas the essential virtue of such pieces is their spontaneity, and this Shelley claims to achieve. More interesting is the question how far such poems will bear scrutiny for meanings, how far such fantasies can be treated as allegorical. This I take to be the question of the last stanza above, and Shelley's answer is rather ambiguous. He begins by warning the reader not to rationalize at all, implying that Wordsworth came to grief by inviting such a reading; but then, in the teasing play with 'love' and 'idolatry', he seems to allow that to look for an allegory is perhaps the best tribute one can give. At any rate it seems plain that 'The Witch of Atlas', like 'Kubla Khan' no less than *Peter Bell*, is a flight of gratuitous fancy, a sort of iridescent bubble in which the reader looks for a 'message' only at his peril.

And of course the poem is all that Shelley says – a wayward fable, set in an unearthly landscape peopled by creatures neither human nor divine. Like *Alastor* and 'The Sensitive Plant', it has no meaning except as a whole. It is one half of a vast metaphor with the human term left out; and this, its meaning for human life, emerges from the shape of the whole or else it is lost for ever. It was lost in *Alastor*, and to give the meaning in an Introduction (as Shelley did then) is not enough. The meaning may fit the myth, but it is not carried in the myth, and one always forgets what *Alastor* is about. 'The Witch of Atlas', which is just as wayward and inhuman, takes on meaning, as much meaning as it can bear without cracking the singing voice. Shelley takes care of the meaning:

> The priests would write an explanation full,
> Translating hieroglyphics into Greek,
> How the God Apis really was a bull,
> And nothing more; and bid the herald stick
> The same against the temple doors, and pull
> The old cant down; they licensed all to speak
> Whate'er they thought of hawks, and cats, and geese,
> By pastoral letters to each diocese.

It is absurd, of course. We cannot really believe that the ideal beauty of the vision means no more in moral terms than the regeneration of religious institutions, and their purification from superstition. But Shelley admits the absurdity, by his verse form, at the same time as he implies that such a change must after all be *part* of any regenerated world. There is no danger of taking this too seriously, and thereby damaging the sheer creative *élan* of the poem. And by thus slipping back, at the end of the poem, into the familiar, even slangy, base style of the prefatory stanzas, Shelley guards this most visionary and fantastic poem from any rough handling. He casts his myth into a sort of rough-hewn cradle of coarse sense. The device is the same as that in 'The Sensitive Plant', except that here Shelley uses the base, where there he used the mean style. To complain that the poem is 'obscure' or 'lacking in human interest' is now out of the question. If one does so, one has missed the point, and made not a mistake only, but a social blunder. To that extent Shelley's is an achievement, once again, of urbanity.

*

The poet I have considered here is a poet of poise and good breeding. Shelley was the only English Romantic poet with the birth and breeding of a gentleman, and that cannot be irrelevant. What is more surprising is the evidence that in other poems Shelley failed chiefly for want of the very tact which is here conspicuous. I am at a loss to explain how a poet so well aware of what he was doing should also have written *The Cenci*. But if urbanity depends on the relation between poet and public, then it may be that Shelley's failures in tact were connected with his being unread and neglected. In her notes on the poems of 1821, Mrs Shelley hinted as much:

Several of his slighter and unfinished poems were inspired by these scenes, and by the companions around us. It is the nature of that poetry, however, which overflows from the soul, oftener to express sorrow and regret than joy; for it is when oppressed by the weight of life, and away from those he loves, that the poet has recourse to the solace of expression in verse.

It is, alas, too true that many of Shelley's poems are the products of self-pity looking for 'solace' or compensation; and it is not strange that the 'slighter and unfinished poems', inspired by 'the companions around us', should be some of Shelley's best work. This is not the poetry 'which overflows from the soul', but the considered expression of an intelligent man.

IV

Hopkins as a Decadent Critic

THERE are many ways of looking at the letters of Gerard Manley Hopkins. To the theologian and musician they can offer as much as to the critic and the prosodist. And anyone interested in the varieties of human friendship will find much to wonder at and admire. It is as a critic, however, that Hopkins is most surprising and most obviously impressive, for it is in his criticism that he is most plainly ahead of his time. His opinions of the verse of his contemporaries chime almost exactly with the views reached, fifty years after his death, by the best modern poets and critics. And this clairvoyance, added to the prestige of his poetry, has made him in certain circles almost above reproach. It will be the object of this essay to point out that while his criticism, especially of poetry, is so influential, it can be dangerous. But because, in other circles, Hopkins as a poet can still be rejected out of hand, it is in place to say at the start that the present writer holds him to be perhaps the greatest Victorian poet, and the best critic of his age after Matthew Arnold. While making these claims, it is only fair to remind the reader that the Victorian age produced little great poetry *in any case*; and also to assure him that if Hopkins is the first critic after Arnold, he may come a long way after.

There is nothing to show that Hopkins's criticism developed very much from first to last. There is no great difference, in substance or in quality, between his first pronouncements and his latest. It is none the less convenient to observe an order roughly chronological, if only because the earliest statement of critical principles is also the most comprehensive. It occurs in a letter to Alexander William Mowbray Baillie, written in 1864, when Hopkins was twenty.[1] In this letter Hopkins divides the language of verse into three kinds. The first is the language of inspiration:

The word inspiration need cause no difficulty. I mean by it a mood of great, abnormal in fact, mental acuteness, either energetic or receptive, according as the thoughts which arise in it seem generated by a stress or action of the brain, or to strike into it unasked.

The second kind of language is Parnassian:

It can only be spoken by poets, but is not in the highest sense poetry. It does not require the mood of mind in which the poetry of inspiration is written. It is spoken *on and from the level* of a poet's mind, not, as in the other case, when the inspiration which is the gift of genius, raises him above himself.

Parnassian is above all distinctive:

Great men, poets I mean, have each their own dialect as it were of Parnassian, formed generally as they go on writing, and at last, – this is the point to be marked, – they can see things in this Parnassian way and describe them in this Parnassian tongue, without further effort of inspiration. In a poet's particular kind of Parnassian lies most of his style, of his manner, of his mannerism if you like.

The third kind of language is treated only in passing:

The third kind is merely the language of verse as distinct from that of prose, Delphic, the tongue of the Sacred *Plain*, I may call it, used in common by poet and poetaster. Poetry when spoken is spoken in it, but to speak it is not necessarily to speak poetry.

There are also, he explains, two sub-kinds, the first Castalian, the second Olympian. Castalian is 'a higher sort of Parnassian', differing from the language of inspiration only because it lacks impersonality, is too characteristic of the writer. As for Olym-

1 Claude Colleer Abbott (ed.), *Further Letters of Gerard Manley Hopkins* (OUP, 1938), pp. 69–73.

pian, 'This is the language of strange masculine genius which suddenly, as it were, forces its way into the domain of poetry, without naturally having a right there. Milman's poetry is of this kind I think, and Rossetti's "Blessed Damozel". But unusual poetry has a tendency to seem so at first.'

It is remarkable how well these principles correspond with those in vogue today among the reviewers. For them 'Delphic' becomes 'poetic diction' (in a derogatory sense); 'Parnassian' is 'a distinctive voice', taken to be an improvement on the first stage; and 'the language of inspiration' is 'the profound impersonality of all art that is truly great'. The course of poetic advancement is often taken in this way to be from the impersonal (= 'undistinguished') through the personal (='distinctive') to the impersonal (='a disembodied voice'). But is it not true that the course may be run without deviating into the personal? that the voice can move from 'undistinguished' to 'distinguished', without once being 'distinctive'? It may seem that in periods when 'poetic diction' was not in such bad odour as it was for Hopkins and is for us, when, in particular, it was accompanied by the idea of 'purity' ('a pure diction'), this possibility was recognized. It is worth while asking whether, if we follow Hopkins in this (as I think we mostly do), we are limiting ourselves to a Victorian view of poetry, or whether we are only acceding to the extinction of a principle which was once fruitful but can be so no longer.

On joining the Society of Jesus, Hopkins destroyed the poetry he had written before 1868, and produced no more for about nine years. As might be expected, his letters in this period contain no criticism. With the reawakening of his creative talent in 1877, criticism engages him again.

In 1878 appeared another guiding principle in Hopkins's criticism, his devotion to Milton:

The same M. Arnold says Milton and Campbell are our two greatest masters of *style*. Milton's art is incomparable, not only in English literature, but, I should think, almost in any; equal, if not more than equal, to the finest of Greek or Roman. And considering that this is shewn especially in his verse, his rhythm and metrical system, it is amazing that so great a writer as Newman should have fallen into the blunder of comparing the first chorus of the *Agonistes* with the opening of *Thalaba* as instancing the gain in smoothness and correctness of versification made since Milton's time . . .[1]

Milton is, for Hopkins, always the final court of appeal. And it is worth remarking that those modern readers who have most readily embraced Hopkins's poetry and his criticism are very often those who have called in question Milton's prestige, or at any rate the fruitfulness of his influence. Hopkins is quite unambiguous. He puts forward Milton, time and again, as a model; and in so doing he flies in the face not only of modern poets – Ezra Pound and T. S. Eliot – but also of Keats and Cowper. In effect, he challenges one of the best authenticated working principles in the English poetic tradition – the principle that Milton, however great in himself, is a bad example for other poets. Was Hopkins alive to certain Miltonic aspects of his own poetry which his modern critics conspire to ignore, or merely cannot see? Of course he was indebted to Milton for the first hints of his novel prosody, and this is certainly one aspect of his art which has not engaged his later readers so much as he expected. But this does not entirely explain the matter; for Milton repeatedly appears in connection with 'Style', and, while this term is never fully explained by Hopkins, it plainly involves for him much more than prosody. It is quite possible of course that the critics may have seen the nature of Hopkins's achievement more clearly than he saw it himself; and that, where he thought himself indebted to Milton, he was mistaken. But for students of his criticism the problem remains. Milton's practice is central to that criticism; and this must make it very different from the criticism of Keats, of Cowper or of Mr Eliot. It is

1 C. C. Abbott (ed.), *The Correspondence of Gerard Manley Hopkins and Richard Watson Dixon* (OUP, 1935), p. 13.

worth asking where and how Hopkins differs from these authorities, and whether he differs for the better or for the worse.

'Miltonic style' soon appears in connection with another important principle, as novel as that of 'Parnassian', the idea of 'inscape':

> No doubt my poetry errs on the side of oddness. I hope in time to have a more balanced and Miltonic style. But as air, melody, is what strikes me most of all in music and design in painting, so design, pattern or what I am in the habit of calling 'inscape' is what I above all aim at in poetry. Now it is the virtue of design, pattern, or inscape to be distinctive and it is the vice of distinctiveness to become queer. This vice I cannot have escaped.[1]

It has been found by critics of Hopkins's poetry that to explain 'inscape' it is necessary to explore the poet's theology and philosophy, especially his admiring study of Duns Scotus. The same, of course, is true of his criticism. Every system of criticism rests, explicitly or not, upon a moral philosophy, and to do justice to the criticism one should ideally set it in that context. On the other hand I am concerned with how far Hopkins's standards of criticism are viable, how far they can be adopted with profit by readers professing quite different philosophies. And for this purpose it is enough to point out that, for Hopkins, since 'it is the virtue of design, pattern, or inscape to be distinctive', this principle is closely related to 'the Parnassian'. Hopkins shows himself here aware of some of the dangers inherent in giving to 'distinctiveness' such value as he does. It is interesting to know how he intended to guard against those dangers, or whether he thought them only a risk that must be run.

To 1870 belong most of the snap judgements that show Hopkins at his best. There is the comment on Swinburne, for instance:

1 C. C. Abbott (ed.), *The Letters of Gerard Manley Hopkins to Robert Bridges* (OUP, 1935), p. 66.

I do not think that kind goes far: it expresses passion but not feeling, much less character. This I say in general or of Swinburne in particular. Swinburne's genius is astonishing, but it will, I think, only do one thing.[1]

Or this on Tennyson:

... there may be genius uninformed by character. I sometimes wonder at this in a man like Tennyson: his gift of utterance is truly golden, but go further home and you come to thoughts commonplace and wanting in nobility (it seems hard to say it but I think you know what I mean). In Burns there is generally recognized a richness and beauty of manly character which lends worth to some of his smallest fragments, but there is a great want in his utterance; it is never really beautiful, he had no eye for pure beauty, he gets no nearer than the fresh picturesque expressed in fervent and flowing language ...[2]

Or the comment on the age:

For it seems to me that the poetical language of an age should be the current language heightened, to any degree heightened and unlike itself, but not (I mean normally: passing freaks and graces are another thing) an obsolete one. That is Shakespeare's and Milton's practice and the want of it will be fatal to Tennyson's Idylls and plays, to Swinburne, and perhaps to Morris.[3]

Or, more generally, on obscurity:

One of two kinds of clearness one should have – either the meaning to be felt without effort as fast as one reads or else, if dark at first reading, when once made out *to explode*.[4]

This certainly does not exhaust the question of how a poet transmits his meanings, but it could hardly be bettered as a handy rule of thumb. In the same way, many readers will admire

1 *Letters to Bridges*, p. 79.

2 Ibid., p. 95.

3 Ibid., p. 89.

4 Ibid., p. 90.

the way the critic goes at once to the heart of the matter in the judgements on his contemporaries. But even here there are puzzling elements. However warmly we may agree that 'the poetical language of an age should be the current language heightened', we are not used to seeing Milton cited as an authority for it. Keats, we remember, discarded the Miltonic 'Hyperion' just because 'English must be kept up'. And in the same way we may be sure that Hopkins is right about Tennyson and yet wonder if he is right about Burns. 'He had no eye for pure beauty . . .' – we suspect that 'pure beauty' never meant anything exact, and we should blush to see it in critical parlance today. Whatever the force of 'pure', we may find it a narrow notion of beauty that cannot find room for 'the fresh picturesque'. And does not such a narrowness reflect upon the critic?

The evidence of Hopkins's own poetry and what we know of his age can help us without much trouble to understand 'inscape' on the one hand, and 'pure beauty' on the other, whatever we may think of their value as critical terms. And his own account of 'Parnassian' and the related categories is sufficiently clear. What gives most trouble is his usage of 'Style'. It recurs in his detailed criticism of poems by Bridges:

And 'pleasurable' is a prosaic word, I think: can you not find something better? It is not a bad word, but it falls flatly. (This reminds me that 'test' is to my ear prosaic in 'Thou didst delight', but could scarcely be changed.) Otherwise the poem is very beautiful, very fine in execution and style. Style seems your great excellence, it is really classical. What fun if you were a classic! So few people have style, except individual style or manner – not Tennyson nor Swinburne nor Morris, not to name the scarecrow misbegotten Browning crew. Just think of the blank verse these people have exuded, such as *Paracelsus, Aurora Leigh*, Baillie's or Bayley's *Festus*, and so on. The Brownings are very fine too in their ghastly way.[1]

1 Ibid., p. 111.

This is very puzzling. 'Style', thus called 'classical' and opposed to 'manner', might seem to approach the Augustan notion of 'a pure diction'. Hopkins applauds both Dixon and Bridges for the beauty of gentlemanly character in all they write, and this might have something to do with a sort of serious urbanity which we can readily associate with such a diction. Moreover, Hopkins is a stickler for propriety, as when he takes Bridges to task for confusing 'disillusion' and 'disenchantment'.[1] But we have already seen that, for Hopkins, 'classical' means 'Miltonic'. And what is more, the compliment is surely a left-handed one, since we have already learnt that what Hopkins values most in poetry is 'inscape', the distinctive. In denying to Bridges 'individual style or manner', Hopkins seems to deny him 'inscape', and plainly the language of Bridges can be neither Castalian nor Parnassian, since these are pre-eminently distinctive. It must be either 'Delphic' or else 'the language of inspiration', and since the complimentary intention is clear, it must be the latter. And indeed since he tries always for 'inscape', and 'inscape' is distinctive, it seems as if in his own poetry Hopkins commits himself to just that Parnassian which elsewhere he relegates to a second rank. This is in effect a *reductio ad absurdum*.

The point becomes a little clearer in a letter to Dixon of 1881, which is the fullest review by Hopkins of the English poetry of his own century:

> The Lake poets and all that school represent, as it seems to me, the mean or standard of English style and diction, which culminated in Milton but was never very continuous or vigorously transmitted, and in fact none of these men unless perhaps Landor were great masters of style, though their diction is generally pure, lucid, and unarchaic.[2]

It is now clear that when Hopkins discerns 'Style', he discerns Miltonic style. It is important that the language of poets should

1 *Letters to Bridges*, p. 121.
2 *Correspondence*, p. 98.

be current and should observe propriety without being prosaic, and most of his contemporaries he thinks fail to observe these rules, but to observe them is not to guarantee 'Style'. What is still wanting appears to be some sort of consistent elevation. If the language has all these, then it may be Miltonic and will therefore be 'Style'. The chief difficulty which remains is Hopkins's assumption that the language of Milton is somehow 'current'; some readers may find this hard to concede.

As 'Style' is one of Milton's virtues, 'inscape' is the other. Now since 'inscape' is distinctive and admirable, and 'Parnassian' is distinctive and regrettable, and since it is absurd to suppose that Hopkins set out to write Parnassian, it follows that 'inscape' has little or nothing to do with language at all, but is a quality of form and design. The poet who seeks 'inscape' (Hopkins himself) must make his language current, proper and clear, and he may even, by adding elevation, attain to 'Style'. (Hopkins, as we have seen, hoped to achieve 'a more balanced and Miltonic style', though he knew his other aim, distinctiveness, made it difficult.) But he has a task above or apart from this, a matter of distinctive formal disposition or moulding.

This notion engages Hopkins more and more:

> In general I take it that other things being alike unity of action is higher the more complex the plot; it is the more difficult to effect and therefore the more valuable when effected. We judge so of everything.[1]

> But how could you think such a thing of me as that I should in cold blood write 'fragments of a dramatic poem'? – I of all men in the world. To me a completed fragment, above all of a play, is the same unreality as a prepared impromptu.[2]

> Now this is the artist's most essential quality, masterly execution: it is a kind of male gift and especially marks off men from women, the begetting one's thought on paper, on verse, on whatever the matter is; the life must be conveyed into the work and be displayed there, not

1 Ibid., p. 113.
2 *Letters to Bridges*, p. 218.

suggested as having been in the artist's mind: otherwise the product is one of those hen's-eggs that are good to eat and look just like live ones but never hatch.[1]

It would be easy and idle to relate the metaphors of this last to 'Time's eunuch' (which occurs in the letters as well as the poem) and to the celibate rule. This train of thought may have had a special significance for the poet. For us, the three passages quoted point in the direction of something lost to English poetry since the Renaissance. We come nearest to what Hopkins meant by 'execution' by recalling Sidney's *An Apologie for Poetrie* or an expression of Gabriel Harvey's – 'excellentest artificiality'. What is meant by 'execution' and 'inscape' is the Renaissance idea of poem as artefact, a shape in space and time, added to creation, thrown out by will and energy, and the more elaborate the better. But if the artefact reappears, it is only with a difference. Sidney's poem was something added to the world, cut loose of its maker, absolute, anonymous, in its own right. The maker's energy was all to the casting forth, the endowment of independent life, the cutting of the threads from maker to made thing. Hopkins's poem on the contrary is to be distinctive; the systematic elaboration, and the setting of self-imposed tasks, generate the energy which throws the poem away from the poet, but only to the end that the reader, admiring the elaborate self-sufficiency, shall infer the energy and the shape of the making mind, and so work back to the poet again. The poet attempts a brilliant finesse. Things turn inside out. If he attains to 'Style', his impersonality is so conspicuous that it becomes his most intriguing personal trait; if he attains to 'inscape', the artificiality, the lack of intimacy, is the most intimate thing in the poem.

Such self-regarding ingenuity may be called decadent. Hopkins wrote in a decadent age, and if he is its greatest poet, he may be so because he cultivates his hysteria and pushes his sickness to

1 *Correspondence*, p. 133.

the limit. Certainly he displays, along with the frantic ingenuity, another decadent symptom more easily recognized: the refinement and manipulation of sensuous appetite. This is an important, perhaps the essential, part of that pure beauty which he recognized in Tennyson and missed in Burns, a quality of hectic intensity. Much of his work, in criticism and poetry alike, is concerned with restoring to a jaded palate the capacity for enjoyment. There is an interesting letter to Dixon, very revealing in this connection:

I remember that crimson and pure blues seemed to me spiritual and heavenly sights fit to draw tears once; now I can just see what I once saw, but can hardly dwell on it and should not care to do so.[1]

And in his latest letters there is a mild controversy with Patmore about Keats:

Since I last wrote I have reread Keats a little and the force of your criticism on him has struck me more than it did. It is impossible not to feel with weariness how his verse is at every turn abandoning itself to an unmanly and enervating luxury. It appears too that he said something like 'O for a life of impressions instead of thoughts'. It was, I suppose, the life he tried to lead. The impressions are not likely to have been all innocent and they soon ceased in death. His contemporaries, as Wordsworth, Byron, Shelley, and even Leigh Hunt, right or wrong, still concerned themselves with great causes, as liberty and religion; but he lived in mythology and fairyland the life of a dreamer. Nevertheless I feel and see in him the beginnings of something opposite to this, of an interest in higher things and of powerful and active thought.[2]

Hopkins, it may be thought, misses the point, which is not that some of Keats's experiences cannot have been innocent, but that the whole of Keats's programme may have been 'vicious'. In his most important poems, the Odes, this is the question which Keats explores.

1 Ibid., p. 38.
2 *Further Letters*, pp. 237, 238.

Of course, it is plain why Hopkins could not agree with Patmore about Keats. His earliest work, the school prize poems, are conspicuously Keatsian, and revel in an excess of sensuous luxury; and of course this luxury is a conspicuous feature of all his verse. It is possible that Hopkins thought to counterbalance this Keatsian effeminacy by the strenuous masculinity of 'inscape'; perhaps for some readers he does so and thereby attains a human mean, not decadent at all. Others again may find the compensating masculinity not in 'inscape' at all but in the taut frame of intellectual argument in all the poems, an important aspect of his poetry which the poet seems to take curiously for granted. (One may suspect that it was this, more than rhythm or diction, which baffled Bridges sometimes; if so, neither Bridges nor Hopkins realized it.) Other readers again may find that 'inscape' and sensuous luxury go together and make the poetry decadent, and that the strict Jesuitical logic, for all its discipline, is not really a sign of health, but only another aspect of that systematizing elaboration which produced the doctrine of 'inscape' and the prosody. One has to leave this margin for difference of opinion, for if 'decadent' occurs in the critic's vocabulary at all, it comes at the point where criticism is not distinguishable from moral philosophy.

At any rate, one cannot read the letters, even where they are concerned with music or the classical studies in the Dorian rhythms, without feeling that the systematic and the elaborate have a value for Hopkins in themselves, and not merely as instruments for reaching after truth. The doctrine of 'inscape' admits as much. His thinking is casuistical. The most remarkable example of the value of the systematic for Hopkins is his letter to Bridges about Whitman:

> Extremes meet, and (I must for truth's sake say what sounds pride) this savagery of his art, this rhythm in its last ruggedness and decomposition into common prose, comes near the last elaboration of mine. For that piece of mine is very highly wrought. The long lines are not rhythm

run to seed: everything is weighed and timed in them. Wait till they have taken hold of your ear and you will find it so. No, but what it *is* like is the rhythm of Greek tragic choruses or of Pindar: which is pure sprung rhythm. And that has the same changes of cadence from point to point as this piece. If you want to try it, read one till you have settled the true places of the stress, mark these, then read it aloud, and you will see. Without this these choruses are prose bewitched; with it they are sprung rhythm like that piece of mine.[1]

The upshot of this is that Hopkins does not use his special rhythms in order to catch the movement of living speech. That is Whitman's policy but it is only Hopkins's starting-point. His rhythms differ from Whitman's (and by implication they are superior to Whitman's) sheerly because they are reduced to or elaborated into a system. Hopkins is systematic where Whitman is casual. And there, in the systematizing, resides the distinctive, the masculine, the 'inscape'.

Surely something the same is true of Hopkins's language. We applaud him, and rightly, for making his language current and refusing archaism. But again that is only the start; the language is anything but current by the time Hopkins has finished with it. And of course that was his doctrine: poetic language must be based on the current speech, but it could be elevated and elaborated ad lib, as, in his view, it was by Milton. He says of Dryden:

I can scarcely think of you not admiring Dryden without, I may say, exasperation. And my style tends always more towards Dryden. What is there in Dryden? Much, but above all this: he is the most masculine of our poets; his style and his rhythms lay the strongest stress of all our literature on the naked thew and sinew of the English language, the praise that with certain qualifications one would give in Greek to Demosthenes, to be the greatest master of bare Greek.[2]

And what he says of Dryden has been applied by admiring

1 *Letters to Bridges*, p. 157.

2 Ibid., pp. 267, 268.

critics to his own poems. But it does not really apply, or only with a difference. 'The naked thew and sinew' is not enough for Hopkins. It has to be crammed, stimulated and knotted together. He has no respect for the language, but gives it body-building exercises until it is a muscle-bound monstrosity. It is the Keatsian luxury carried one stage further, luxuriating in the kinetic and muscular as well as the sensuous. Word is piled on word, and stress on stress, to crush the odours and dispense a more exquisite tang, more exquisite than the life. To have no respect for language is to have none for life; both life and language have to be heightened and intensified before Hopkins can approve them. He has been praised more warmly still: it is contended that his use of language is Shakespearian. Certainly Shakespeare shows similar audacity. But the cases are not parallel. For Shakespeare there was not, in this sense, a language to respect. It was still in the melting-pot, fluid, experimental and expanding rapidly. Even in their speaking, Shakespeare's contemporaries were at liberty to coin, convert, transpose and cram together. Hopkins, like Doughty, treats nineteenth-century English as if it were still unstable and immature.

I think this is a true description of Hopkins's poetry, but to prove it one would need to move from point to point through several poems. At least such a view of language, poetic function and human experience is implied in the system of criticism. That system (and, though it is available in fragmentary form, it is truly systematic), however it may touch at several points upon modern criticism, is violently at odds with what distinguished later poets have laid down in theory or implied in critical practice. The gulf between Hopkins and Mr Pound, for instance, or Mr Eliot, is very wide, and can be shown most neatly perhaps by comparing the attitudes taken by the three poets towards Dante. For both Eliot and Pound, Dante has been consistently a pole of reference, in Mr Eliot's specially limited sense 'a classic', and for both poets he has been in particular a model of poetic diction:

The border line between 'gee whizz' and Milton's tumified dialect must exist. (Dante, in *De Volgari Eloquio*, seems to have thought of a good many particulars of the problem.)[1]

The language of each great English poet is his own language; the language of Dante is the perfection of a common language.[2]

Hopkins's solitary comment on Dante is perhaps the most astonishing judgement in all three volumes of the letters:

This leads me to say that a kind of touchstone of the highest or most living art is seriousness; not gravity but the being in earnest with your subject – reality. It seems to me that some of the greatest and most famous works are not taken in earnest enough, are farce (where you ask the spectator to grant you something not only conventional but monstrous). I have this feeling about *Faust* and even about the *Divine Comedy*, whereas *Paradise Lost* is most seriously taken. It is the weakness of the whole Roman literature.[3]

It is true that Hopkins's judgement does not turn upon Dantesque diction, but seems rather related to the doctrinal differences between Scotist and Thomist. Nevertheless the judgement, from a Jesuit poet, is remarkable. And of course it is plain that there is, in Hopkins's criticism, no room for such a notion as 'the perfection of a common language' or for highly rating a language which strikes a mean between current slang and Miltonic elevation. When Hopkins writes of a mean style he means the Miltonic style, and when he writes of 'pure diction' he means no more than observation of propriety. When he esteems gentlemanliness or 'character' in the writing of Bridges and Dixon, he means neither Arnold's urbanity nor the Aristotelian mean, but 'character' in the sense of 'a man of character', i.e. something built up and maintained by the will. Even 'the language of the poetic plain', we remember, is called 'Delphic', that is, vatic, esoteric and elevated.

1 *Letters of Ezra Pound*, p. 349.
2 T. S. Eliot, 'Dante', in *Selected Essays* (Faber, 1934), p. 252.
3 *Letters to Bridges*, p. 225.

It is true, of course, that not only Hopkins but all the critics of his period were far from esteeming or even recognizing 'pure diction' in this sense. But Hopkins is further from it even than his contemporaries. The last passage quoted, for instance, makes play with what is obviously Hopkins's version of the 'high seriousness' of Arnold; and this may serve to remind us that in Hopkins's lifetime Arnold was the critic who came nearest to the idea of 'the perfection of a common language'. Arnold made the idea a principle in the criticism of prose, excluding it from poetry. His most elaborate statement of this position occurs in 'The Literary Influence of Academies', where he finds that Attic prose is valuable because it maintains a valuable urbanity, the tone and spirit of the centre as opposed to the provincial spirit. He finds that there is a strong tradition of such prose writing in France, but he seeks it in vain in England, where the masters of prose style (Jeremy Taylor, Burke, Ruskin, Kinglake) employ a rhetorical 'poetic' prose. English prose comes nearest to the Attic model in Addison or (in the critic's own day) Newman. Hopkins valued Arnold's criticism and rebuked Bridges for calling him 'Mr Kid-glove Cocksure'. He mentions 'The Literary Influence of Academies' in a letter of 1864 to Baillie:

You must also read, if you have not done so, Matthew Arnold on 'The literary influence of Academies' in the August *Cornhill*. Much that he says is worth attention, but, as is so often the case, in censuring bad taste he falls into two flagrant pieces of bad taste himself. I am coming to think much of taste myself, good taste and moderation, I who have sinned against them so much. But there is a prestige about them which is indescribable.[1]

It is more than twenty years later that he gives what is obviously his considered rejoinder to Arnold's argument. It occurs in a letter to Patmore:

... when I read your prose and when I read Newman's and some other modern writers' the same impression is borne in on me: no matter how

1 *Further Letters*, p. 74.

beautiful the thought, nor, taken singly, with what happiness expressed, you do not know what *writing prose* is. At bottom what you do and what Cardinal Newman does is to think aloud, to think with pen to paper. In this process there are certain advantages; they may outweigh those of a perfect technic; but at any rate they exclude that; they exclude the belonging technic, the belonging rhetoric, the own proper eloquence of written prose. Each thought is told off singly and there follows a pause and this breaks the continuity, the *contentio*, the strain of address, which writing should usually have.

The beauty, the eloquence, of good prose cannot come wholly from the thought. With Burke it does and varies with the thought; when therefore the thought is sublime so does the style appear to be. But in fact Burke had no style properly so called: his style was colourlessly to transmit his thought. Still he was an orator in form and followed the common oratorical tradition, so that his writing has the strain of address I speak of above.

But Newman does not follow the common tradition – of writing. His tradition is that of cultured, the most highly educated, conversation; it is the flower of the best Oxford life. Perhaps this gives it a charm of unaffected and personal sincerity that nothing else could. Still he shirks the technic of written prose and shuns the tradition of written English. He seems to be thinking 'Gibbon is the last great master of traditional English prose; he is its perfection: I do not propose to emulate him; I begin all over again from the language of conversation, of common life.'

You too seem to me to be saying to yourself 'I am writing prose, not poetry; it is bad taste and a confusion of kinds to employ the style of poetry in prose: the style of prose is to shun the style of poetry and to express one's views with point.' But the style of prose is a positive thing and not the absence of verse forms and pointedly expressed thoughts are single hits and give no continuity of style.[1]

Plainly Hopkins now so highly values 'inscape', elevation and distinctiveness that they are to be a principle of prose no less than poetry. The comments on Burke are quite unambiguous: Hopkins censures him because, when his thoughts were not

1 Ibid., pp. 231, 232.

sublime, neither was his style. This is as far as may be from what is almost taken for granted today, the principle that, in any sort of writing, that style is best which transmits most accurately the thought or the feeling of the writer.

As might be expected, Hopkins's judgements of his contemporaries are in general less acceptable to modern opinion when he speaks of prose writers than when he judges the poets. Stevenson is his hero:

In my judgement the amount of gift and genius which goes into novels in the English literature of this generation is perhaps not much inferior to what made the Elizabethan drama, and unhappily it is in great part wasted. How admirable are Blackmore and Hardy! Their merits are much eclipsed by the overdone reputation of the Evans-Eliot-Lewis-Cross woman (poor, creature! one ought not to speak slightingly, I know), half real power, half imposition. Do you know the bonfire scenes in the *Return of the Native* and still better the sword-exercise scene in the *Madding Crowd*, breathing epic? or the wife-sale in the *Mayor of Casterbridge* (read by chance)? But these writers only rise to their great strokes; they do not write continuously well; now Stevenson is master of a consummate style and each phrase is finished as in poetry.[1]

The condescension to George Eliot of course has probably more to do with her sexual conduct than with her writing. Stevenson's 'consummate style' is chiefly a matter of 'word-painting'.[2] This narrow idea of the functions of prose style corresponds to the narrowness of that 'pure beauty' which excluded Burns.

In 1886 'inscape' is still the ultimate criterion. The lack of it is damning to Sir Samuel Ferguson, for instance:

. . . for he was a poet; the *Forging of the Anchor* is, I believe, his most famous poem; he was a poet as the Irish are – to judge by the little of his I have seen – full of feeling, high thoughts, flow of verse, point, often fine imagery and other virtues, but the essential and only lasting

1 *Letters to Bridges*, p. 238, 239.
2 Ibid., p. 267.

thing left out – what I call *inscape*, that is species or individually-distinctive beauty of style . . .[1]

Plainly 'inscape' is the clue to whatever is still puzzling in Hopkins. And it is not necessary to examine its philosophical basis in his thought or its manifestation in his poems. It is time to ask what it means in simple terms of human personality. 'Inscape' is, we remember, specifically a Miltonic virtue. Now on Milton the man as distinct from the poet, there is only one comment among all the letters. It was made in 1877 to Bridges:

Don't like what you say of Milton, I think he was a very bad man: those who contrary to our Lord's command both break themselves and, as St Paul says, consent to those who break the sacred bond of marriage, like Luther and Milton, fall with eyes open into the terrible judgement of God.[2]

It does me little credit, perhaps, that I find here an anticlimax little short of comical. Of course 'the sacred bond of marriage' is an important matter. And I can well understand anyone, especially a Roman Catholic, who finds Milton 'a very bad man'; but I do not expect to find him called a bad man only in the sense that George Eliot is 'a bad woman'. I expect to find the verdict go against Milton on more general and comprehensive grounds, precisely as a type of the extreme Protestant. One thinks to find the characteristic formulae of later Catholic writers – 'individualism', perhaps, or 'humanistic arrogance', all that aspect of Milton which has to do with his ambivalent treatment of the Lucifer figure. This is conspicuous by its absence from all Hopkins's comments on Milton. And it is not hard to see why. Hopkins's theory and his practice point in one direction. Put together such recurrent terms as 'inscape', 'sublime', 'distinctiveness', 'masculinity', 'character', and one is forced to the conclusion that it was just this – Milton's egotism, individualism and arrogance –

1 *Further Letters*, p. 225.
2 *Letters to Bridges*, p. 39.

which made him, for Hopkins, the model poet. His own poetry and his own criticism proceed from the single assumption that the function of poetry is to express a human individuality in its most wilfully uncompromising and provocative form. His is the poetry and the criticism of the egotistical sublime. Dixon answered the contention that poetry was incompatible with membership of the Society of Jesus by saying he could not see how one vocation could clash with the other. It was true, so long as the poet's vocation was conceived as Dixon conceived of it. But Hopkins knew better, and he was right too. He conceived of poetry as self-expression at its most relentless, as a vehicle for the individual will to impose itself on time. Between that and any sort of Christian calling there could be no compromise at all.

V

Landor's Shorter Poems

To C. H. Herford, in 1897, it seemed that 'Landor was . . . on the whole the greatest prose writer of the age of Wordsworth; and, after Wordsworth, Coleridge, Byron, Shelley, and Keats, he was its greatest poet'.[1] Whatever may be thought of Landor's prose, it would be hard to find anyone today to endorse the claim that, as a poet, he was greater than Scott, Clare, Crabbe, Hogg or Darley – all poets with whom Herford deals. I find him inferior to every one of these poets; but my intention here is not to gird at Herford or to sneer at Landor. For the latter has an importance out of proportion with his meagre achievement. At a crucial stage in the English poetic tradition he struck out alone a path of interesting and sensible experiment; and in deciding what chance there was of success, and where and how the experiment failed, we touch upon matters of importance for the writing of poetry at any time.

What Landor stood for in the writing of poetry can be seen from one of his more distinguished poems, 'To Wordsworth':

> He who would build his fame up high,
> The rule and plummet must apply,
> Before he try if loam or sand
> Be still remaining in the place
> Delved for each polisht pillar's base.
> With skilful eye and fit device
> Thou raisest every edifice,
> Whether in sheltered vale it stand
> Or overlook the Dardan strand,

1 Herford, *Age of Wordsworth*, p. 283.

Amid the cypresses that mourn
Laodameia's love forlorn.

The advice is sufficiently trite. It appears less so in the rather better verse of the 'Epistle to the Author of *Festus*':

Some see but sunshine, others see but gloom,
Others confound them strangely, furiously;
Most have an eye for colour, few for form.
Imperfect is the glory to *create*,
Unless on our creation we can look
And see that all is good; we then may rest.
In every poem train the leading shoot;
Break off the suckers. Thought erases thought,
As numerous sheep erase each other's print
When spungy moss they press or sterile sand.
Blades thickly sown want nutriment and droop,
Although the seed be sound, and rich the soil;
Thus healthy-born ideas, bedded close,
By dreaming fondness perish overlain.

This is far more provocative, challenging as it does that other precept of the period, to 'load every rift with ore'. And yet the principle applied in the lines to Wordsworth and in these to Bailey is identical. We find it more provocative here because, in addressing Wordsworth, Landor uses a trite architectural metaphor for quite commonplace ideas about the need for structure in longer poems; whereas in the lines to Bailey he seems to imply that a short poem requires structure no less. And we are more willing, I think, to consider the structure of an ode or an epic than of a lyric or epigram. Just for that reason, perhaps, it is more salutary to examine Landor's theory and practice in his shorter poems. And I shall here not trouble myself with *Gebir* and the longer narratives, except to record my opinion that these poems, like the shorter ones, have been overrated by Herford and others.

To begin with, it is not hard to see why we fight shy of Landor's theories about the structure of short poems. For when Landor insists that 'ideas' must be disposed carefully about the poem, not crowded one upon another, he raises at once the question of a staple language in which those 'ideas' may be set. The staple of a poem, in this sense, is the diction of the poem. And problems of poetic diction are particularly difficult in the period of the Preface to *Lyrical Ballads*. Critics have never reached agreement about the rights and wrongs of Wordsworth's remarks on diction, and as a result no one has examined with any thoroughness the diction of our Romantic poets. This has prevented us esteeming, as we should, such different achievements as *The White Doe of Rylstone* and 'The Witch of Atlas'. For Landor's principles of disposition seem to me self-evidently right; and it follows that poetic diction, in the sense of a staple language for the poet, is a burning question for poets and readers in any age.

Landor's practice is another matter. The very lines in which he expounds his theory show how far he was from putting it into practice. To begin with, his word 'ideas' is peculiar, since any logical arrangement of words has meaning, and in that sense contains ideas. He cannot mean what he seems to say, that the staple, the gold ring in which the gems are set, shall be devoid of ideas, hence meaningless. And I infer that by 'ideas' Landor means rather what older critics called 'figures'. In other words, we are to find 'ideas' in this sense wherever we find in a poem any conscious rhetoric, any attempt to be striking, concentrated or elaborate beyond what we expect from conversational prose. As a matter of fact, the lines from the 'Epistle to the Author of *Festus*' are themselves highly figurative, in the way they seem to condemn. And only four of them can be said to contain no images:

> Most have an eye for colour, few for form.
> Imperfect is the glory to *create*,

Unless on our creation we can look
And see that all is good; we then may rest.

Here, then, if anywhere, we should find the staple language, that poetic diction which Landor seems to demand, in which figures ('ideas') shall be disposed. Yet here the language is quite indiscriminate. The first line is notably conversational, the second, with its italic, even more so. But the third and fourth, with their presumptuous echo from Genesis, are elaborate, rhetorical and literary. How can this be a staple language, or a pure diction, when in the space of four lines it veers so giddily from high to low? It betrays in particular a bewildering insecurity of *tone*. At one moment the poet is addressing us amicably in the study; at the next, he is thundering from a rostrum. How can we know how to take him? What tone can we adopt in reading the poem aloud? The golden ring is cracked; and, however fine the brilliants, we can only be distressed.

This seems to me the besetting sin of all Landor's writing, something which cancels out all his other virtues. And nearly always Landor courts disaster, as here by the italic, so elsewhere by passages of direct speech. This is the case, for instance, in the much-anthologized 'Faesulan Idyll':

I held down a branch
And gather'd her some blossoms; since their hour
Was come, and bees had wounded them, and flies
Of harder wing were working their way thro'
And scattering them in fragments under-foot.
So crisp were some, they rattled unevolved,
Others, ere broken off, fell into shells,
For such appear the petals when detacht,
Unbending, brittle, lucid, white like snow,
And like snow not seen thro', by eye or sun:
Yet everyone her gown received from me
Was fairer than the first. I thought not so,
But so she praised them to reward my care.
I said, 'You find the largest.'

'This indeed,'
Cried she, 'is large and sweet.' She held one forth,
Whether for me to look at or to take
She knew not, nor did I; but taking it
Would best have solved (and this she felt) her doubt.

No doubt one censures this most sharply by pointing to the inept handling of the blank verse measure. But if we try to look at it still from the standpoint of diction, we have to find much to admire. The language is prosaic in the best sense, carrying precise observation – 'working their way thro''; and the same language is used to a different end in the last lines, where it renders with some subtlety a moment of human contact. Even the Miltonic Latinism 'unevolved' could be saved by the strong coarseness of 'rattled'. It is true that the comparison with shells and snow is less happy, its would-be precision all on the surface. But what damns the passage is the inserted exchange of direct speech. Everything is more conversational than the conversation.[1] The movement of real speech is trimmed and elevated, as if the context were more lofty than it is. And yet the poem began loftily enough:

Here, where precipitate Spring, with one light bound
Into hot Summer's lusty arms, expires . . .

The truth is that Landor merely takes no care for any consistent tone of discourse.

As a matter of fact, despite his advice to 'train the leading shoot', Landor was always prone to lose the thread of his poems, even in more obvious ways. In a poem addressed to satire, which contains more promising lines (for, like Shelley, Landor had satirical talent, but despised it), the failure with direct speech only aggravates a trailing-off into obscurity:

1 Mr. F. W. Bateson suggests that 'You find the largest' is genuinely colloquial, if it is an imperative, as he thinks it is. This had not occurred to me; I had taken it to mean 'Oh, you are only looking at the big ones'. At any rate we can agree that the reply is stilted.

Byron was not *all* Byron; one small part
Bore the impression of a human heart.
Guided by no clear love-star's panting light
Thro' the sharp surges of a northern night,
In Satire's narrow strait he swam the best,
Scattering the foam that hist about his breast.
He who might else have been more tender, first
From Scottish saltness caught his rabid thirst.
Praise Keats . . .
'I think I've heard of him.'
'With you
Shelley stands foremost.'
. . . And his lip was blue . . .
'I hear with pleasure any one commend
So good a soul; for Shelley is my friend.'
One leaf from Southey's laurel made explode
All his combustibles. . . .
'An ass! by God!'

This is mere doodling. It would be hard to find anything less classical, in Landor's or any other sense.

It is unfair, perhaps, to recall it. For we can adapt Herford's verdict on *Gebir* and say of its author that 'though hardly a great poet, he is full of the symptoms of greatness'. Nothing could be much more damaging or sadder; for, as Herford also says, 'It is characteristic of Landor that he is great in detail rather than in mass'.[1] In other words, the poet who tried above all things for the poem as an artefact, a whole thing cut loose from its maker, emerges as a true poet only in fragments and snatches. It is for this reason that one turns back through Landor's poems, coming across distinguished phrases by the way, and thinking, 'Surely I have misjudged him'. But one never has. On rereading, the poem does not improve; it is still disastrously uneven, in the rough, unshaped. The fine writing remains irrelevant; it never adds up to an effect.

1 Herford, op. cit., p. 273.

This difficulty should not arise so sharply with the epigrams. And the best of these are very good:

> Clap, clap the double nightcap on!
> Gifford will read you his amours,
> Lazy as Scheld and cold as Don;
> Kneel, and thank Heaven they are not
> yours.

But this, it will be said, is to miss the point. His epigrams are important – the argument runs – because they retrieve the epigram from flippancy and make it once again a serious vehicle, as in *The Greek Anthology*. Well, I should like to think so. But, in the first place, flippancy can be serious in one sense where a solemn triviality is not. Such graceful marginalia as the lines 'With Petrarca's Sonnets' or 'On Catullus' are all very well in their way, but not serious in the sense that posterity need remember them. There are other epigrams that offer to be serious in the sense that they are momentous statements, and these that are serious in every sense often fail of their effect in the same way as the longer poems, on the score of diction.

Leaving aside the marginalia, Landor's epigrams can be divided for convenience into three classes. There are, in the first place, the compliments ('Dirce', for instance, and most of the poems to Ianthe). Then there are traditional commonplaces, to be expressed in novel ways, with a seeming finality ('Rose Aylmer', 'The Leaves are falling; so am I'). And finally there are poems which offer to be 'discoveries', original in theme but expressed in traditional form. These last two classes may correspond to the two functions of wit, as distinguished by Johnson in 'The Life of Pope'.

The most famous example of the first class is the epigram on 'Dirce':

> Stand close around, ye Stygian set,
> With Dirce in one boat conveyed!

> Or Charon, seeing, may forget
>   That he is old, and she a shade.

In the classical examples of such compliments, from the seventeenth and eighteenth centuries, we find the effect depends upon combining daring hyperbole with imperturbable urbanity:

> To her, whose beauty doth excell
>   Stories, wee tosse theis cupps, and fill
>   Sobrietie, a sacrifice
> To the bright lustre of her eyes.
> Each soule that sipps this is divine:
> Her beauty deifies the wine.

'Urbanity' begs at once the question of diction. For to explain how these trivia seem momentous we have to give to 'urbanity' the meaning that Arnold gave to it, in 'The Literary Influence of Academies', when he spoke of it as the tone or spirit of the centre, embodying the best of a civilization. There, of course, he spoke of such urbanity as an attribute of the best prose, and thought it no business of the poet. But such centrality seems the virtue of a pure diction in poetry, as of an Attic style in prose. And one distinguishes between Landor's compliment and Carew's by saying that in the latter speaks the voice of Caroline culture, whereas in Landor's verses nothing speaks but the voice of the poet himself. It could not be otherwise, for there was for Landor no Regency or Victorian culture to speak through his mouth, as Caroline culture spoke through Carew. Carew knew where he could find the best thought and feeling of his age – at Great Tew, or Hampton Court. It was embodied in a society, the best society of his time. By Landor's time, to speak of 'the best society' required quotation marks. What was accounted the best was plainly not the best; and to find the best one went to Venice or Fiesole, Hampstead or Ravenna, where one found not a society but a cluster of cliques. One has to say that by Landor's day to turn an elegant compliment and make momentous poetry of it was no longer a possibility; and of course it has never been possible since.

The same is true of the second class of Landor's epigrams, his attempts at 'what oft was thought but ne'er so well expressed'. To make poetry out of moral commonplace, a poet has to make it clear that he speaks not in his own voice (that would be impertinent) but as the spokesman of a social tradition. Hence the importance of the Horatian imitation for Pope, or the imitation of Juvenal by Johnson. By employing those forms and modes, the poets spoke out of a tradition which was not merely literary; for the reading of Horace and Juvenal was a tradition of social habit in the audience they addressed, which was also the society for which they spoke. The Greek epigram was no substitute. And when Landor treats a traditional commonplace ('Past ruin'd Ilion Helen lives', 'The Leaves are falling; so am I', 'There is a mountain and a wood between us'), his achievement seems frail and marginal, chiefly because he does not show, in the form he chooses, how traditional, how far from original, is what he wants to say. The difficulty appears very clearly in respect of what is probably the most famous of all the epigrams:

> I strove with none, for none was worth my strife;
> Nature I loved, and, next to Nature, Art;
> I warmed both hands before the fire of life;
> It sinks, and I am ready to depart.

Landor realized the enormity of Byron's demands for admiration, and here I think he meant to avoid it, making instead a dignified *apologia pro vita sua*, like Swift's at the end of 'Verse on the Death of Dr Swift'. But instead he falls between two stools; for we do not feel, as we feel with the traditional forms of apologia, that the apologist makes a case for his own life only as one version of the universal human predicament. It is not at all clear that Landor does not regard his own life and his own nobility as something unique and special. And the reader can therefore be excused for thinking that, in the four lines of Landor's epigram and the umpteen lines of *Manfred*, the attitude is the same – exorbitant, immature and self-pitying.

There remains the third sort of epigram, which I have called 'Discoveries'. I have in mind the use made of this idea by De Quincey, in respect of Wordsworth:

> . . . the author who wins notice the most, is not he that perplexes men by truths drawn from fountains of absolute novelty – truths as yet unsunned, and from that cause obscure; but he that awakens into illuminated consciousness ancient lineaments of truth long slumbering in the mind, although too faint to have extorted attention. Wordsworth has brought many a truth into life both for the eye and for the understanding, which previously had slumbered indistinctly for all men.

Like Wordsworth, Landor does not discover 'truths drawn from fountains of absolute novelty'. Perhaps Shelley does. At any rate Landor occasionally makes discoveries of the Wordsworthian sort, not 'what oft was thought but ne'er so well expressed', but what was never consciously thought before, nor ever expressed. Even here, I think, he tries more often than he suceeds. But sometimes he can make genuine discoveries, especially about movements of the mind:

> Something (ah! tell me what) there is
> To cause that melting tone.
> I fear a thought has gone amiss
> Returning quite alone.

In this field urbanity is of no account, as the name of Wordsworth may remind us. For it is achievement of this sort which preserves many of Wordsworth's early poems, where the diction is eccentric and the versification barely adequate. So, in the poem quoted, the diction of the first two lines is faded and decadent, but this is important only because it leads us to expect something quite different from what we are given thereafter. In other words it makes the discovery more sudden and surprising.

Perhaps for this reason the lines have been found obscure, but their bearing is plain enough. Landor catches in a touching metaphor the experience of breaking off a line of thought, surprised by a melancholy reflection. He explains the shadow falling across the face of his companion by the supposition that a thought has 'gone amiss' (i.e. broken off the train of thought of which it was a link) and 'returned alone', or, as the common metaphor has it, 'brought home' to the thinker a melancholy truth. The poem, one could say, is an exploration and a discovery of what we mean when we say 'The truth was brought home to me'. To give form to an experience so fugitive yet so permanently human seems to me an achievement of a high order. Unfortunately I can think of only one other case in which Landor does something comparable, in his poem 'For an Urn in Thoresby Park'.

There is considerable pathos in the story of Landor's life, so devoted, so disinterested, and to so little end. It is interesting and important chiefly because his attempt to put the clock back shows how inevitable was the Romantic revolution in poetic method and the conception of the poet's function. The poets had to undertake to make discoveries of truth, in some sense novel, because the poetry of truths already acknowledged depended upon conditions which no longer obtained. To make poetry out of traditional commonplace or personal compliment the poet had to write in and for a homogeneous society acknowledging strong and precise traditions of literature and manners. His awareness of such a society as his audience gave the poet the sureness of tone which comes out of a pure diction and achieves urbanity. When Landor attempted this, all the odds were against him. No such society and no such audience existed. And, as a result, the great poets of the age were great in quite novel ways. Wordsworth, for instance, eschewed urbanity and made a virtue of provincialism. Shelley set out to be the discoverer in an absolute sense. Keats, when he was not the discoverer, evaded the question of a staple language by figurative luxury. And when the poets needed to be urbane (as in *Don Juan*, or at the end of 'The Witch of Atlas'), they sought no longer an impossible purity of diction, but a sort of calculated impurity; so that urbanity since has always been ironical. Landor is the type of the poet who refuses to acknowledge the temper of his age. There is a certain magnificence in his obstinate wrong-headedness; but it did not go to produce important poems.

APPENDIX A

Pathos and Chastity in Thomas Gray and Thomas Parnell

I HAVE tried to show that Goldsmith and Wordsworth are at one in asserting that highly figurative writing is more inimical to the pathetic strain than to the sublime. Like most of the contentions of criticism, this cannot be proved. But it may be worth while to present an example which seems to bear out this contention.

Goldsmith admired the work of Thomas Parnell, a neglected minor poet of Pope's circle;[1] and he thought Parnell's 'Night-Piece on Death' superior to Gray's *Elegy in a Country Churchyard.* Johnson disagreed politely, and no doubt we must side with him, for Gray's poem is a more ambitious piece. But certainly Parnell avoids some of the traps into which Gray falls.

William Empson criticizes a stanza from the *Elegy*:

> Full many a gem of purest ray serene
> The dark, unfathomed caves of ocean bear;
> Full many a flower is born to blush unseen
> And waste its sweetness on the desert air.

Mr Empson points out that 'a gem does not mind being in a

1 There is a fatuous crib from Parnell in Goldsmith's *Threnodia Augustalis.* Death speaks in Parnell's 'Night-Piece':

> When Men my Scythe and Darts supply,
> How great a King of Fears am I!

And Goldsmith starts a song:

> When vice my dart and scythe supply
> How great a king of terrors I! . . .

cave and a flower prefers not to be picked; we feel that the man is like the flower, as short-lived, natural and valuable, and this tricks us into feeling that he is better off without opportunities'.

Parnell's version of the 'village Hampdens' is as follows:

> The flat smooth Stones that bear a Name,
> The Chissel's slender Help to Fame,
> (Which ere our Sett of Friends decay
> Their frequent Steps may wear away.)
> A middle Race of Mortals own,
> Men, half ambitious, all unknown.

While it may be true, as Johnson says, that Parnell's verse falls short of Gray's in 'dignity, variety and originality of sentiment', it has here the advantage of keeping the subject soberly in view. If the line read '*un*ambitious' the way would be clear: 'Unworried by worldly competition, these men were happy'. Or if it read '*all* ambitious', it would spark another ready response: 'Men in this humble sphere are worldly as we are, and we, like them, shall be unknown'. Gray, while purporting to say the second, really says the first. Parnell's prosaic 'half-ambitious' says neither, and his pathos is free of any trickery. The treacherous ambiguity comes in with the metaphors.

APPENDIX B

'Strength' and 'Ease' in Seventeenth-century Criticism

SOME of our difficulty in dealing with the abundant good verse of the first part of the seventeenth century derives from the poverty of literary criticism in this period. Outside Jonson's *Discoveries* and Hobbes's essay on *Gondibert* we look in vain for anything to tell us how the men of the period regarded the poetry they and their contemporaries were writing. And as there is no way of taking this poetry on its own valuation, we have to provide scales of our own – 'Cavalier lyrists', 'metaphysicals', 'the marinist tradition', 'the line of wit'. None of these labels would have made sense to any of the poets to whom we attach them.

If there is no criticism in the period, there are clues to be found in the poetry itself to two terms which would have made sense to them. From title-pages, poems of dedication, and votive offerings to poetic masters, we can extricate the terms 'strength' and 'ease'; and we can deduce that it was in these terms that the poets discussed their own and each other's verse. Our difficulty lies in trying to define, on this meagre and fragmentary evidence, what was meant by each of these words. And in the case of 'ease' this question is probably insoluble, since the meaning appears to fluctuate between a smooth fluency in numbers and a quite different, though related, quality of social demeanour, the *sprezzatura* of Castiglione and the Sidneyan ideal, a potent influence at least as late as Lovelace. 'Strength' can be defined more closely, and it is in 'strength' that I am chiefly interested; but since the terms are frequently opposed, and the one seems to strike off from the other, it seems advisable to try to trace them both together.

In *Discoveries*, Jonson censures both extremes, both too much strength and too much ease. You shall have, he says:

> others, that in composition are nothing, but what is rough, and broken: *Quae per salebras, altaque saxa cadunt*. And if it would come gently, they trouble it of purpose. They would not have it run without rubs, as if that stile were more strong and manly, that stroke the eare with a kind of uneven(n)esse. These men erre not by chance, but knowingly, and willingly; they are like men that affect a fashion by themselves, have some singularity in a Ruffe, Cloake, or Hat-band; or their beards, specially cut to provoke beholders, and set a marke upon themselves. They would be reprehended, while they are look'd on. And this vice, one that is in authority with the rest, loving, delivers over to them to bee imitated: so that oft-times the faults which he fell into, the others seeke for: This is the danger, when vice becomes a Precedent.
>
> Others there are, that have no composition at all; but a kind of tuneing, and riming fall, in what they write. It runs and slides, and onely makes a sound. Womens-Poets they are call'd: as you have womens-Taylors.
>
> They write a verse, as smooth, as soft, as creame;
> In which there is no torrent, nor scarce streame.
>
> You may sound these wits, and find the depth of them, with your middle finger. They are Creame-bowle, or but puddle deepe.[1]

This position, from which not 'strong', 'manly', 'rough' on the one side, nor 'smooth', 'easy', on the other, are praiseworthy in themselves, was probably given lip-service throughout the period.

Towards the end of the century, Jonson is echoed by Dryden in *Of Dramatick Poesie*. Crites declares that he has 'a mortal apprehension of two poets':

1 Ben Jonson, *Works*, ed. Herford and Simpson, vol. viii (OUP, 1947), p. 585.

''Tis easy to guess whom you intend,' said Lisideuis; 'and without naming them, I ask you, if one of them does not perpetually pay us with clenches upon words, and a certain clownish kind of raillery? if now and then he does not offer at a catachresis or Clevelandism, wresting and torturing a word into another meaning: in fine, if he be not one of those whom the French would call *un mauvais buffon*; one that is so much a well-willer to the satire, that he spares no man; and though he cannot strike a blow to hurt any, yet ought to be punished for the malice of the action, as our witches are justly hanged, because they think themselves so; and suffer deservedly for believing they did mischief, because they meant it.' 'You have described him,' said Crites, 'so exactly, that I am afraid to come after you with my other extremity of poetry. He is one of those who, having had some advantage of education and converse, knows better than the other what a poet should be, but puts it into practice more unluckily than any man; his style and matter are everywhere alike: he is the most calm, peaceable writer you ever read: he never disquiets your passions with the least concernment, but still leaves you in as even a temper as he found you; he is a very Leveller in poetry; he creeps along with ten little words in every line, and helps out his numbers with *For to*, and *Unto*, and all the pretty expletives he can find, till he drags them to the end of another line; while the sense is left tired half way behind it: he doubly starves all his verses, first for want of thought and then of expression; his poetry neither has wit in it, nor seems to have it; like him in Martial:

Pauper videri Cinna vult, et est pauper.'[1]

Dryden's prose is more loose-limbed, and his fancy more fantastic, but it is plain that his two 'extremities of poetry' are roughly the same as Jonson's.

Between Jonson's essay and Dryden's, this notion of a balance to be struck between too much strength and too much ease was the principle on which all critical perspective was aligned. The terms 'soft' or 'smooth' and 'strong' were habitually opposed:

1 W. P. Ker (ed.), *Essays of John Dryden*, vol. i (OUP, 1900), pp. 31, 32. The two poets discussed are identified as Robert Wild and (perhaps) Flecknoe.

His Muse is soft, as sweet, and though not strong,
Pathetic, lively, all on fire, and young.[1]

But the poets can be seen to group themselves, according as they more esteem the strong and masculine style or the smooth and easy. And these groupings are not always those wished upon the poets by later historians.

A spokesman of those poets who most admired ease may have been Suckling. In 'Sessions of the Poets', he censures Godolphin for his 'strength':

During these troubles in the Court was hid
One that Apollo soon mist, little Cid;
And having spied him, call'd him out of the throng,
And advis'd him in his ear not to write so strong.

This attitude is shared by Earle, discussing Lord Falkland: 'Dr Earle would not allow him to be a good poet, though a great witt; he writ not a smoth verse, but a great deal of sense.'[2]

It is not surprising, on the other hand, that Godolphin appears as the spokesman of the 'strong', using the term as one of unqualified praise:

This Work had been proportion'd to our Sight,
Had you but knowne with some allay to Write,
And not preserv'd your Authors Strength and Light.

But you so crush those Odors, so dispense
Those rich perfumes, you make them too intense
And such (alas) as too much please our Sense.

We fitter are for sorrows, then such Love;
Iosiah falls, and by his fall doth move
Teares from the people, Mourning from above.

1 'L. B.', prefatory poem to *Arcadius and Sepha* by William Bosworth, 1651, in G. Saintsbury (ed.), *Minor Poets of the Caroline Period*, vol. ii, p. 528.

2 Aubrey, 'Life of Falkland', in *Brief Lives.*

> Iudah, in her Iosiah's Death, doth dye,
> All Springs of grief are opened to supply
> Streames to the torrent of this Elegy . . .[1]

And again later in the same poem:

> Others translate, but you the Beames collect
> Of your inspired Authors, and reflect
> Those heavenly Rais with new and strong effect.

The disagreement between these two bodies of opinion did not remain so gentlemanly and mild. Spirits became partisan, and as usual when controversy becomes a little heated both opinions became distorted and extreme. From the first, other terms began to cluster around 'strength' on the one hand, 'ease' on the other. 'Ease' degenerated into 'smoothness':

> Sucklyn and Carew, I must confess, wrote some few things smoothly enough, but as all they did in this kind was not very considerable, so 'twas a little later than the earliest pieces of Mr Waller.[2]

And 'strength', which had from the first been connected with 'the masculine style',[3] now became the same as 'Clevelandism':

> And now instead of that strenuous masculine style which breatheth in this author, we have only an enervous effeminate froth offered, as if they had taken the salivating pill before they set pen to paper. You must hold your breath in the perusal lest the jest vanish by blowing on.[4]

When, as we saw from Dryden, 'Clevelandism' became a term of reproach, 'strength' too was a term thoroughly in disrepute:

1 'To my very much honoured Friend Mr George Sandys upon his Paraphrase on the Poeticall Parts of the Bible', in William Dighton (ed.), *The Poems of Sidney Godolphin* (OUP, 1931), p. 66.
2 Preface to *Posthumous Poems of Edmund Waller*, 1690.
3 Cf. Carew on Donne, 'An Elegie upon the Death of Dr Donne'.
4 Preface to 'Clievelandi Vindiciae', 1677, in Saintsbury, op. cit., vol. iii, p. 18.

To this palpable darkness I may also add the ambitious obscurity of expressing more than is perfectly conceived or perfect conception in fewer words than it requires, which expressions, though they have had the honour to be called strong lines, are indeed no better than riddles, and, not only to the reader but also after a little time to the writer himself, dark and troublesome.[1]

And soon 'strength' became a simple gibe:

He'll take a scant piece of coarse Sense, and stretch it on the Tenter-hooks of half a score Rhimes, until it crack that you may see through it, and it rattle like a Drum-Head. When you see his Verses hanged up in Tobacco-Shops, you may say, in defiance of the Proverb, that the weakest does not always go to the Wall; for 'tis well known the Lines are strong enough, and in that Sense may justly take the Wall of any, that have been written in our Language.[2]

It becomes obvious that the confusions engendered by this word 'strength' are becoming unmanageable. Hobbes, Jonson, Godolphin and the anonymous apologist for Cleveland seem not to be speaking of the same thing. And what are we to make of such collocations as 'the strength of his fancy'?

The strength of his fancy, and the shadowing of it in words, he taketh from Mr Marlow in his Hero and Leander . . .[3]

Confusion is worse confounded when, in the next century, Pope and Dr Johnson are found applauding Denham as 'strong':

The 'strength of Denham' which Pope so emphatically mentions, is to be found in many lines and couplets, which convey much meaning in few words, and exhibit the sentiment with more weight than bulk.[4]

And for chaos to come again, we may cite John Drinkwater:

1 Thomas Hobbes, essay on *Gondibert*, 1651.
2 Samuel Butler, *Characters*, ed. A. R. Waller (CUP, 1908), p. 52.
3 'R. C.' To the Reader, prefixed to *Arcadius and Sepha*, 1651, in Saintsbury, op. cit.
4 Dr Johnson, 'Denham', in *Lives of the Poets*.

'Apollo', says Suckling in a doggerel passage of the 'Sessions of the Poets', calling 'little Cid' 'out of the throng', advised him 'not to write so strong'. Unless the warning had some special allusion that now escapes us, Apollo could not well have talked greater nonsense. Violence is the quality furthest removed from Godolphin's reserved and modest muse. A little access of vigour was what he most needed. Not vigour of conscience or invention, but of speech. He remained his own debtor for an occasional transport of vehemence that might have loosened up the whole current of his poetry.[1]

Although we may not hope to be able to pin down every usage, we may come near to the 'special allusion' which escaped Mr Drinkwater.

For at least it is apparent that whatever 'strength' may be, it is not what Drinkwater supposes, 'a transport of vehemence that might have loosened up the whole current'. 'Strength' is not a 'loosening' but a 'tightening'; it is a matter of compression and concentration. And Johnson therefore used the word with propriety when he applied it to Denham, and disengaged it from the hyperbolical conceit with which it had been identified. Donne achieves concentration by way of hyperbole, Denham by means of syntax. And both are 'strong'.

1 John Drinkwater, Introduction to *Poems of Godolphin*, p. xi. It may be remarked that the other side of the controversy is also fruitful of confusions, though not to such an extent. Thus, in respect of the 'ease-smoothness-sweetness' group of terms, it may be pointed out that in seventeenth-century parlance it is possible for verse to be easy, smooth and laboured all at once. 'Laboured' is not a term of dispraise; cf. Saintsbury, op. cit., vol. ii, p. 529: 'On these laboured poems of the deceased Author, Mr William Bosworth'.

[illegible]

[illegible] passage in the [illegible] of the [illegible]

[illegible]

Although we may not need to [illegible] the [illegible] to the [illegible] which [illegible]

[illegible]

[illegible]

ARTICULATE ENERGY

An Inquiry into the Syntax of English Poetry

Introduction

THIS book is built on a very simple plan. Its earlier sections are devoted to examining three main authorities in the field of poetic theory, each of which offers, explicitly or by implication, a theory about the nature and function of syntax in poetry. Then I try to discover, simply from the reading of certain poems, the different ways in which syntax can contribute to poetic effect; and I think I show that none of the theories will quite meet the case, because the contributions of syntax are more various and often more subtle than any one of them can allow. The remainder of the book attempts to show how this discrepancy between theory and practice can obstruct our reading, and sometimes also our writing, of poetry. In case the first sections should be dry and laborious reading, I have tried here also to introduce into the exposition and criticism of theory some passages and even whole sections of a more practical kind. This has the advantage of criticizing the theories by showing how their principles work out when adopted and applied in critical practice.

I am grateful to Douglas Brown, Professor H. O. White and John Broadbent for helpful criticism of earlier versions of the whole work or of sections from it. And I am particularly indebted to G. Warren Shaw for permission to incorporate some of the fruits of his researches into the attitude taken up towards poetic syntax by poets and readers in the eighteenth century.

Preface to the 1975 edition

My first book of criticism, *Purity of Diction in English Verse*, was a thinly disguised manifesto. Though this second book grew quite immediately out of that first one – from the realization that syntax was part and parcel of diction – *Articulate Energy* was or became a quite different sort of book. Whatever polemical motives I had when I started it were soon lost sight of as I recognized the excitingly unmapped territory I had blundered into. As I began drawing the map, the work became ever more truly what I finally described it as: an Enquiry, from which whatever partialities and prejudices I started with were gradually eliminated. Reading it over now, I still find that it has that character, genuinely an investigation by a student who has no axes to grind.

Not unnaturally, however, people who were kind enough to read the two books one after the other, and to read my poems too, supposed that there was a manifesto hidden in this book as in the earlier one. They wanted to see me as taking sides, with Pope and Yeats and perhaps Auden, against Pound and perhaps Eliot. And so these friends of mine were disconcerted and even annoyed when a few years later I devoted a book to Pound's poetry – a book which, though it failed to please the really committed Poundians on either side of the Atlantic, on the other hand was certainly too sympathetic towards Pound, and too admiring of him, to please most British readers. And I compounded my offence later by giving respectful attention to later American poets working the Poundian vein, Charles Olson for instance, who went even further than Pound in disrupting and distorting formal syntax. Where did I stand, or where do I (for the question is still put to me)? It is not easy to answer this question without sounding self-righteous, without saying for instance that poetry, even the poetry of the last hundred years, is too wide and various a territory, and too important for the survival of our civilization, for 'taking sides' to be an adequate response to it. It is a field of human study, in which bluff common sense and evangelizing fervour are as inadequate and obstructive as they are in any other field; the coolness and impartiality which we associate with the idea of *enquiry* are as much the rules of the game in this study as in others. (Which is *not* to say that such investigations can be; or should be, 'scientific'; nor is it to advocate a limp eclecticism.)

However, my friends who looked in *Articulate Energy* for a manifesto, and thought they found one, deserve a less lordly answer. The subject of the book is a limited one: syntax in poetry. Although I was surprised and a little alarmed, as I worked at it, to find how many other aspects of poetry I had to touch upon, it remains true that there are whole dimensions of poetry as we have it, which had to be left out of account altogether. The histrionics of Yeats, the magnanimity of Pound – these were matters that just did not come up for discussion. And so it was entirely feasible and proper for me to prefer Yeats's handling of syntax to Pound's (as I did and do), while keeping to myself certain reservations about other aspects of these two poets' work – reservations which in a final account would tilt the balance of my sympathies the other way. My book was an investigation of poetic method, not an estimate of poetic achievements.

The older one gets, the easier it should be to maintain the impartiality of the true enquirer. But testiness too is something that comes with age. And so if I were to write the book now, it would be a testier performance, and the worse for that. As my friend Ted Weiss has written, 'though with twenty years elapsed, symbolism . . . hardly dominates today', the Anglo-American poetic scene is more than ever dominated by 'the intuitive, the improvisatory, the fragmentary, as against reason, syntax, order'. If *Articulate Energy* reads quaintly now, it may be because of its author's ingenuous assumption that Wordsworth and Pope – Pope! – were not just standard authors reeking of the library and the examination-hall, but living presences in our poetry, challenging emulation and guiding practice. Twenty years have made a great and woeful difference here: they have seen a rapid and strident advance of the perennial and parochial fallacy that our own predicament, 'the modern', is unprecedented; and accordingly the historical perspective of the poet and his readers has been drastically foreshortened. Nowadays we travel light. It sometimes seems that the most ancient author in the English language whom we acknowledge as a living presence is ... William Blake. And even so, the Blake thus recognized as 'relevant' is the author of *The Four Zoas* and *America: A Prophecy*, certainly not the master of poetic syntax whom I honour in Chapter VII. If an unprejudiced Enquiry into poetic method were undertaken nowadays, how could it be presented to an English-speaking audience which has settled all the troublesome questions in advance, by ruling nine-tenths of the evidence inadmissible?

Some things in the book strike me now as unsatisfactory. In Chapter V the one test case that I take from Shakespeare is not enough to vindicate Ernest Fenollosa's contentions about him, though I proceeded as if it were. Verse that is spoken by a *dramatis persona* in a fully specified dramatic situation requires, in any case, that the student take into account many more considerations than I was prepared to allow for. Then, the one comment that I permit myself on William Carlos Williams seems to me now to be wide of the mark, and in any case Williams's handling of syntax deserves more than an insolent swipe in passing. I still think that Williams's precedent and his precepts have exerted, and still exert, a lamentable influence, especially in the U.S.; and that no one is more responsible for what I have called the foreshortening of historical perspectives since 1955. But another whole book would be required to substantiate this, and it is not one that I would care to write, for Williams is in many ways a very winning figure and I am affected by how much his poetry means to my American friends. It was his ambition to write an American poetry that should sever all ties with English poetry, and in this he succeeded; it is not surprising therefore that a British reader, even one like myself who has read some of his poems with pleasure, should regard his work as a whole with alarm and even a sort of rancour. I ought to have left him alone; his work has nothing to do with an enquiry into the syntax of *English* poetry.

On the other hand I am quite impenitent about Dylan Thomas's sonnets, written according to principles which seem to me radically vicious. But I do something disingenuous when, in Chapter X, I slide from making this point into what looks like a discussion of Rimbaud. Thomas may have been what he called himself with bitter self-mockery, 'the Rimbaud of Cwmdonkin Drive'; but this is not to say that the author of *Les Assis* and *Les Chercheuses de Poux* was the Dylan Thomas of Charleville. I can excuse myself by saying that the Welsh name and the French one were twenty years ago connected on just these lines, as by Elizabeth Sewell in a passage I discuss, and that I was considering the image of Rimbaud created by such critics, rather than Rimbaud himself. But this is not a good excuse. The least one can say is that, if indeed Thomas and Rimbaud do write themselves into the same vicious *impasse*, Rimbaud had set out from a place altogether more sane and robust and precociously splendid than any imaginative stage known to Thomas.

Some of the most careful readers of *Articulate Energy* have fastened upon those pages where I speak of a tacit compact or contract between writer and reader, and have suggested, more or less gently, that this was a graceful delusion of the mid-1950s when some of us dreamed of reconstituting a literary world like that of the eighteenth century, when author and reader alike agreed about what experiences should be brought into the public domain, what others should remain covert. (I have in mind particularly Patrick Swinden's penetrating essay, 'English Poetry'.[1]) I never knew anyone at that time who laboured under that delusion. Instead there were certain writers who agreed with themselves to write *as if* such contracts existed between writer and reader, although they knew that they didn't exist, and couldn't. This is a quite different matter: a deliberate stratagem, undertaken so as to will into being conditions which ought to exist, but don't. And for those of us who have survived as writers from the 1950s into the 1970s it is still the only honourable stratagem that we can practise – to act *as if* the writer and his readers were still the civilized people that they may have ceased to be.

What seems to be never recognized is that some contract *must* exist between the poet and his readers, a contract which, if the poet suppresses it from his mind when he writes his poems, at least must be in his mind when he publishes them. The reader who pays hard cash for a book of poems, and then spares the time to look at what he's bought, certainly does so in the expectation of getting some return for his trouble. One remembers the perhaps legendary Frenchman in the boulevard café who in the 1920s greeted Cocteau with 'Étonne-nous, Monsieur Jean!' If the reader, when he opens a book of poems, does not look to it for the range of variously noble pleasures which the doctrine of the *genres* led him to expect, then he opens it 'looking for kicks'. 'Étonne-nous, Monsieur Jean . . .', 'Blow my mind, man!' A poet like Ted Hughes, who in the 1950s plainly rejected the terms of the contract accepted by the Movement poets of that era, did not thereby free himself of any contractual obligations whatever. He accepted instead, as he may have learnt afterwards with dismay, the terms of that grosser contract which put him on a par with Mick Jagger – as of course Allen

1 In C. B. Cox and A. E. Dyson (ed.), *The Twentieth Century Mind: History, Ideas and Literature in Britain*, vol. iii (OUP, 1972).

Ginsberg did also, at about the same time. Ezra Pound, who first loosened and then rewrote the traditional contract so as to weigh it towards the writer and against the reader, would be appalled to find that the new form of contract in effect makes the writer wholly the slave and creature of his public – a mass-public, swayed by it knows not what, capable of responding only to the grossest stimuli, at once fickle and predictable, exacting as only the undirected can be. Yet this is what has happened. And the 1960s, that hideous decade, showed what was involved: the arts of literature were enlisted on the side of all that was insane and suicidal, without order and without proportion, *against civilization*. Charles Olson in his last years was appalled by the stoned and bombed-out zombies who flocked to hear him read and lecture. *That* was not the public he thought he had been addressing! But once the poet abandons the traditional forms of contract he has no control over who shall countersign the document that is his poem.

And yet in the 1960s and today, not all poets who abandon or disrupt syntax do so for aggressive or egotistical reasons. There are some who would claim by doing so to celebrate through imitation certain natural or cosmic processes which know nothing of transitive or intransitive, of subjects, verbs or objects:

> What strikes me is how openly placed the poem is to receive whatever fruits are ripe. Mostly up to now the forms have been very tight, with theology to match and the life within purged from these two margins. And now he can hardly finish a sentence! I can't help thinking of some sweet rain falling steadily over the fields, gracefully immune to human denial; and JR moved even more than moving others, the elegist turning to psalms.[1]

Such humility as is expressed here, such gentleness and self-effacement in poets, may be grounded in self-deception; and in

1 From advance publicity (1973) by the *Grosseteste Review* for John Riley's *Ways of Approaching*; a comment by J. H. Prynne on Riley's long poem, *Czargrad*.

any case the suppression or subversion of syntactical order may not be a necessary or logical consequence of such a sense of the poet's role. But clearly, perverse or not, this is something more admirable than the strident self-aggrandizement which leads other poets to cultivate a superficially similar dishevelment – 'he can hardly finish a sentence!' And indeed, I nowadays detect, under provocation from such a statement as this, another vast reach of my subject which was wholly out of my ken in 1955: how differently syntax in poetry must be regarded when poem-making is considered as a religious (celebratory) activity, rather than an ethical one. I am not much better equipped now to deal with this range of possibilities than I was in 1955; for, as J. H. Prynne rightly hints, the question is really a theological one – whether leading the chance congregation in worship isn't the priestly function, not a poetical one.

I have changed my mind? My friends seem to think I have, not once but several times. If I have, it is nothing to be ashamed of. But it seems to me that I have not. What I wrote in 1955, I stand over now. Then what I said seemed to be timely; now it has, to my eyes, an air more forlorn. But I stand over it.

Stanford, California — Donald Davie

I

Syntax as Unpoetical: T. E. Hulme

I

IN 1902, Hugo von Hofmannsthal, then twenty-eight, published a work in prose called *The Letter of Lord Chandos.*[1] This purports to be a letter written to Francis Bacon by an Elizabethan nobleman, explaining why the writer has fallen silent and dropped out of the literary life in which (as we are to understand) he had already made his mark in his youth. It is generally conceded that this is Hofmannsthal's rendering of a similar crisis in his own life, a crisis which silenced him, not completely indeed, but as a lyrical poet. For the rest of his life Hofmannsthal was occupied with prose and with drama, no longer with self-sufficient poetry. *The Letter of Lord Chandos* is not a plain allegory, and it is difficult, perhaps impossible, to describe the crisis Hofmannsthal writes about in any other way than as he renders it himself. Here I am interested in only one aspect of what happens to Lord Chandos or what happened to Hofmannsthal.

Near the beginning of the letter, Chandos speaks of his state of mind in the days of his productive youth:

> And out of Sallust, in those happy, stimulating days, there flowed into me as though through never-congested conduits the realization of form – that deep, true, inner form which can be sensed only beyond the domain of rhetorical tricks: that form of which one can no longer say that it organizes subject-matter, for it penetrates it, dissolves it, creating

1 Hugo von Hofmannsthal, *Selected Prose*, tr. Mary Hottinger and Tania and James Stern (Routledge, 1953), pp. 129–41.

at once both dream and reality, an interplay of eternal forces, something as marvellous as music or algebra. This was my most treasured plan.

This introduces at once a fancy which will recur many times in the course of this study – the notion of a literary form 'as marvellous as music or algebra'. This was of course an ideal of the symbolist poets, and it is not surprising that it should be in the minds of all the post-symbolist generations, up to our own day. But different writers and thinkers respond to the idea in different ways. For some it is a will-o'-the-wisp which can lead nowhere; for some it is a baleful phantom, a nightmare; for some to whom it remains an ideal, it is all the more attractive for being unattainable, an object of wistful yearning; others believe it is attained in every successful poem. Having connected literature with music, it is natural to go on and relate it to other arts, to sculpture, painting, architecture; so Chandos compares the structure of Latin prose with the architecture of Palladio. On the other hand, if literature can be connected with mathematics, how shall it be related to science? And here again, there are many answers. Science can join hands with literature over mathematics as a bridge; or it can glare at literature over mathematics as a gulf; or mathematics can be lumped with the sciences away from literature; or it can be embraced by literature and denied to the sciences; or poetry and science can fight back to back, against the mathematical abstractions that threaten both of them. This is a world, in fact, of large gestures, sweeping statements, rash conclusions, not a field for the timid or the scrupulous.

Not that this applies to Hofmannsthal. His *Letter of Lord Chandos* is a work of art, not a treatise, and if we take it as a treatise, we do so at our peril, and must take the consequences.

Chandos, then, goes on to describe the state of despondency and sterility into which his buoyant arrogance has declined:

At first I grew by degrees incapable of discussing a loftier or more general subject in terms of which everyone, fluently and without hesitation, is wont to avail himself. I experienced an inexplicable distaste for so much as uttering the words *spirit*, *soul*, or *body* . . . the abstract terms of which the tongue must avail itself as a matter of course in order to voice a judgement – these terms crumbled in my mouth like mouldy fungi.

This first stage of the distemper, of which the symptom is distaste for abstract terms, comes to a head when Chandos, trying to scold his small daughter for lying, finds it impossible to distinguish, or at any rate to communicate the distinction, between truth and falsehood. This grows until the simplest propositions of common gossip seem to him 'indemonstrable, as mendacious and hollow as could be'. In this stage:

For me everything disintegrated into parts, those parts again into parts; no longer would anything let itself be encompassed by one idea. Single words floated round me; they congealed into eyes which stared at me and into which I was forced to stare back – whirlpools which gave me vertigo and, reeling incessantly, led into the void.

Chandos attempts to cure himself by recourse to the Ancients – not to Plato, but to Seneca and Cicero, writers notable for 'the harmony of their clearly defined and orderly ideas'. But in vain:

These ideas, I understood them well: I saw their wonderful interplay rise before me like magnificent fountains upon which played golden balls. I could hover around them and watch how they played, one with the other; but they were concerned only with each other, and the most profound, most personal quality of my thinking remained excluded from this magic circle.

The connection with syntax should now be clear. In his youthful buoyancy Chandos saw language as above all an instrument of articulation, a way of establishing relationships, like the harmonies of music and the equations of algebra. Syntax is one of the ways in which language is able to do this. Hence, when Chandos loses his nerve (if we may put it like that), he loses, in fact, his faith in syntax. The only language he can trust is a language broken down into units of isolated words, a language which abandons any attempt at articulation, because that articulation seems to take place only inside a closed system – 'they were concerned only with each other'.

In *The Letter of Lord Chandos* this change in his attitude to language is only one aspect, perhaps no more than a symptom, of a change in his attitude to experience. In his youth, he explains, he had been sure of the harmonious relationship existing between apparently quite disparate fields of experience. This I think is the point of the period setting, for, as Hofmannsthal implies, the pastoral convention is a good example of this confidence. So too of course is the figure of Bacon himself, 'the last man' (so we say in the lecture hall) 'to take the whole of human knowledge for his province', and, we may add, to take it *as* a whole. What is more, human experience was also articulated, as it were, in depth: Chandos meant to decipher the ancient fables and myths, confident (like George Chapman) of reducing them all to one articulated system. 'At other times I divined that all was allegory and that each creature was a key to all the others; and I felt myself the one capable of seizing each by the handle and unlocking as many of the others as were ready to yield.' In his later phase Chandos feels drawn to dwell upon things in themselves and in isolation. In this way, sometimes, he can attain a conviction of harmony throughout nature. But this is of a different sort; it is, specifically, unutterable, the product of momentary sympathy with another form of life in all its uniqueness and otherness. These moments, when they come, are ecstatic, but also brief, fitful, unpredictable. It seems that they leave behind them no residue of confidence; and the tenor of life between these revelations is distracted and inert.

Hofmannsthal, it should be realized, by creating the *persona* of Chandos, avoids committing himself on the whole issue. His detachment may even be ironical: the point may be (though I do not think it is) that the youthful confidence of Chandos was an illusion well lost; hence that syntax is a snare and a sham, and that truth is only to be found in the isolated 'thing'.

2

SOME ten or more years later, the English philosopher T. E. Hulme used the analogy of language and algebra in a quite different way:

In prose as in algebra concrete things are embodied in signs or counters which are moved about according to rules, without being visualized at all in the process. There are in prose certain type situations and arrangements of words, which move as automatically into certain other arrangements as do functions in algebra. One only changes the Xs and the Ys back into physical things at the end of the process. Poetry, in one aspect at any rate, may be considered as an effort to avoid this characteristic of prose. It is not a counter language, but a visual concrete one. It is a compromise for a language of intuition which would hand over sensations bodily. It always endeavours to arrest you, and to make you continuously see a physical thing, to prevent you gliding through an abstract process. It chooses fresh epithets and fresh metaphors, not so much because they are new, and we are tired of the old, but because the old cease to convey a physical thing and become abstract counters. A poet says a ship 'coursed the seas' to get a physical image, instead of the counter word 'sailed'. Visual meanings can only be transferred by the new bowl of metaphor; prose is an old pot that lets them leak out. Images in verse are not mere decoration, but the very essence of an intuitive language. Verse is a pedestrian taking you over the ground, prose – a train which delivers you at a destination.[1]

This passage, and others like it from Hulme, have had a very great influence upon English and American poets, and upon their readers, since *Speculations* was first published, in 1924. It is therefore a great pity that these writings were left by their author fragmentary and unrevised; for Hulme's looseness in the use of words like 'abstract', 'concrete', 'embodied', 'visualized' has survived as a persistent 'woolliness' ever since and has, as we shall see, brought a needless muddle into the question of poetic syntax. If Hulme had lived to revise this material, this looseness

1 T. E. Hulme, *Speculations* (Routledge, 1924), pp. 134, 135.

no doubt would have been cleared away, and it should not blind us to the great power, clarity and independence of his thought. What is more to the point here is the handful of excellent poems Hulme left behind him, which prove that when he spoke of the language of poetry he spoke with first hand experience.

It is plain that Hulme has more in common with the later Lord Chandos than with the earlier. And it is worth noting that, like Hofmannsthal, he had abandoned writing poetry long before his death (according to Epstein, 'this seemed to him too facile'), and also that, according to Sir Herbert Read, Hulme's *magnum opus* was to be 'a personal philosophy, cast into an allegorical form perhaps analogous to Nietzsche's *Zarathustra*, and having as its final object the destruction of the idea that the world has unity, *or that anything can be described in words*'[1] (my italics). Yet Hulme nowhere realizes, or nowhere acknowledges, that in his view of poetic language there is no place for syntax. That this is the case should be clear to common sense, even without the parallel with Lord Chandos; but to establish the fact more firmly we need to realize what lies beneath Hulme's view of poetry, his adherence to the philosophy of Bergson. The passage I have quoted comes from the essay 'Romanticism and Classicism', but it is reproduced, almost word for word, in another called 'Bergson's Theory of Art'; and it is there that it falls into place in the whole pattern of Hulme's thought.

It is probably due to Hulme that much modern criticism is Bergsonian, perhaps without knowing it. When, for instance, John Crowe Ransom writes that the poet's is a world of 'stubborn and contingent objects', with a sign up, 'This road does not go through to action; fictitious', he is writing quite in the Bergsonian spirit. Bergson distinguishes between the roads that go through to action and those others, such as the poet's, that do not, in terms of extensive and intensive manifolds, respectively. Hulme's essay 'Intensive Manifolds' is devoted to explain-

1 T. E. Hulme, op. cit., p. xiv.

ing these terms, but their relevance to literature is brought out in 'Romanticism and Classicism', when Hulme discusses Coleridge's use of the word 'vital':

. . . Coleridge uses it in a perfectly definite and what I call dry sense. It is just this: A mechanical complexity is the sum of its parts. Put them side by side and you get the whole. Now vital or organic is merely a convenient metaphor for a complexity of a different kind, that in which the parts cannot be said to be elements as each one is modified by the other's presence, and each one to a certain extent is the whole. The leg of a chair by itself is still a leg. My leg by itself wouldn't be.

Now the characteristic of the intellect is that it can only represent complexities of the mechanical kind. It can only make diagrams, and diagrams are essentially things whose parts are separate from another. The intellect always analyses – when there is a synthesis it is baffled. That is why the artist's work seems mysterious. The intellect can't represent it. This is a necessary consequence of the particular nature of the intellect and the purposes for which it is formed. It doesn't mean that your synthesis is ineffable, simply that it can't be definitely stated.

Now this is all worked out in Bergson, the central feature of his whole philosophy. It is all based on the clear conception of these vital complexities which he calls 'intensive', and the recognition of the fact that the intellect can only deal with the extensive multiplicity. To deal with the intensive you must use intuition.[1]

There is more about 'intensive manifolds' in the essay of that name. There too we find a fuller treatment of the opposite to this, the extensive manifold:

It is necessary then to show exactly in what way Bergson thinks that our ordinary methods of explanation distort reality. The process of explanation itself is generally quite an unconscious one. We explain things and it never strikes us to consider what we have done. We are as it were *inside* the process, and we cannot observe it, but you may get a hint of its nature by observing its effects. In any explanation you start off with certain phenomena, and you transform them into something else and say: 'This is what really happens.' There is something about

1 Ibid., pp. 138, 139.

this second state that satisfies the demands of your intellect, which makes you say: 'This is perfectly clear.' You have in your mind a model of what is clear and comprehensible, and the process of explanation consists in expressing all the phenomena of nature in the terms of this model. I ought to say here that I am speaking not of ordinary explanation, but of explanation when it has gone to its greatest lengths, which is when it has worked itself out in any completed science like mechanics.[1]

My point is that syntax is, on this showing, an extensive manifold; and since poetry must deal with intensive manifolds, it follows that in Hulme's view poetry has no use for syntax.

We can clinch this as nearly as possible when we find Hulme making an excursion into etymology:

The question arises: Why is the intellect satisfied in this way? The answer to this is quite simple and can be got from the etymology of the words which indicate explanation. Explanation means *ex plane*, that is to say, the opening out of things on a plain surface. There is the phrase, *the chestnut explains its leaves*, i.e. unfolds them. Then the French word is *expliquer* (*explico*), to unfold. The process of explanation is always a process of unfolding. A tangled mass is unfolded flat so that you can see all its parts separated out, and any tangle which can be separated out in this way must of course be an extensive manifold.[2]

The same equation (explaining = unfolding) occurs in Ezra Pound, at one time an associate of Hulme's, when he compares Confucius with Aristotle: 'Give the Greek points on explanatory elaborations. The explicitness, that is literally the unfoldedness, may be registered better in the Greek syntax, but the loss must be counted.'[3] Syntax assists explanation, but explanation is unfolding, and intensive manifolds, which should be poetry's main concern, cannot be unfolded; hence it appears that syntax is out of place in poetry.

1 T. E. Hulme, op. cit., pp. 175, 176.
2 Ibid., p. 177.
3 *Guide to Kulchur* (Faber, 1938), p. 279.

3

There is an excellent poem by Terence Tiller which expresses the view of life recommended by Hulme and Bergson, and endured, towards the end, by Hofmannsthal's Lord Chandos. (Its true paternity, I should guess, is to be found in Rilke.) And it shows too what is likely to happen to syntax in poems that are written in this spirit. It is called, 'Substitutes':

> Squeezing the private sadness until words
> pearl round it, and all images become
> the private sadness and the life; and a name
> blood. Or flowering like a bride towards
> the object, amorous of image, a home:
> giving oneself to symbols; feeding myths.
>
> There is one house beyond opposing paths.
> Pelican or vampire is the same.
>
> Only by going in and not around;
> pulsing with stone's cold veins; duck's world,
> rock's world;
>
> Sifting the air as trees; long as the wind;
> sucking the air as wheat; become a field.
>
> No myth will ever come to any good:
> but biting the wasp's apple; being blood.

To refuse to articulate is itself articulation; we issue the statement that we shall issue no more statements. Hence Mr Tiller's poem closes on a full sentence. But where he wants to convey the 'going in and not around', he has to dislocate the syntax of his verses.

There is poetry of the present age which goes much further than this in abnegating syntax. But it is more important to realize that syntax may have gone from a poem even when all the syntactical forms in the poem are perfect and correct. If this were not the case, Hulme would have had to repudiate all the poetry written before his own day, because it is a fact that nearly all such poetry observes the forms of syntax, the forms of unfoldedness, of the extensive manifold. In fact Hulme makes no such repudiation, nor is there any need why he should. There is no harm in syntactical forms, so long as their function is perverted, so long as they are emptied of the significance they have in scientific explanation.[1] It might seem, for instance, that syntax goes out of a poem along with punctuation; but this is not the case. A poet who does without syntax may well be reluctant to write without punctuation; for (to take it on the most elementary level) the different lengths of pause signified by comma, colon, and full stop are invaluable aids to the control of rhythm. Hence the poet may construct a complex sentence, not because the terms in the sentence are to be articulated subtly and closely, but just because he wants at that point a rhythmical unit unusually elaborate and sustained. In this case articulation is by rhythm, and syntax only *seems* to be doing the articulating; it is a pseudo-syntax, a play of empty forms.

One way, then, to empty syntactical forms of their significance is to make them subservient to a very heavy rhythmical pattern. There are subtler ways of 'emptying'. Thus T. C. Pollock remarks, 'Full-sentence statement is now the favoured symbolic pattern in civilized speech, especially in civilized writing, so that there exists in the minds of most educated people what we may call *an expectation of the sentence*, which results in a sense of frustration or bafflement if the words they hear or see are not arranged in conventional sentence-patterns . . .'[2] Hence it would be possible for a poet to set up such frustration in his readers only so as to reap the fuller reward when, at the end of a poem or passage, he resolves them. It would be possible to argue that

1 This is a point missed by Mr Howard Nemerov in an otherwise excellent brief discussion of this question with reference to the poetry of Dylan Thomas ('The Generation of Violence', *Kenyon Review*, Summer 1953, pp. 477, 478).

2 T. C. Pollock, *The Nature of Literature*, p. 75.

Terence Tiller places a 'full-sentence statement' at the end of his poem not because what he has to say demands that form, but so as to induce in the reader a sense of welllearned composure after the frustrations caused by the incomplete syntactical forms of the earlier lines.

Again, no one maintains that syntax, as the grammarian understands the term, is the only means available to poetry for articulating experience. There is, for instance, the sort of irrational articulation that goes on in dreams. This, it could be argued, is a sort of articulation that does not involve, in Hulme's terms, an 'extensive manifold'. By exploiting to the full an articulation analogous to that of dreams, the poet can make the articulations of syntax, even while their forms are retained, no more than a phantasmal play on the surface of his poem. Then the true articulation takes place by magical or dreamlike associations of one image with another; a word in one sentence reaches out to embrace another two sentences away, and the relationship thus established makes the relation of each word to the others in its sentence seem thin and illusory. So, once more, the forms of syntax are emptied of significance.

Of great interest in this connection are the admirable speculations of Elizabeth Sewell on the literature of nonsense. Hulme remarks, 'As an example of the kind of thing which the intellect does consider perfectly clear and comprehensible you can think of a lot of pieces on a draught board.'[1] Games like draughts or chess are perfect examples of extensive manifolds, an exercise of sheer articulation. So Elizabeth Sewell writes of Lewis Carroll,[2] 'Chess and language seem to have been united in some way in Carroll's mind, as if it might be possible to manipulate words according to the principles of a game of chess, which are those of logic.' Hence she finds in Carroll's writing passages where the syntactical possibilities of language have been exploited so far as to usurp all others:

1 T. E. Hulme, op. cit., p. 176.

2 'Bats and Tea-Trays: A Note on Nonsense', *Essays in Criticism*, I, 4, 376–86.

> If I or she should chance to be
> Involved in this affair,
> He trusts to you to set them free,
> Exactly as we were.

But this, as Miss Sewell points out, is unrepresentative because it is too easy. The point of the game is to defeat the dream on its own grounds, by using 'words referring to concrete things', words which are the material of dreams, yet which shall, by skilful handling, deny to dream any foothold:

> Nonsense has to make a simple universe from material which is complex and subject, in part at least, to a force whose main activity lies in weaving networks of relations, establishing associations, identifying one element with another and both with the mind in which this process is going on, observing strange and multiple likenesses, creating the never-stable complex which is the typical product of the dreaming mind. To prevent this happening, Nonsense can do only one thing: select and organize its words in such a way as to inhibit as far as possible the dreaming mind's tendency towards the multiplication of relations. The Nonsense universe must be the sum of its parts and nothing more. There must be no fusion and synthesis, no calling in of the dream faculty to lend to the whole so formed new significances beyond the grasp of logic.

Elizabeth Sewell goes on to show in detail how Lear and Carroll go about this game. Carroll's world is as far as possible from the world of dreams. His language is the apotheosis of syntax, and there is no wonder that Miss Sewell should have moved from considering Carroll to the symbolist poet Valéry.

Now the poet who distrusts syntax has only to reverse this process. As the nonsense poet will exclude wherever possible the articulations of dream, a poet like Hulme or Tiller will build up the structure of dream in order to break down or to emasculate the logical articulations of syntax.

4

I GET the impression that Hulme's views about the nature of poetical language are the ideas most generally current, almost the standard ideas, among poets and their readers today, at least in the English-speaking world. We still generally assume that it is the poet's duty to exclude abstractions in favour of concretions:

> For it is part of the business of poetry to peel off the woolly overcoats of language and to break through to the bare and physical sense: the poet will seldom use an abstract word like 'dynamic'; instead, he will discover a music or an image that concretely imitates a dynamic happening.[1]

As I have hinted, because Hulme originally used these terms loosely, they are frequently 'woolly' today. One example is the use of 'specific', often going along with 'concrete' as a term of approval. Yet, as T. C. Pollock points out, 'Abstract and generalized linguistic forms are more useful than are concrete for making specific references.'[2] Such examples could be multiplied, and may appear in due course. On the other hand, later writers have abandoned the Bergsonian element in Hulme's vocabulary, while often retaining, tacitly or unconsciously, his Bergsonian assumptions.

1 W. R. Rodgers, 'Speak and Span', *New Statesman and Nation*, Dec. 15, 1951, p. 704.
2 T. C. Pollock, op. cit., p. 75.

II

Syntax as Music: Susanne Langer

WHEN Susanne Langer's *Philosophy in a New Key* was published at Harvard in 1942, it attracted little attention. Nine years later Sir Herbert Read thought this neglect comparable to the neglect of Kierkegaard's works when they first appeared.[1] No doubt the comparison is designedly provocative; but if it is extravagant, it is not ludicrous. For *Philosophy in a New Key* is indeed a remarkable book. It ranges through many fields of speculation and knowledge, and that, I suspect, is why it was neglected; only a committee could review it properly. But one need not be an expert in any of these fields to be astonished and delighted by its grand synoptic sweep and the vigour and lucidity of its style.

I make no pretensions here to consider it as a whole. I want to examine it from only one point of view, in the light of Sir Herbert Read's claim, 'For the first time we have a theory which accounts satisfactorily for all forms of art.' And, to narrow the matter still further, I seek to examine this from the standpoint of only one form of art, the art of poetry.

A glance at the index advises us that if Susanne Langer has accounted for poetry, along with the other muses, she has done so very succinctly. And when we turn to such comments as there are, to find in the conjuror's hat only that dowdy old rabbit, 'significant form', we may well feel we can direct the author to I. A. Richards's *Principles*, and be done with it.

But this would be a mistake. Sir Herbert Read has not been gulled, and this is not just another system of aesthetics compiled

1 Sir Herbert Read, 'The Language of Symbols', *World Review*, Sept. 1951, pp. 33–6.

by the professional philosopher, one of those books that would be so admirable if only we could be sure that the author had ever enjoyed a poem, a sonata or a painting. Susanne Langer takes her Clive Bell with reservations; and in taking over his phrase she transforms it – chiefly because the analogy she proposes for poetry is not so much painting or ceramics, as music. As a result 'significant form' comes back into the arena of serious discussion. And so does another old tag that has faded and rubbed smooth, Walter Pater's pronouncement, 'All the arts aspire to the condition of music.' Both these must now be taken seriously; for what in Pater was cryptic, what in Bell was vague, becomes by this handling crisp and definite.

The force of the argument, as Mrs Langer presents it, is in her grasp of what it feels like to listen to music. This is an author who *has* enjoyed a sonata. She has enjoyed poems too, but it is the music we must start with. Because she can recreate the effect music has on the listener, we are prepared to go with her when she asks what music means, to him and to us.

What is the meaning of music? There is a passage in *The Waves* where Rhoda, having heard of the unexpected death of a friend, seeks consolation in a concert:

> Then, swollen but contained in slippery satin, the seagreen woman comes to our rescue. She sucks in her lips, assumes an air of intensity, inflates herself and hurls herself precisely at the right moment as if she saw an apple and her voice was the arrow into the note, 'Ah!'
>
> An axe has split a tree to the core; the core is warm; sound quivers within the bark. 'Ah!' cried a woman to her lover, leaning from her window in Venice. 'Ah, ah!' she cried, and again she cries 'Ah!' She has provided us with a cry. But only a cry. And what is a cry? Then the beetle-shaped men come with their violins; wait; count; nod; down come their bows. And there is ripple and laughter like the dance of olive trees and their myriad-tongued grey leaves when a seafarer, biting a twig between his lips where the many-backed steep hills come down, leaps on shore.
>
> 'Like' and 'like' and 'like' – but what is the thing that lies beneath

the semblance of the thing? Now that lightning has gashed the tree and the flowering branch has fallen and Percival, by his death, has made me this gift, let me see the thing. There is a square; there is an oblong. The players take the square and place it upon the oblong. They place it very accurately; they make a perfect dwelling-place. Very little is left outside. The structure is now visible; what is inchoate is here stated; we are not so various or so mean; we have made oblongs and stood them upon squares. This is our triumph; this is our consolation.[1]

This conveys admirably the paradox of musical effect, which is, on the one hand, oppressively emotional (blurted out, a cry, or a moan), on the other hand, as rigorously dry and abstract as Euclid. What is the link between these two elements? – a link, not in time, though Mrs Woolf presents them in sequence, but in the total impression of any musical work? The link, clearly, is some sort of articulation, when the fiddles begin to weave in and out; not quite the articulation of narrative, though it may evoke narratives as fanciful similes, but more like the articulation of a painting, although it takes place in time, with first one thing then another, as a painting does not.

Such is Mrs Langer's account of the effect of music. The crudest idea of musical meaning is that any piece of music expresses an emotion – this is a joyful piece, this one is sad; this is a cry of joy, this is a moan of pain. But the same piece may be joyful to one person, sorrowful to another. At the other extreme the purist cries that music is shape, pattern, which means nothing but itself; but this is belied by the universal experience that music *does* stir the emotions, *is* tinged with feeling, *does* speak to us as to active and suffering persons. A true account of musical effect must include both these elements; and Mrs Langer does so by saying that '*what music can actually reflect is only the morphology of feeling*', not this feeling or that (though this one and that one swim up for an instant now here, now there), but feeling in itself, its structure. And as Mrs Langer says, a joyful and a

1 Virginia Woolf, *The Waves* (The Hogarth Press, 1946), pp. 115, 116.

sorrowful feeling may have the same morphology. Its burden is, as she says, 'in very naïve phrase, a knowledge of "how feelings go"'. And it is there, in the 'going' – in presenting how feelings are built up, how they branch and fork and coalesce – that we find the articulating back and forth that is music's life:

> Articulation is its life, but not assertion; expressiveness, not expression. The actual function of meaning, which calls for permanent contents, is not fulfilled; for the *assignment* of one rather than another possible meaning to each form is never explicitly made.

In saying this Mrs Langer uses 'meaning' in a specially restricted sense. She certainly does not want to dismiss music as meaningless. This labour of articulation is meaning enough, she thinks, and rational meaning too; for the whole brunt of her argument is directed against thinkers like Russell, Carnap and Wittgenstein, for whom the arts are welcome enough so long as they remain in the world of the emotive, outside the pale of reason. This is the point of her chapters on semantics, on folklore and ritual. For 'the new key' of her title is the idea of symbol – this is the key that is to open new philosophical doors; and the arts, she argues, use symbols no more than language does, and no less rationally, though in a non-discursive, a 'presentational' way.

This is the thorniest part of the book, though still absorbing and still beautifully lucid. For present purposes we need only realize that for Mrs Langer language is a discursive symbolism, where music is a presentational symbolism; and that poetry, as an art, in this resembles music more than it resembles the language of speech or of prose. This she explains as follows:

> Though the *material* of poetry is verbal, its import is not the literal assertion made in the words, but *the way the assertion is made*, and this involves the sound, the tempo, the aura of associations of the words, the long or short sequences of ideas, the wealth or poverty of transient imagery that contains them, the sudden arrest of fantasy by pure fact, or of familiar fact by sudden fantasy, the suspense of literal meaning by

a sustained ambiguity resolved in a long-awaited keyword, and the unifying, all-embracing artifice of rhythm. (The tension which music achieves through dissonance, and the reorientation in each new resolution to harmony, find their equivalents in the suspensions and periodic decisions of propositional sense in poetry. Literal sense, not euphony, is the 'harmonic structure' of poetry; word-melody in literature is more akin to tone-colour in music.)[1]

The first thing to say of this is that Mrs Langer knows what it is like to read and enjoy a poem, just as she knows what it is like to hear and enjoy a sonata. Her account is true to the features of experience. As a result she avoids the traps set for the poet who does not know music 'from the inside', for the musician who does not know poetry 'from the inside', and for the aesthetician who too frequently knows neither.

When poets say that poetry is or ought to be like music, they often turn out to have only a naïve idea of what music is. They take such musical freaks as the imitations of cuckoo calls, or clocks, or peals of bells, as if they were central to music's nature; and so build up a theory of poetry around the equally freakish poetical device of onomatopoeia. Or else they take music to be 'a cry' ('But only a cry? And what is a cry?'), and when they say that poetry is or ought to be like music, they mean by that that the only genuine poem is the lyric, and that a poem is 'lyrical', other things being equal, when it displays a profusion of vocatives and a punctuation consisting of exclamation marks, dashes, and rows of dots. (This is the sort of thing we find, not only in late-Victorian conservatives, but in an aggressive modernist like William Carlos Williams.) Very frequently nowadays the two ideas, of poetry as cry and poetry as onomatopoeia, come together, as in *Finnegans Wake*, where the language is onomatopoeic on the one hand, on the other the metaphorical crying language of Vico's 'Age of Giants'. So they come together for

1 Susanne Langer, *Philosophy in a New Key* (Harvard, Second Edition, 1951), pp. 260, 261.

W. R. Rodgers.[1] And Hopkins's theory of 'inscape', and Rilke's doctrine that things utter themselves through us, can be used in a similar way, to make of poetry an onomatopoeic cry. At the other extreme comes 'la poésie pure', with its poems, like Edith Sitwell's early pieces, that are sheer constructs of euphony, supposedly as drained of all emotive reference as (on this purist view) music is.

What distinguishes Mrs Langer's from all these other accounts of the poetry–music relationship is her insistence on music as pre-eminently articulation. In her view a poem is like a piece of music in that it articulates itself; and in thus establishing internal relations, establishes also relations of feeling, building up the structure, the morphology of feeling, and telling us 'what it feels like to feel'. In other words the central act of poetry as of music, is the creation of syntax, of meaningful arrangement. And hence (this seems to me the most salutary implication) the unit of poetry is not the 'passage', but *the poem*.

And yet the syntax we speak of here is not the syntax of prose, that is a part of formal grammar. There is no need for the poet to preserve even *the forms* of prose syntax; and as a result we must not suppose, whenever we find a poet who dislocates prose syntax, that we have to deal with the poetry of the blurted-out ejaculation, the cry. The dislocated syntax of Ezra Pound in the *Cantos* may look like the dislocated syntax of William Carlos Williams, but in fact the *Cantos* are, or are meant to be, articulated most closely. They are articulated, however, by a syntax that is musical, not linguistic, by 'the unifying, all-embracing artifice of rhythm', understood in its widest sense to mean not only the rhythm that rides through tempo and metre in the verse paragraph, but also the rhythmical recurrence of ideas hinted at in one canto, picked up in another much later, suspended for many more, and so on.[2] The *Cantos* indeed fit Mrs Langer's account very well.

1 Rodgers, 'Speak and Span'.

2 See Hugh Kenner, *The Poetry of Ezra Pound* (Faber, 1951), pp. 112–15, 274–85.

But there are poets whose poetry 'aspires to the condition of music', but who nevertheless preserve the forms of linguistic syntax, as Pound does not. And it is these poets who are provided for in Mrs Langer's parenthesis. It is their poetry, not Pound's, of which one may say that 'The tension which music achieves through dissonance, and the reorientation in each new resolution to harmony, find their equivalents in the suspensions and periodic decisions of propositional sense in poetry.' Perhaps the clearest example of a poet of this sort is Valéry. I happened to read Elizabeth Sewell's *Valéry* at about the same time as Mrs Langer's book, and the poet's view of poetry chimed in so well with the philosopher's that one would think the latter had written with this poet, of all others, in mind. Valéry saw very clearly that music is not a cry, but above all an articulation: 'The pythoness could not dictate a poem. Only a line – that is to say a unit – and then another. This goddess of the continuum is incapable of continuity.'[1] And *La Jeune Parque* was first envisaged as 'an operatic recitative, à la Gluck: 30 or 40 lines in one long phrase almost; and for contralto voice.'[2]

But it is time to unravel the implications of Mrs Langer's persuasive formulation. And they are clear enough. In her view the poet suspends the propositional sense through a long verse period, not because the sense has to be qualified before it can be completed, but so as to achieve 'the tension which music achieves through dissonance'; and he decides the sense, bringing the period to a close, not because he is now prepared to commit himself to an assertion, but just to find an equivalent for music's 'reorientation in each new resolution to harmony'. The whole play of literal meaning, in fact, is a Swedish drill, in which nothing is being lifted, transported or set down, though the muscles tense, knot and relax as if it were. This is what Mrs

1 Quoted by Elizabeth Sewell, *Paul Valéry: The Mind in the Mirror* (Bowes, 1952), p. 28.

2 Quoted in *Times Literary Supplement*, Aug. 22, 1952, review of *Lettres à Quelques-Uns*.

Langer means by saying that 'Literal sense . . . is the "harmonic structure" of poetry.'

Milton can be taken on Mrs Langer's terms:

It is only in the period that the wavelength of Milton's verse is to be found: it is his ability to give a perfect and unique pattern to every paragraph, such that the full beauty of the line is found in its context, and his ability to work in larger musical units than any other poet – that is to me the most conclusive evidence of Milton's supreme mastery. The peculiar feeling, almost a physical sensation of a breathless leap, communicated by Milton's long periods, and by his alone, is impossible to procure from rhymed verse.[1]

So long as Milton does not 'justify God's ways to man', but only, quite precisely, 'goes through the motions', we can read him as if he were Valéry, and Mr Eliot can admire him.

It is plain that Mrs Langer's sort of poetry, where it retains forms of prosaic syntax, only *seems* to make use of them. And to that extent the things it says are still, in the time-honoured phrase, pseudo-statements. Mrs Langer insists that they are not 'pseudo' in the way that I. A. Richards supposed; they are not irrational and crudely emotive like a strangled cry, the hoot of an owl, or the howl of a wolf. The statements of poetry, in her account, are like the statements of music, rational and meaningful as the hub or nest of articulations. But to the common reader the statements of poetry, even on this showing, are still 'pseudo', though in a different way. They are pseudo-statements in that they do not mean what they say; the poet will not stand by them, nor take his stand upon them. 'The actual function of meaning, which calls for permanent contents, is not fulfilled; for the *assignment* of one rather than another possible meaning to each form is never explicitly made.'

Mrs Langer's position on this matter is made very plain in a passage from her more recent book, *Feeling and Form*:

1 T. S. Eliot, *Milton*, the British Academy Lecture.

. . . all poetry is a creation of illusory events, even when it looks like a statement of opinions philosophical or political or aesthetic. The occurrence of a thought is an event in a thinker's personal history, and has as distinct a qualitative character as an adventure, a sight, or a human contact; it is not a proposition, but the entertainment of one, which necessarily involves vital tensions, feelings, the imminence of other thoughts, and the echoes of past thinking. Poetic reflections, therefore, are not essentially trains of logical reasoning, though they may incorporate fragments, at least, of discursive argument. Essentially they create the *semblance* of reasoning; of the seriousness, strain and progress, the sense of growing knowledge, growing clearness, conviction, and acceptance – the whole experience of philosophical thinking.

Of course a poet usually builds a philosophical poem around an idea that strikes him, at the time, as true and important; but not for the sake of debating it. He accepts it and exhibits its emotional value and imaginative possibilities. Consider the Platonic doctrine of transcendental remembrance in Wordsworth's 'Ode: Intimations of Immortality' . . .[1]

Here Mrs Langer, the disciple of Cassirer, stands shoulder to shoulder with T. E. Hulme and the other disciples of Bergson. Miss Rosemond Tuve has pointed out that, for the latter, poetry has to do with 'a man having thoughts', not with 'the thoughts a man had'; and on this showing Mrs Langer agrees with them. For her, too, when a poet seems to speak about the thoughts he has had, he is really speaking about himself in the process of having them. And so, when the poet uses the syntactical form of the logical proposition, this form is empty, phantasmal, a sleight of hand. Thus Susanne Langer and T. E. Hulme by very different routes reach the same conclusion: that the syntactical forms used in poetry may or may not be identical with those of prose; but that, where they are identical, this identity of form masks an entirely different function.

1 Susanne Langer, *Feeling and Form* (Routledge, 1953), p. 219.

III

Syntax as Music in the Poetry of Thomas Sackville

IF we reject Mrs Langer's analysis as a full account of the nature of poetic syntax, we have still to acknowledge that to take the play of syntax on her terms can illuminate certain poetic effects which previously could not be rationalized. It is worth taking a case which shows the advantages, if also the limitations, of examining poetic syntax from her point of view. This will be all the more effective if we find a case quite remote in time and kind from symbolist and post-symbolist verse. I propose to examine from this point of view two poems by Thomas Sackville from the sixteenth-century *A Mirror for Magistrates.*

Sackville, in one of the best passages of the 'Complaint of Henrie Duke of Buckinghame' (which seems to me, incidentally, quite as good as the better known 'Induction') rings the changes, through several stanzas, on one simple but effective syntactical arrangement. In stanzas 142 and 143, Buckingham is made to apostrophize Rome and reproach her for her ungrateful treatment of the patriot Camillus:

> Rome thou that once advaunced up so hie
> thie staie, patron, and flour of excelence
> hast now throwen him to depth of miserie
> exiled him that was thie hole defence
> ne comptes it not a horrible offence
> to reaven him of honnour and of fame
> that wan yt the whan thou had lost the same.
>
> Behold Camillus he that erst revived
> the state of Rome that dienge he did find
> of his own state is now alas deprived

> banisht by them whom he did thus detbind
> that cruell age unthankfull and unkind
> declared well their fals unconstancie
> and fortune eke her mutabilitie.

The construction 'exiled him that was thie hole defence' is natural enough and would go unnoticed were it not echoed almost at once:

> to reaven him of honnour and of fame
> that wan yt the whan thou had lost the same

and echoed again in the next stanza:

> banisht by them whom he did thus detbind.

The little tune comes again and again, restated in each of the next three stanzas. Buckingham apostrophizes Scipio, who:

> art now exild as though thow not deserved
> to rest in her whom thow had so preserved.

He turns again on Rome:

> Ingratefull Rome hast shewed thie crueltie
> On him by whom thow livest yet in fame.

And finally, approving Scipio's contemptuous gesture:

> his cinders yet lo doth he them denie
> that him denied amongst them for to die.

The sentence itself has a little tragic plot, with the peripeteia at the turn on the relative pronoun. As Miss Rosemond Tuve has said so well, to handle syntax with this nicety is to come as near as may be to the impossible ideal of a silent eloquence. And this is a way of handling syntax for which neither Hulme nor Mrs Langer makes provision.

On the other hand, there is, in the 'Complaint', a justly famous lyrical digression on sleep and night (stanzas 159–61).

While the beauty and pathos of these stanzas is acknowledged, I do not know that anyone has tried to account for their powerful effect, coming where they do. To do so, one needs to quote not the three stanzas alone, but a block of seven; and then to have recourse to Mrs Langer:

> For by this wretch I being strait bewraied
> to one John mitton shreif of shropshere then
> all sodenlie was taken and convaied
> to Salsburie with rout of harnest men
> unto King Richard ther encamped then
> fast by the citie with a mightie host
> withouten dome wher hed and lief I lost.
>
> And with those wordes as if the ax even there
> dismembered had his hed and corps apart
> ded fell he doune and we in wofull feare
> amasd beheld him when he wold revart
> but griefes on griefes stil heapt about his hart
> that still he laie sometime revivd with pain
> and with a sigh becoming ded againe.
>
> Mid night was come and everie vitall thing
> with swete sound slepe their wearie lims did rest
> the bestes were still the litle burdes that sing
> now sweteli slept beside their mothers brest
> the old and all were shrouded in their nest
> the waters calm the cruell seas did cesse
> the woods and feldes and all things held their peace
>
> The golden stars weare whirld amid their race
> and on the erth did laugh with twinkling light
> when ech thing nestled in his resting place
> forgat daies pain withe plesure of the night
> the hare had not the gredy houndes in sight
> the ferfull dere of deth stode not in doubt
> the partridge dremd not of the sparhaukes fote
>
> The ouglie bear now minded not the stake
> nor how the cruel mastives did him tere

the stag laie stil unroused from the brake
the fomie bore ferd not the hunters spere
al thing was stil in desert bush and brere
with quiet hart now from their travels cest
soundlie they slept in midst of all their rest.

Whan Buckingham amid his plaint opprest
with surging sorowes and with pinching paines
in sorte thus sowned and with a sigh he cest
to tellen furth the trecherie and the traines
of Banaster which him so sore distraines
that from a sigh he fals in to a sound
and from a sound lieth raging on the ground

So twitching wear the panges that he assaied
and he so sore with rufull rage distraught
To think upon the wretche that him betraied
whome erst he made a gentleman of nought
That more and more agreved with this thought
he stormes out sights and with redoubled sore
Shryke with the furies rageth more and more.

It is plain that if a modern editor were to punctuate this, he would make one sentence of stanza 157 (the first quoted) and probably of 158 also. Stanza 159, however, contains six sentences, 160 has four, 161 has five, 162 and 163, resuming the narrative, seem to make up one sentence between them. In fact, it seems to be Sackville's normal procedure to make the metrical unit (the stanza) the grammatical unit also. From this flowing melody, it is easy for Sackville to modulate into a plangent strain by putting into the stanza several short and simple, poignant sentences. (Of course this does not 'explain' the effect; not all the eloquence is silent, and we certainly need Dr Swart's[1] admirable account of Sackville's diction.)

It is plain that we have, in Sackville's lyrical digression on

1 J. Swart, *Thomas Sackville: A Study in Sixteenth-Century Poetry* (Groningen, 1949).

sleep, a clear example of the sort of poetic syntax that Susanne Langer led us to envisage. We admitted as much by the musical analogy we had to use – 'From this flowing melody, it is easy . . . to modulate into a plangent strain.' This, of course, is something that could have occurred to any critic, whether he had read Susanne Langer or not. (In fact, I had noted it in just those terms before reading *Philosophy in a New Key*.) But this is true, I suggest, only because Sackville is working on a large scale and the machinery of his effects is correspondingly massive. The example is an obvious one; but it seems clear that effects no different in kind can be detected, once we are prepared for them, within the compass of a sonnet. And this is the value of Mrs Langer's note about musical equivalents for 'the suspensions and periodic decisions of propositional sense in poetry'.

What Sackville has to say in the stanzas about night does not exact from him the peculiar syntactical arrangements he finds for it. On the contrary, the first two of the stanzas we quoted, being simple narrative, seem to demand a syntax much simpler than the complex sentences Sackville finds for them:

> For by this wretch I being strait bewraied
> to one John mitton shreif of shropshere then
> all sodenlie was taken and convaied
> to Salsburie with rout of harnest men
> unto King Richard ther encamped then
> fast by the citie with a mightie host
> withouten dome wher hed and lief I lost.

There is no articulation of meaning (e.g. of cause and effect) to compel each clause to grow out of the one before it, as each one does. Of course the syntax and the sense are not at odds, as they would have been, for instance, if we were here learning for the first time of Buckingham's death by execution. (If that had been the case, then to put the momentous information in a last subordinate clause would give it a ludicrous air, as of a careless afterthought – there is a passage in Wordsworth's 'Vaudracour and Julia' where this happens.) Still the sense does not demand a particular syntactical form, in the way that Camillus and Scipio demand the syntax Sackville gives them. The arc of their career in public life is the arc described by the sentences which describe it – 'banisht by them whom he did thus detbind.' Here the turn on the pronoun is not a matter of convenience but of necessity, if the curve of syntax is to reproduce the curve of destiny.

The distinction is not a fine one, though here it may seem to be niggling. Camillus and Scipio ride through on a syntax which is the authentic thing, which does what it appears to do. The syntax of the stanzas on night and sleep appears to be collecting *exempla*; in fact, it is the servant of a plangent rhythm, stopping and starting as the rhythm commands.

Of course I have used a musical metaphor for the Camillus–Scipio passage also. The recurrent syntactical arrangement is 'a little tune'. But this is natural. Just as Sackville takes care in the 'Induction' not to let his syntax come to blows with his sense, so here in the 'Complaint' he takes care to profit by his fidelity to the sense, to make music on a recurrent motif. No doubt in the greatest poetry sense and music go together so closely that it is impossible to say that one came before the other. Nevertheless the distinction remains, and I insist it is a crucial one.

This use of 'music' – 'the music of the poem' – is far from satisfactory. To speak of 'sense and music' in a poem is not a great deal better than saying 'sense and sound', a phrase time-honoured in other connections but quite out of place here. The trouble is that music can be heard, and so, when we speak of the music of verse, we think at once of those elements in poetry – phonetic and rhythmical – that likewise appeal to the ear. But when we speak of music in relation to poetic syntax, we mean something that can be appreciated in silent reading without the reader having to imagine how the poem would sound if it were uttered aloud. This is a silent music, a matter of tensions and resolutions, of movements (but again not rhythmical movements) sustained or broken, of ease or effort, rapidity or languor. What we mean, in fact, is *empathy*. Empathy occurs in our response to the plastic arts when 'we feel ourselves occupying with our senses the *Gestalt* of the rising column or the spatial design of a picture.'[1] Sir Herbert Read warns us regarding empathy, that 'in general our use of the word in literary criticism can only be analogical.' Yet he agrees that 'there may be a true empathic relationship to the sound and shape of a poem – our response to metre, for example.' It is Susanne Langer's achievement to have shown that our response to syntax can be 'a true empathic relationship' also.

Perhaps this appears most clearly in respect of pace. We are accustomed to think, quite rightly too, that trisyllabic metre is more rapid than the iambic:

> The Assyrian came down like the wolf on the fold,
> And his cohorts were gleaming in purple and gold.

We certainly get the impression, which may even be true to fact, that in reading these lines (even silently) we have read twenty-four syllables in the time we take, in iambic verse, for sixteen. Hence we call it rapid. But now consider Pope:

> The thriving plants ignoble broomsticks made,
> Now sweep those Alleys they were born to shade

Here too, in this iambic verse, we get an impression of rapidity, but of a quite different sort. This is rapid because it expresses so much in so short a time. The rapidity of Byron is a rapid movement of lips and tongue; Pope's rapidity is a rapid movement of the mind. Pope's rapidity we perceive by empathy; Byron's we do not.

T. S. Eliot has remarked, 'I know . . . that a poem or a section of a poem tends to appear first in the shape of a rhythm before developing into words, and that this rhythm is capable of giving

1 Sir Herbert Read, 'The Critic as Man of Feeling', *Kenyon Review*, XII, 4, p. 577.

birth to the idea and the image.' And Schiller says, 'When I sit down to write a poem, what I most frequently see before me is its musical element and not a clear idea of the subject, about which I am often not entirely clear myself.' Both these statements are cited by Daniel-Henry Kahnweiler, in his book on Juan Gris,[1] at a point where he is arguing that Gris, too, got the first idea for a canvas in terms of a spatial rhythm. This rhythm, worked out in preliminary drawing and then transferred to the canvas, produced shapes which were only at a relatively late stage in the composition 'modified' (to use Gris's own term) into the semblance of a guitar, a bowl of fruit, a coffee-mill, or whatever else.

If Kahnweiler is right, certainly Gris's procedure is precisely analogous to what both Schiller and Eliot record as their own ways of going to work. Yet 'rhythm' and 'musical element' are not necessarily the same thing. Whatever Schiller meant by 'musical element', we cannot help but relate it to what has just been established as the soundless music of poetic syntax.

Interesting in this connection is a passage some pages earlier in Kahnweiler's book (pp. 100–101), where he considers Thierry-Maulnier's remark on rhythm in poetry, to the effect that 'it only exists where the repeated and regular shocks of an exact mechanism maintain the soul in a sort of vigilant torpor like the mysterious receptivity of a medium, so that everything is excluded which is not the pure suspense in anticipation of the unforeseeable.' The trouble with this is the emphasis on regularity, which seems to reduce rhythm to metre. Ignore this (as Kahnweiler for his quite different purposes has to do), and the 'exact mechanism', producing 'the pure suspense in anticipation of the unforeseeable', could be taken to describe a piece of complex poetic syntax no less than a piece of complex and sounding rhythm. Indeed such syntax *is* rhythm, but soundless.

1 Daniel-Henry Kahnweiler, *Juan Gris: His Life and Work*, tr. Douglas Cooper (Lund, 1947), p. 104

And after all, the rhythm in the head of the poet before he starts to write is soundless in any case. We need Thierry-Maulnier's expressions to define the effect of such elaborate poetic syntax as that of F. T. Prince in his 'Epistle to a patron'.[1] The sounded rhythm of that poem is very loose indeed. It can afford to be, but only because the unsounded rhythm of the syntax is so elaborately strict.

Thus, if all poems are born as rhythms, then some, it seems, may be born as rhythms of ideas, that is, as patterns of syntax rather than patterns of sound. And this would make of syntax the very nerve of poetry.

1 See *post*, p. 280.

IV

Syntax as Action: Ernest Fenollosa

I

I HAVE spoken, in discussing Sackville, of a sentence as having a tragic plot. This idea I owe to a cryptic comment by Mr H. M. McLuhan on some lines of Pope, and to some illuminating pages in Hugh Kenner's *Poetry of Ezra Pound.* With the latter as my clue (I am much indebted to Mr Kenner), I traced this notion back to Ernest Fenollosa's essay on 'The Chinese Written Character as a Medium for Poetry'. And this is the next document I want to consider.[1]

In the period when Ezra Pound was 'spotting the winners' with such astonishing consistency, he came across the work of the orientalist Ernest Fenollosa, and subsequently prepared for publication this essay discovered among Fenollosa's papers after his death in 1908. It has never had the recognition it deserves. For Pound's flair had not deserted him. He subtitles the essay, 'An Ars Poetica', and the claim is no presumptuous one. In its massive conciseness, Fenollosa's little treatise is perhaps the only English document of our time fit to rank with Sidney's *Apologie*, and the Preface to *Lyrical Ballads*, and Shelley's *Defence*, the great poetic manifestos of the past. This is a matter of intrinsic value, not historical importance. For while the essay has already been influential (chiefly through the agency of Pound), it has not yet exerted the influence it deserves. We know as we read, in default

1 All quotations are from the edition by John Kasper, New York, in the Square Dollar series, where Fenollosa's essay appears along with two translations from Confucius by Ezra Pound.

of any historical evidence, that this is a great seminal work, speaking with the authority of a devoted and passionate solitary thinker.

Syntax, we have argued, is a silent eloquence, not in any hyperbolical sense, but quite literally. For syntax, we have shown, can be rapid, for instance, in a way that has nothing to do with rapid movements of lips and tongue as we read, or imagine ourselves reading, aloud. If we approach Fenollosa from this point, the relevance of his essay is apparent from the start. For the problem with which he begins is as follows: Is there anything in common between 'The curfew tolls the knell of parting day', and the Chinese line, consisting of five characters the sound of which is unknown, 'Moon Rays Like Pure Snow'? If there is something in common between them, then this (so Fenollosa audaciously suggests) may be taken as the essential element in poetic form.

He answers his own question by saying that what they have in common is a sort of significant sequaciousness, 'the transference of force from agent to object'. For 'we do not always sufficiently consider that thought is successive, not through some accident or weakness of our subjective operations but because the operations of nature are successive.' And, 'one superiority of verbal poetry as an *art* rests in its getting back to the fundamental reality of *time*.' Fenollosa points out that music does this, but painting does not.

According to Fenollosa, the uniquely poetical value of Chinese rests in its combining this temporal (sequacious) feature with the density and angularity of 'things', the peculiar contribution of painting and sculpture. It is thus, as it were, both music and painting. In the Chinese sentence 'Man Sees Horse', we perceive that

> Chinese notation is something much more than arbitrary symbols. It is based upon a vivid shorthand picture of the operations of nature. In the algebraic figure and in the spoken word there is no natural connection

between thing and sign: all depends upon sheer convention. But the Chinese method follows natural suggestion. First stands the man on his two legs. Second, his eye moves through space: a bold figure represented by running legs under an eye, a modified picture of an eye, a modified picture of running legs, but unforgettable once you have seen it. Third stands the horse on his four legs.

Fenollosa, of course, reproduces the Chinese characters in question, and from them one sees clearly that the characters are as he says stylized pictures from nature, yet set in motion, moving pictures, musical and graphic at once.

Fenollosa goes on to show that this obtains inside the single character, no less than in the syntactical arrangements of several characters together:

A true noun, an isolated thing, does not exist in nature. Things are only the terminal points, or rather the meeting points, of actions, cross-sections cut through actions, snapshots. Neither can a pure verb, an abstract motion, be possible in nature. The eye sees noun and verb as one: things in motion, motion in things, and so the Chinese conception tends to represent them.

> The sun underlying the bursting forth of plants = spring.
> The sun sign tangled in the branches of the tree sign = east.
> 'Rice field' plus 'struggle' = male.
> 'Boat' plus 'water' = boat-water, a ripple.

Pound gives, as an example of this noun-verb in English, 'dog *attending* man = dogs him'.

What is the moral of this for poetry in English? Fenollosa argues that English is like Chinese in lacking inflections, and that English poets can therefore learn from Chinese usage.

As regards syntax, the moral that Fenollosa draws from Chinese usage is this: the uniquely poetic, because uniquely truthful, syntactical form is the transitive sentence:

The sentence form was forced upon primitive men by nature itself. It was not we who made it; it was a reflection of the temporal order in causation. All truth has to be expressed in sentences because all truth is the *transference of power*. The type of sentence in nature is a flash of lightning. It passes between two terms, a cloud and the earth. No unit of natural process can be less than this. All natural processes are, in their units, as much as this. Light, heat, gravity, chemical affinity, human will, have this in common, that they redistribute force. Their unit of process can be represented as:

term		transference		term
from	→	of	→	to
which		force		which

If we regard this transference as the conscious or unconscious act of an agent we can translate the diagram into:

agent → act → object

In this the act is the very substance of the fact denoted. The agent and the object are only limiting terms.

It seems to me that the normal and typical sentence in English as well as in Chinese expresses just this unit of natural process. It consists of three necessary words: the first denoting the agent or subject from which the act starts, the second embodying the very stroke of the act, the third pointing to the object, the receiver of the impact. Thus:

Farmer pounds rice

the form of the Chinese transitive sentence, and of the English (omitting particles), exactly corresponds to this universal form of action in nature. This brings language close to *things*, and in its strong reliance upon verbs it erects all speech into a kind of dramatic poetry.

According to Fenollosa, the 'unpoetical' intransitive verbs in English should in poetry be made transitive, wherever possible. Even negations in his view are really active, because in nature force is required to annihilate, and a negation can therefore, and should, be expressed poetically by a transitive verb. Finally the mere copula 'is' should be avoided, and transitive verbs substituted:

There is in reality no such verb as a pure copula, no such original conception; our very word *exist* means 'to stand forth', to show oneself by a definite act. 'Is' comes from the Aryan root *as*, to breathe. 'Be' is from *bhu*, to grow.

As regards the choice of single words other than verbs, Fenollosa draws from Chinese the rule that such other parts of speech should always manifest their origin in verbs, as it seems Chinese words do. Pound gives one of the relatively rare examples of such a verbal family in English: the verb, to shine; the adjective, shining; the noun, shine or sheen. So in Chinese a seeming noun, 'farmer', is a verb, 'one who farms'. A seeming adjective, 'bright' = 'which shines'. Prepositions: 'off' = what is thrown away from; 'by' = what is used to effect something; 'to' = what falls towards. Conjunctions: 'and' = to be included under one; 'or' = to partake; 'if' = to permit. Even pronouns are the same: thus Chinese has five forms of 'I', differing according to the sort of thing 'I' is set to do.

So far, says Fenollosa, for poetry of the seen; what of the poetry of the unseen, which deals with 'lofty thoughts, spiritual suggestions, and obscure relations'? He deals with this in the way we might expect, appealing to etymology to show that the abstract words used for these topics have their root 'in direct action'. It is the poet's duty to reveal these concretions at the base of any abstract word, even as he uses it. This is one of the less original parts of the essay, though expressed with great force and beauty. Fenollosa points out that it is easy, in a phonetic language like English, to overlook the metaphorical roots of the abstract word, and hence to blur 'the ancient lines of advance'. It is much harder for a Chinese to miss them, painted into the character.

2

It will be apparent that in his dislike of a language of 'arbitrary symbols' such as algebra, in his pleasure when language comes 'close to *things*', in his use of etymology to establish concretions under abstractions, Fenollosa is ranged with T. E. Hulme rather than Susanne Langer. But he goes far beyond Hulme in that he finds room in his theory for a syntax that is not mere formalism. It is true that he has room for only one syntactical form, a very simple one; but most people would agree that this syntactical form is the basis of all the rest; and, such as it is, it is absolutely central to Fenollosa's conception of poetic language. It was the great disadvantage of Hulme's system that it found no room for syntax at all; from his point of view poetry could only grow more and more inarticulate until at last it fell silent altogether. Fenollosa, as insistent as Hulme that poetry should get close to 'things', realized as Hulme did not that 'things' were bundles of energies, always on the move, transmitting or receiving currents of force. Hence syntax was necessary to poetry.

Hulme and Fenollosa differ more profoundly. Fenollosa is a humanist. His appeal is always to 'nature'. He will accept no vindication of syntax short of that which makes it the Aristotelian imitation of a natural process. Moreover he appeals to nature in a pre-Wordsworthian way. His 'nature' is the nature of John Locke. This is the clue to his audacity, which is often breathtaking. He makes the astounding claim to establish a norm, a single authentic pattern, for all human thought – the pattern of the transitive sentence. He takes for granted what Hulme, holding fast to original sin, could never admit, that 'there is no disharmony between man and the outside world', that 'they are both on the same level, on which man feels himself one with nature and not separate from it.'[1] It would, for instance, be possible to attack Fenollosa's system at the root, by objecting that as man is

1 T. E. Hulme.

an immortal spirit, it is no way to the perfection of language or of any other human institution to make it conform to the patterns of fallen nature. It seems that Fenollosa never conceived of such an objection. His humanist convictions, rare in his own day and rarer still in ours, give to his thought a clarity and an assurance that is positively Augustan. This eighteenth-century air is no accident, as we shall see.

Hulme in effect excludes syntax from poetry altogether. Fenollosa admits it, and values it highly, but only so long as it preserves a primitive austerity. He finds no more room than Hulme does for an elaborate verbal syntax analogous to the mathematical syntax of modern physics. Things, Fenollosa had said, are only 'the terminal points . . . of actions', but in the act he corrected himself – 'or rather meeting-points'. The correction gives the show away. If the action goes on after the end of the sentence, if it was already approaching before the sentence began, then to begin the sentence with an agent, to end it with an object, is a quite arbitrary carving out of an artificial unit from what is a continuous flow. And the argument, from the imitation of a natural process, falls to the ground.

3

IT may be naïve of me to read Fenollosa *au pied de la lettre*, but he seems to be sufficiently categorical. He delivers a number of precepts: that the good poet will use, wherever possible, the full sentence driving through a transitive verb; that he will avoid, wherever possible, the copula; that he will rearrange, wherever possible, negations, so as to use a positive verb of negation; that he will avoid intransitive verbs; that he will be fond of verbs and cut down as far as possible the use of other parts of speech;[1] that

1 Cf. Gumilev, 'Thought is movement, and poets should use verbs and not adjectives,' quoted by Marc Slonim, *Modern Russian Literature: From Chekhov to the Present* (OUP, 1953), p. 214.

when he uses an abstract word he will draw attention, by his use of it, to its etymological growth out of concrete actions; that in using parts of speech other than verbs he will choose wherever possible words that reveal in themselves verbal elements or origins. That is enough to be going on with; and I now propose to see what happens to our reading of certain poems when we approach them with these precepts in mind. But I must first say something of a critic who has been before me in applying Fenollosa's speculations to the criticism of poetry.

Few people have looked at Fenollosa and those who have, have seen him through the spectacles of Ezra Pound. Pound has shown himself far more interested in Fenollosa's observations on the structure of words than in what he says about the structure of sentences. In Fenollosa's treatise these two bodies of reflections hang together, but it is possible, if one considers one without the other, to make them thrust against each other. Hence it comes about that Pound, who has done so much to dislocate and disrupt syntax in poetry, has been able, in doing so, to appeal to Fenollosa's authority. Fenollosa breaks down the Chinese ideogram for 'red' into 'Rose: Iron Rust: Cherry: Flamingo'. And he puts this forward as the product of a way of thinking preferable to our way of abstraction, which explains red as colour, colour as vibration, vibration as a mode of energy, and so on, moving ever further away from the perception of concreteness. But Fenollosa never suggests that this way of thinking is preferable to the way of thinking that produces the sentence. Quite the contrary: Fenollosa values as highly the way of thinking by sentences as the way of thinking by ideogram. He holds up Chinese as a model, because in that language the two ways of thinking work together. Pound, on the other hand, attempts to substitute thinking by ideogram for thinking by sentences; and the work of articulation that is done by syntax he hands over, in his own poetry, to the element of rhythm (in its widest sense). Hence it comes about that so long as we see Fenollosa only in Pound's terms, we only squint at him.

I find this squint in the work of Hugh Kenner.[1] Mr Kenner is at his best in his chapter on 'The Moving Image'. When he comes to ideogram, to which he gives much fuller attention, he draws out a central thread in Fenollosa's thought, the Aristotelian doctrine of *mimesis*, especially as it is related to the Aristotelian encomium of metaphor:

> Metaphor, as Aristotle tells us in another place, affirms that four things (*not* two) are so related that A is to B as C is to D. When we say 'The ship ploughs the waves', we aren't calling a ship a plough. We are intuitively perceiving the similarity in two dissimilar actions: 'The ship does to the waves what a plough does to the ground.'[2]

As Mr Kenner rightly says, this is at odds with our common conception of metaphor as combining only two terms, 'tenor', and 'vehicle'. But already the critic contradicts himself. As he says, 'We are intuitively perceiving the similarity in two dissimilar actions.' Yet when he contends that metaphor relates four things rather than two, it is precisely this similarity that is scanted. The metaphor relates not two things, nor four either, but six: the plough, the ship, the ground, the waves, *the action of ploughing, the action of sailing*. Fenollosa, who insists so loudly on the importance of verbs, and the distinctions between them, is here called in to justify a view of metaphor which reduces all transitive verbs to a colourless 'doing to'.

The consequences of this appear when Mr Kenner considers a poem two lines long:

> Swiftly the years beyond recall.
> Solemn the stillness of this spring morning.

He comments:

> Two experiences, two concretions of emotion, are juxtaposed to yield the proportion, 'My feelings of transience are held in tension with my

1 Kenner, *Poetry of Ezra Pound*.
2 Ibid., p. 87.

desire to linger amid present pleasures, as the flight of time is in tension with the loveliness of this spring morning.' The presence of two purely emotional components among the requisite four does not differentiate this in principle from the entirely 'objective' metaphor, 'The ship ploughs the waves.'[1]

No; but the absence of two components out of the requisite six – this does make a difference. What are missing are the verbs, hence the syntax. Where the verbs should be, the ploughing or the sailing, we have only the yawning vagueness of 'held in tension with'. Significantly what we get is only a state, an immobile grouping, not an action, a dynamic transference of energy. As Mr Kenner says, 'The Chinese ideograph . . . deals in exceedingly condensed juxtapositions.' And in this he says it is 'like the metaphor'. But on Fenollosa's showing, the Chinese sentence does not 'deal in juxtapositions' any more than the English sentence does. It does not just put things together, it moves from one to another, knitting webs of force. And if Aristotle's example is to be taken as the type of the metaphor, then it seems to resemble the sentence more than the ideograph.

1 Ibid., p. 90.

V

Syntax as Action in Sidney, Shakespeare, and Others

I

WHAT happens if we read some well-known poems with Fenollosa's injunctions in mind? It is worth stopping to see, but, to be fair to Fenollosa, we ought to realize that the exercise is purely experimental. We read in this way simply to see what happens, what conclusions we are led to about the value of the poems in question. The question whether we endorse these conclusions or reject them shall for the moment be waived altogether.

I have chosen for the purpose a group of poems, or passages of poetry, mostly from the sixteenth century and mostly about sleep. The first of them is a famous sonnet by Sidney:

> Come, Sleep! O sleep, the certain knot of peace,
> The baiting-place of wit, the balm of woe,
> The poor man's wealth, the prisoner's release,
> The indifferent judge between the high and low;
> With shield of proof shield me from out the press
> Of those fierce darts Despair at me doth throw:
> O make in me these civil wars to cease;
> I will good tribute pay if thou do so.
> Take thou of me smooth pillows, sweetest bed,
> A chamber deaf to noise and blind to light,
> A rosy garland and a weary head.
> And if these things, as being thine in right,
>   Move not thy heavy grace, thou shalt in me,
>   Livelier than elsewhere, Stella's image see.

According to Fenollosa the natural norm for syntax, and hence the poetic ideal, is: *term from which→transference of force→term to which*; or, *agent→act→object*. Of this there is hardly anything in Sidney's poem; where such straightforward transference of energy is in sight, Sidney avoids it by juggling with word order – 'I will good tribute pay'. The imperative or permissive verbal forms, however natural to the invocation, do not conform to this pattern; and the pervasive grammatical device is the arrangement of the catalogue, of phrases connected only by commas, each standing for the mere copula.

Sleep does not, as with Shakespeare, 'knit up the ravelled sleeve of care'; it simply *is* 'the certain knot of peace'. The sense, we may say, is the same, but in Shakespeare the force is transferred temporally through the transitive verb; Sidney's copula evades the transference of energy, and is static, asserting an equivalence, where Shakespeare's verb is dynamic, an imitation of action. In the same way, Sidney's sleep does not 'bait'; it is a baiting-place. It does not soothe; it is not even 'a soothing', but a balm. It does not enrich the poor man; it is not even 'his riches', but his wealth. It does not free the prisoner; it is his release. It does not judge; it *is* a judge.

Fenollosa would economize on prepositions, but Sidney dwells on them: not 'from', but 'from out the press of'. 'Press' to mean 'throng' is a noun Fenollosa should admire, for it incorporates much verbal energy; but in applying it to darts Sidney applies the word to just that kind of throng – a flying cloud – where its verbal force is unacceptable and has to be suppressed by the reader from his attention.

'Smooth pillows', 'sweetest bed', 'chamber', 'garland' and 'weary head' repeat the merely copulative arrangement of the first lines – but with a difference. Fenollosa had written of 'the tyranny of mediaeval logic':

According to this European logic, thought is a kind of brickyard. It is baked into little hard units or concepts. These are piled in rows according to size and then labelled with words for future use. This use consists in picking out a few bricks, each by its convenient label, and sticking them together into a sort of wall called a sentence by the use either of white mortar for the positive copula 'is', or of black mortar for the negative copula 'is not'. In this way we produce such admirable propositions as 'A ring-tailed baboon is not a constitutional assembly'.

Let us consider a row of cherry trees. From each of these in turn we proceed to take an 'abstract', as the phrase is, a certain common lump of qualities which we may express together by the name cherry or cherryness. Next we place in a second table several such characteristic concepts: cherry, rose, sunset, iron-rust, flamingo. From these we abstract some further common quality, dilutation or mediocrity, and label it 'red' or 'redness'. It is evident that this process of abstraction may be carried on indefinitely and with all sorts of material. We may go on for ever building pyramids of attenuated concept until we reach the apex 'being'.

But we have done enough to illustrate the characteristic process. At the base of the pyramid lie *things*, but stunned, as it were. They can never know themselves for things until they pass up and down among the layers of the pyramids. The way of passing up and down the pyramid may be exemplified as follows: we take a concept of lower attenuation, such as 'cherry'; we see that it is contained under one higher, such as 'redness'. Then we are permitted to say in sentence form, 'Cherryness is contained under redness', or for short, '(The) cherry is red'. If, on the other hand, we do not find our chosen subject under a given predicate we use the black copula and say, for example, '(The) cherry is not liquid'.

Now it is plain that Sidney's 'smooth pillows', his 'sweetest bed', and the rest are things which, in Fenollosa's vivid phrase, have been 'stunned'. They are not metaphors for sleep, nor, in any precise sense, symbols of sleep; they are particulars of the abstraction sleep. And it is natural to connect this with the role of the mistress in the Petrarchan sonnet. The mistress of the Petrarchan or Platonic love poet is, through a sonnet sequence, stunned time and again, attenuated more and more, until all that is left of her is an abstract 'worthiness'. Sometimes, when the poet complains of her cruelty, she is abstracted further still, into the ultimate abstraction 'being'. What began as a living woman is squeezed out until it is a pinpoint target for the lover's will.

Altogether, it seems indisputable that Sidney's poem, under Fenollosa's scrutiny, will come off very badly indeed. It is poetry where the verb is evaded whenever possible.

2

A POEM of roughly the same period as Sidney's and on the same subject is Daniel's 'Care-charmer Sleep'. This too begins with a clutter of phrases in opposition, apparently simple copulas:

> Care-charmer Sleep, son of the sable Night,
> Brother to death . . .

But this is different from anything in Sidney's poem. Sleep, Night and Death are not particulars of one stunning abstraction. Nor, on the other hand, is Sleep going to do anything to Night or to Death, as Sidney's sleep was going to knot peace and bait wit, until prevented by having its verbs wrenched from it one by one. There is no conceivable verb that could convey the relation of Sleep to Night, or of Sleep to Death. Yet these relationships are being established, by the copulas understood and the metaphor (not a very lively one) of family kinship. The relationship established is a correspondence, not an equivalence. Night is the sleep of the world; death is the sleep of the soul. Articulation is effected, but no force is expended for none is needed.

Fenollosa had declared that 'thought is successive . . . because the operations of nature are successive.' But these lines belie him. This is a sort of thought that does not go by sequence in time; if it did, it could be expressed in sentences. Daniel starts with Sleep and goes on to Night and Death, but he could equally well have started with Night or with Death (as other poets did), for in fact the three things come together. When we talk about this sort of thing we use a metaphor from space, not from time: Sleep corresponds, *on one level*, to Death, *on another level*. Yet this too is only a makeshift. As Bergson says, 'We think in terms of space – the insurmountable difficulties presented by certain philosophic problems arise from the fact that we separate out in space, phenomena which do not occupy space.' And the poet himself needs no spatial metaphors. What we have to deal with, in fact, is articulation not by syntax, neither narrative syntax like Fenollosa's nor the propositional syntax of the logician, but by dream or myth, alogical and mysterious. It is plain that the sentence, 'Death is sleepy', though propositional in form, is not a true proposition, which can be achieved by running up and down Fenollosa's pyramids. On the other hand it cannot be transformed into the narrative sentence that Fenollosa asks for, transmitting energy through a transitive verb. It seems, therefore, that the copula, in a sentence of this sort, does not deserve the opprobrium that Fenollosa heaps on it – unless, of course, one describes the statement, and Daniel's verses, as nonsense; in which case a lot of similar statements, from verse of all periods, must go through the window after it.

It is well established that a great deal of Elizabethan thought was of this kind, perceiving correspondences on different 'levels'. This thing on one level corresponds to that thing on another, level above level, microcosm inside macrocosm, sphere outside sphere. It often seems there is no movement in 'the Elizabethan world-picture'; or what movement there is, is movement that cancels itself out, like the dance in which the dancer ends where he started, or the circular motion of the sphere which returns upon itself. It was an age that appreciated Spenser's ingenious and radical dislocation of narrative order in *The Faerie Queene*. The timeless and motionless painted emblem, or the dance in which time and motion abrogate themselves, seem to be better media than language for expressing some characteristically Elizabethan attitudes. Certainly, if one accepts Fenollosa's version of the functions of language and syntax in poetry, that is the conclusion one is forced to. According to Fenollosa, a verb denotes the action of a mind or a body or a force, in time. If one believes that significant action occurs outside the dimension of time ('reality' being 'timeless'), and that the significant acts of the mind – those by which it apprehends reality – are escapes out of time into eternity, one's use of language will obviously not conform to Fenollosa's pattern.

This is the case, for instance, with a genuinely mystical poet like Henry Vaughan:

> Dear Night! this world's defeat;
> The stop to busy fools; care's check and curb;
> The day of spirits; my soul's calm retreat
> Which none disturb!
> Christ's progress, and His prayer-time;
> The hours to which high Heaven doth chime.
>
> God's silent, searching flight;
> When my Lord's head is filled with dew, and all
> His locks are wet with the clear drops of night;
> His still, soft call;
> His knocking time; the soul's dumb watch,
> When spirits their fair kindred catch.

This begins with copulas like Sidney's and proceeds to copulas like Daniel's; and it is essential to the persuasive effect that the syntactical form should be the same throughout. Night is 'care's check and curb' as Sleep is 'the baiting-place of wit'. But Night is not *the time of* God's flight; it *is* that flight, by the same dream logic that produced for Daniel, 'Sleep is the brother of Death'. And for Vaughan as for Daniel the syntactical form of *the sentence* is out of the question. This admitted, the poem answers Fenollosa's prescriptions very well. Far more than Sidney, Vaughan uses nouns full of verbal energy: 'stop', 'check', 'curb', 'watch'. In this way he expends great positive energy in expressing negations. To quote Fenollosa, 'all apparently negative or disruptive movements bring into play other positive forces. It requires great effort to annihilate.'

3

Our next example shall be from Shakespeare. Fenollosa observed:

I have seldom seen our rhetoricians dwell on the fact that the great strength of our language lies in its splendid array of transitive verbs, drawn both from Anglo-Saxon and from Latin sources. These give us the most individual characterizations of force. Their power lies in their recognition of nature as a vast storehouse of forces. We do not say in English that things seem, or appear, or eventuate, or even that they are; but that they *do*. Will is the foundation of our speech. We catch the Demi-urge in the act. I had to discover for myself why Shakespeare's English was so immeasurably superior to all others. I found that it was his persistent, natural, and magnificent use of hundreds of transitive verbs. Rarely will you find an 'is' in his sentences. 'Is' weakly lends itself to the uses of our rhythm, in the unaccented syllables; yet he sternly discards it. A study of Shakespeare's verbs should underlie all exercises in style.

Plainly Fenollosa chooses Shakespeare as the case on which his argument may rest. Shakespeare should bear him out, if any can:

O sleep! O gentle sleep!
Nature's soft nurse, how have I frighted thee,
That thou no more wilt weigh my eyelids down
And steep my senses in forgetfulness?
Why rather, sleep, liest thou in smoky cribs
Upon uneasy pallets stretching thee,
And hushed with buzzing night-flies to thy slumber,
Than in the perfumed chambers of the great,
Under the canopies of costly state,
And lulled with sound of sweetest melody?
O thou dull god! why liest thou with the vile
In loathsome beds, and leav'st the kingly couch
A watch-case or a common 'larum bell?
Wilt thou upon the high and giddy mast
Seal up the ship-boy's eyes, and rock his brains

> In cradle of the rude imperious surge,
> And in the visitation of the winds,
> Who take the ruffian billows by the top,
> Curling their monstrous heads, and hanging them
> With deafening clamour in the slippery clouds,
> That with the hurly death itself awakes?
> Canst thou, O partial sleep! give thy repose
> To the wet sea-boy in an hour so rude,
> And in the calmest and most stillest night,
> With all appliances and means to boot,
> Deny it to a King? Then, happy low, lie down!
> Uneasy lies the head that wears a crown.

Shakespeare begins, like Sidney and Daniel, with a phrase in opposition, a copula. Sleep is 'Nature's soft nurse'. But the stock correspondence (Sleep = Death) is held in abeyance through many lines, and when it comes, it is as paradox and hyperbole – 'That with the hurly death itself awakes'. The lines are full of energy. Sleep, the negation of activity, is presented as supremely active. ('It requires great effort to annihilate.') So Sleep weighs eyelids, steeps senses, seals eyes, and rocks brains. The word 'leav'st' transfers energy to three things at once, to the King's couch, the watch-case, and the 'larum bell. This ability to affect at once things so widely different quite belies the not very energetic sense of the word in common usage, and makes 'leaving' a very positive action indeed. Moreover, this energy is noisy; this is the pervasive paradox by which sleep is invoked in lines which crash and reverberate with the tolling of bells, the ticking of watches, the buzzing of flies, the clamour and hurly-burly of a storm at sea.

The whole drift of the passage, its literal sense and its metaphorical effect, is towards denying what Sidney took for granted, that a certain range of things are particulars which may stand for 'sleep', the abstraction – pillows, for instance, garlands, and beds. Once sleep is seen, as Shakespeare sees it, to be an energy, then it is seen more truly in terms of the most refractory things on which that energy plays, or (more truly still) in verbs which denote the ways that energy expends itself.

Thus Shakespeare does all that Fenollosa says. He bears him out completely. And yet there are, even here, syntactical elements for which Fenollosa makes no provision. There is, for instance, the chain of interrogations. As we have seen and as Fenollosa led us to expect, each block of verse that concludes with a question mark has the force not of an interrogation, but of a narrative statement. What we take in, as we hear these lines declaimed from the stage, is a series of moving images, little narratives. We watch sleep doing things; we do not enquire, as the question marks suggest that we do, why sleep refuses to do these things in the presented instance. These are, as we say, rhetorical questions. That is to say, the interrogative forms are the empty or emptied forms of a pseudo-syntax. The true syntax is narrative; only the pseudo-syntax is interrogative. It is significant that we should call such pseudo-questions 'rhetorical'. As we shall see, rhetoric is traditionally the province of pseudo-syntax; our expression 'rhetorical question' testifies to our acknowledgement of that.

The last of the questions is, or may be, different. The King may pause after it, enquiring of his own state of mind, 'Is it true I am to get no sleep tonight? Am I in the least sleepy?' No, he realizes, he is not; and yes, sleep can deny itself to him. So the question is answered, and he heaves himself out of bed with 'Uneasy lies the head that wears a crown.' If the episode is acted in this way, then the last question is a true question, not, like those before it, the repetition and variation of a rhythmical pattern, or so many screws to press up the tension of the hearer. In this way the last question is not a rhetorical question, because it waits upon an answer. And its interrogative syntax is authentic. It must be so, I think, and this must be the correct way of playing it, because the language is different from that of the questions that precede it. Gone are the concretions. Instead, 'an hour so rude', 'the calmest and most stillest night', 'with all appliances and means to boot' – the language is abstract and generalized.

Again, 'Uneasy lies the head that wears a crown.' Kings do not sleep in their crowns, and the image of their doing so is comical. Fortunately we are not in danger of making an image, because by this time the language has been let down so far from concreteness that we see the crown not as a thing at all, but as a symbol. Yet this is a sentence with a plot. Like Sackville's sentences about Camillus and Scipio, it changes direction dramatically on the relative pronoun, as does Cowper's couplet about the Israelites, where the relative pronoun is understood:

> And had the grace in scenes of peace to show
> The virtue they had learned in scenes of woe.

Shakespeare's line has gone over into the language as a maxim, like Chaucer's 'high senténce', a meaning of 'sentence' that Fenollosa might have done well to consider. If we cut out of poetry all statements such as this, because they are 'abstractions', we cut away all that part of poetry that has gone into the store of folk wisdom. The sentence enacts the thing it says, but not in any way that Fenollosa acknowledges.

4

I CANNOT leave this excursion into sixteenth- and seventeenth-century poetry without pointing out that there are many poems of this period which lean on what Fenollosa calls 'the discredited, or rather useless, logic of the Middle Ages', far more heavily and patently than even Sidney's sonnet on Sleep. An example is the same poet's 'Because I oft in darke abstracted guise' (*Astrophel and Stella*, xxvii), which Miss Rosemond Tuve shows to be framed throughout on the pattern of a Ramist argument. I can be brief here, for Miss Tuve has made the point at length. Such a poem, if we approach it from Fenollosa's point of view, offers us nothing whatever:

It is necessary to get rid of the modern notion that 'logic' in a poem will make it either coldly unimaginative or pedantically 'abstract', if one is to notice without prejudice the relations between the poems these men wrote and the training they were given in logical invention.[1]

Miss Tuve asks us only 'to notice without prejudice'. To enjoy and respond is another matter again, and it is no good pretending that we can with ease persuade ourselves to respond to such movements of thought as 'natural'. On the other hand there is evidence that they were natural enough to Sidney; and, if we allow Fenollosa to persuade us there is only one 'natural' movement of mind, we are blinded not only to the ways of thinking of the modern physicist, but to the ways of thinking of the Elizabethan gentleman. The loss may well be ours. I can just conceive, though I cannot share, a state of mind to which the turns and swerves of syntax in Sidney's sonnet would be as delightful and as meaningful as the turn on the pronoun in 'Uneasy lies the head that wears a crown.'

Astrophel and Stella, xxvii, is a pure example. Worse distortions occur in our reading when we come across logical syntax and abstractions in poems that, on other counts, we enjoy and want to admire. Then we either ignore the obtrusive logic, or we explain it away by supposing the poet's tone is ironical, so that he is mocking the logical syntax even as he uses it. (It is worth noting here that, to the purist, wherever there is irony, there must be pseudo-syntax, because an ironical statement belies its own syntax, meaning something other than what the syntax says. The exaggerated value placed on irony in modern criticism is either a cause or a symptom of our dislike of authentic syntax in poetry.) Both these manoeuvres occur in our reading of Donne. It has become a commonplace that Donne 'exhibits a Shakespearian use of language', and this is true in many ways. Certainly it is true of Donne by contrast to Milton, and the comment was first

1 Rosemond Tuve, *Elizabethan and Metaphysical Imagery: Renaissance poetic and twentieth-century critics* (Univ. of Chicago, 1947), p. 320.

made in the course of that comparison. But it is certainly not true if it is taken to mean that Donne works in terms of the moving image, as we have seen Shakespeare working in Henry IV's apostrophe to sleep. Much modern criticism of Donne takes 'Shakespearian' in that sense. R. A. Brower, for instance, says of Donne's 'Extasie', 'Certainly our sense of a finely ordered experience owes much to the clarity of this logical and dramatic design and to the fine tact with which it is expressed.'[1] But that is as near as we get to any examination of Donne's syntax, and Mr Brower goes on to extricate instead 'the peculiar sequence of metaphors that make up its key design'.

Fortunately I do not need to labour this point. Miss Tuve has been before me again, in showing how critics enamoured of the word as 'thing' (and at this point Hulme and Fenollosa stand together) must distort Donne and Herbert no less than Sidney and Spenser: 'Donne is especially careful to indicate how we are to conceive the relation of smaller units to the structure of a whole. Such writing utilizes rather than avoids conceptual language.'[2] And again, discussing Donne's statement of his poetic function as he conceives of it (at the end of 'The Second Anniversary'): 'Like most Elizabethan comment, it asks us to read poems as though language were not a tool for announcing facts about a particular *thou* or *I* in their character of particular phenomena, but a medium for intimating and ordering significances which particulars shadow forth.'[3] There is no need to point out that, if this element is to be found in Donne, Fenollosa could only turn down his thumbs.

5

ENOUGH has been said to show that if we take Fenollosa

1 R. A. Brower, *The Fields of Lights* (OUP, 1951), p. 80.
2 Tuve, op. cit., p. 178.
3 Ibid., p. 179.

seriously, we shall find ourselves rejecting as 'unpoetic' the greater part of what has been most admired in the poetry of the sixteenth and seventeenth centuries. This is something not much short of a ***reductio ad absurdum***. Yet Fenollosa's success with Shakespeare suggests that his views are not so much incorrect as incomplete. And the impression of solitary originality remains; for Fenollosa puts into our hands a wholly new technique, and in some cases it pays enormous dividends. No one before Fenollosa looked at Shakespeare as he has done, and Shakespeare, looked at in this way, shines out magnificently alive.

VI

Syntax as Action in Eighteenth-century Poetic Theory

To recapitulate: Hulme would banish syntax from poetry; Mrs Langer would banish it but would retain its forms while perverting their function, so as to make syntax into music; only Fenollosa would retain syntax and set great store by it. Does he stand quite alone in this? So far as I can see, in his own age and ever since, he does. But I have remarked that the temper of his mind was Augustan. Is there, then, in Augustan criticism a theory of poetic syntax which does not make syntax into music?

There is. It is the tradition of 'the strength of Denham'. When Pope exhorts his readers to

> praise the easy vigour of a line
> Where Denham's strength and Waller's sweetness join,

few of them nowadays understand what he means. With 'vigour' for a clue, most of them will suppose that Pope meant by 'strength' what Jeffrey meant when he said of the 'very sweet verses' of Samuel Rogers:

> They do not, indeed, stir the spirit like the strong lines of Byron, nor make our hearts dance within us, like the inspiring strains of Scott.[1]

But no one could call Denham's poetry stirring, and Jeffrey, when he distinguishes the sweetness of Rogers from the strength of Byron, does not mean quite the same as Pope does when he

1 Francis Jeffrey, *Essays from 'The Edinburgh Review'*, ed. H. Bennett (Hudson, 1924), p. 112.

distinguishes the sweetness of Waller from the strength of Denham. In the criticism of the eighteenth century, 'strength' has nothing to do with ardour or emotional pressure; it goes along with 'sense':

> Our great Forefathers in Poetic Song
> Were rude in Diction, tho' their sense was Strong . . .[1]

> Unpolish'd Beauties grac'd the artless Song,
> Tho' rude the diction, yet the Sense was Strong . . .[2]

. . . we may still discern that his sense was strong, and his wit genuine.[3]

Certainly, if we try to distinguish in poetry between the sense of a passage and the feeling that informs it, we shall not get very far. Nevertheless there is obviously a difference, even when we talk of poetry, between strong feelings and strong sense. It is significant that 'strong feelings' is still a normal expression in modern English, where 'strong sense' is not. That in itself suggests that we are dealing with something for which the name has been lost. So too, perhaps, has the relish for it, the capacity for enjoying or even for perceiving it. And in so far as we can distinguish between the sense of a poetic passage and its feeling, what we are looking for belongs to the first of these, to the conveying by poetry of paraphrasable meanings.

What must a poet do, then, in this part of his undertaking, to earn from an eighteenth-century critic the complimentary comment that 'his sense was strong'? We go first to the fountainhead, to Denham himself:

> Nor are the nerves of his compacted strength
> Stretched and dissolved into unsinewed length . . .[4]

1 Jabez Hughes, *Verses occasion'd by reading Mr Dryden's Fables* (1721).

2 Julia Madan (1721), quoted C. F. E. Spurgeon, *500 Years of Chaucer Criticism and Allusion*, vol. i (OUP, 1921), p. 362.

3 Robert Alves (1794), quoted Spurgeon, op. cit., p. 495.

4 'To Sir Richard Fanshawe on his translation of *Pastor Fido*' (1648).

The rhymes 'strong/long' and 'strength/length' become a commonplace:

> To mend one Fault, he makes a hundred more:
> A verse was weak, you turn it much too strong,
> And grow obscure, for fear you should be long . . .[1]

But this is more than a verbal tic, taken from the Rhyming Dictionary:

. . . Virgil, who is all great and majestic etc., requires great strength of lines, weight of words, and closeness of expressions . . .[2]

> By striving to be short they grow Obscure;
> And when they would write smoothly they want
> Strength . . .[3]

. . . illustration would impair the strength and render the sentiment too diffuse and languid . . .[4]

'Strong sense', we perceive, is 'compacted' and 'short'. It requires 'closeness of expressions'. And it vanishes when expressions are too 'long' and too 'diffuse'.

Examples could be multiplied. These should suffice to prove that 'strength', as the eighteenth century understood it, was the ability to crowd much meaning into a short space. We may fairly assume that it is the ability manifested by Pope in his lines on Peterborough:

> And HE, whose lightning pierc'd th' Iberian Lines,
> Now forms my Quincunx, and now ranks my vines,
> Or tames the Genius of the stubborn plain,
> Almost as quickly as he conquer'd Spain.

This is Sackville's Camillus and Scipio all over again, their rise and fall graphed, like Peterborough's, in the rush, the check, and the retreat of the sense through one rapid clause. This is

1 John Ozell, *Boileau his Works made English* (1711).
2 Luke Milbourne (1698).
3 Earl of Roscommon, *Ars Poetica* (1680).
4 John Newbery, *The Art of Poetry on a New Plan* (1762).

narrative. No different in principle is the argumentative verse of the *Essay on Man*:

> Bring then these blessings to a strict account;
> Make fair deductions; see to what they mount;
> How much of other each is sure to cost;
> How each for other oft is wholly lost;
> How inconsistent greater goods with these;
> How sometimes life is risk'd, and always ease:
> Think, and if still the things thy envy call,
> Say, would'st thou be the Man to whom they fall?

This is the strength that resides in expressions which are 'short', 'compacted', 'close'. And this therefore is the poet who was welcomed:

> Hail Bard unequall'd in whose deathless line
> Reason and wit with strength collected shine.[1]

This is he of whom it is said, in the same poem:

> Each Roman's force adorns his various page;
> Gay smiles, collected strength, and manly rage.

'Collected' is another word to go with 'compacted', 'close'.

But this, it may be thought, is nothing new. All critics in all ages have censured the poetry that is diffuse, or at least announced their preference for its opposite:

> The question of how concentrated a poem ought to be seems to me of the same order as how strong you like your tea. Along with most of my contemporaries I like it fairly strong . . .[2]

Is not this modern critic's 'strength' the same as Denham's, Roscommon's, Milbourne's, Julia Madan's? I think it is not. For it is certainly true that most of us like the meanings of poetry to

1 Dr John Brown, D.D., 'On Satire', *Dodsley's Miscellany* (1745).
2 Graham Hough, 'The Scalpel and the Scales', *The Listener*, Aug. 28, 1952.

be 'concentrated'. But 'concentration' is not necessarily 'compactness'. Concentration can come by many ways into poetry, down the avenues of dream, through the keyhole of innuendo, sidling through the false walls of irony, or shooting through a trapdoor from the cellarage of the unconscious. But none of these has much to do with 'closeness of expressions', just as none of them has much to do with what has been quoted from Pope. 'Strength', in other words, is close and compact syntax, neither more nor less.

And it is too a virtue of authentic syntax, not of the pseudo-syntax that is music. For a verse is strong only if it has 'strong sense'. Let syntax be never so close, unless it is truly carrying 'weight of words' it cannot be 'strong'. To be 'strong', poetic syntax must bind as well as join, not only gather together but fetter too. The actual function of meaning, 'which calls for permanent contents', *must* be fulfilled. Verse may be 'strong' or it may 'aspire to the condition of music'; it cannot do both.

This 'strength' hardly appears in nineteenth-century criticism. The word is used as frequently as ever, but it is much harder to be sure what it means. Maria Edgeworth writes in 1810: 'I do not like Lord Byron's *English Bards and Scotch Reviewers*, though, as my father says, the lines are very strong, and worthy of Pope and *The Dunciad*.'[1] This is probably strength as understood by Dryden and Johnson, not as understood by Jeffrey. And fifteen years later Miss Edgeworth was still using the old distinction between 'strength' and 'ease':

You have probably seen in the papers the death of our admirable friend Mrs Barbauld. I have copied for you her last letter to me and some beautiful lines written in her eightieth year. There is a melancholy elegance and force of thought in both. Elegance and strength – qualities rarely uniting without injury to each other – combine most perfectly in her style . . .[2]

1 Augustus J. C. Hare (ed.), *The Life and Letters of Maria Edgeworth*, vol. i (1894), p. 172.
2 Ibid., vol. ii, p. 132.

So too in Crabbe, so often capable of admirably close syntax, it is not surprising to find a laboured imitation of Denham:

> Gay spite of time, though poor, yet well attired,
> Kind without love, and vain if not admir'd.[1]

This is meant to call to mind the hackneyed lines from *Cooper's Hill*, 'which', says Johnson, 'since Dryden has commended them, almost every writer for a century past has imitated'. Obviously Crabbe knew the tradition, and was writing in it. But when *Blackwood's* in 1817 says of Byron, 'strength, vigour, energy are his attributes', we no longer know whether this is the strength of Pope and Dryden, on the one hand, or of Jeffrey and Oliver Elton on the other.

And it is not surprising that just at this period the tradition should become hard to follow. As I shall suggest later, Coleridge is an authority more ambiguous than T. E. Hulme, for instance, realized. But we can agree with Sir Herbert Read[2] that once the idea of 'organic form' was broached, poetic syntax began to move into the orbit of music and away from 'strong sense'. Wordsworth's revision of *The Prelude* is similarly, among other things, a movement from syntax to pseudo-syntax. And in fact the whole Romantic movement in poetry tended to minimize the responsibilities of poetry towards what the Augustan critics understood as 'sense'. Symbolism, from this point of view, only pushes to a logical extreme the implications of Romantic poetic theory. It was the Romantics who first suggested, by implication, that syntax could have only a phantasmal life in poetry.

Particularly interesting from this point of view are Byron and Landor. Landor is the less important, but in all fairness his case must be mentioned, for his work represents one of the traps into which the pursuit of 'strength', in the old sense, could lead the poet. As late as 1863, Landor was writing:

1 *The Borough* (1810), Letter XV.
2 Sir Herbert Read, *The True Voice of Feeling* (Faber, 1953).

> Poets as strong as ever were
> Formerly breath'd our British air:
> Ours now display but boyish strength,
> And rather throw themselves full length.
> Waller was easy, so was Sedley,
> Nor mingled with the rhyming medley . . .[1]

These wretched verses are one among many examples of the importance for Landor of the old distinction between 'strength' and 'ease'. Yet the merest glance at any of Landor's heroic poems will show that he achieved close syntax indeed, but at an exorbitant cost. For his is not after all the strength of Denham, of Pope, of Crabbe, but the strength of Milton. In order to get syntactical closeness, Landor treats the English language as if it were Latin. And even if we make Milton himself a special case, it must be admitted as a rule that 'strength' is not worth this sort of sacrifice. Nevertheless, in Landor can be found at times something approaching Pope's 'thriving plants ignoble broomsticks made', that 'sweep those Alleys they were born to shade'. The fate of Goliath is mirrored, though clumsily, in syntax:

> From the brook,
> Striking another such, another day,
> A little pebble stretcht the enormous bulk
> That would have fill'd it and have turned its course.[2]

Byron is the crucial case. Byron is 'strong', so everyone in his own day agreed. But he is strong in both ways, in the Augustan way and the Romantic; so when Jeffrey says that Byron is 'strong', and when Richard Lovell Edgeworth says so, they do not mean the same thing. The shift of meaning in the term is nowhere so clear as when different comments on Byron's verse are set side by side. Accordingly, in Byron, syntax turns into

1 S. Wheeler (ed.), *The Poetical Works of Walter Savage Landoer*, vol. ii (OUP, 1937), p. 439.
2 *Siege of Ancona*, Act IV, Sc. 2.

pseudo-syntax before our eyes. His housemaid who has risen in the world 'dines from off the plate she lately wash'd' and 'rules the circle which she served before'. But, turned a governess, she finds her charge too innately good for her to spoil:

> Foil'd was perversion by that youthful mind,
> Which Flattery fool'd not, Baseness could not blind,
> Deceit infect not, near Contagion soil,
> Indulgence weaken, nor Example spoil,
> Nor master'd Science tempt her to look down
> On humbler talents with a pitying frown,
> Nor Genius swell, nor Beauty render vain,
> Nor Envy ruffle to retaliate pain,
> Nor Fortune change, Pride raise, nor Passion bow,
> Nor virtue teach austerity – till now.[1]

The little rhythm, common in Pope and inherent in a common syntactical arrangement, grows more and more emphatic as sound usurps sense, or as sound drags the sense behind it, until it rises to a crescendo and roll of drums: '– till now'. What began as syntax has become music – not, as it happens, very subtle music, but that is beside the point.

A truly learned critic, no doubt, could write the full history of poetic syntax in English, a history to which I have contributed here no more than the sketch of a single chapter. But the point I want to make is this: in the seventeenth and eighteenth centuries poets acted on the assumption that syntax in poetry should often, if not always, carry a weight of poetic meaning; in the nineteenth and twentieth centuries poets have acted on the opposite assumption, that when syntactical forms are retained in poetry those forms can carry no weight. I have sought only to make these assumptions explicit, so that we may know just what we are doing, and what we are turning our backs upon, when we agree with the symbolists that in poetry syntax turns into music. Is Pope's handling of poetic syntax really so irrelevant to

1 'A Sketch' (1816).

the writing of poetry today? And are we really so sure of ourselves that we can afford to break so completely with the tradition he represents?

VII

Varieties of Poetic Syntax

(i) *Introduction: Grammar and Logic*

I. A. RICHARDS maintains[1] that grammar often violates logic. In this he challenges J. S. Mill who held that it does not. Richards points out:

> Socrates is wise,
> Wisdom belongs to Socrates

are two different word patterns; the same form of thought might use either.

But the only 'forms of thought' that Richards recognizes are those of logic. And it may be true that what is the same form of thought to the logician may divide into two quite distinct 'forms of thought' for the poet. It is not hard to imagine poetic contexts in which one of the word patterns about Socrates might recommend itself to the poet where the other wouldn't. In such a case the poet would find himself siding with the grammarian against the logician.

This possibility of setting grammarian and logician at odds is seldom realized by apologists for poetry. A good example of this is T. E. Hulme, who implies that since poetry is illogical in its methods, it is therefore ungrammatical, in particular non-syntactical.

On the other hand this point was well taken by Ernest Fenollosa, who unfortunately has been much less influential than Hulme on later literary criticism. He puts poet with grammarian,

1 I. A. Richards, *Interpretation in Teaching* (Routledge, 1938), pp. 284, 285.

as against logician. It is true, however, that the ally he seeks for the poet is an ideal grammarian who has broken for good the alliance with logic. Moreover, Fenollosa is not interested in 'forms of thought', or rather he is interested in 'forms of thought' only where they parallel forms of non-mental existence. Such are, he maintains, the forms of thought truly apparent in grammar as it has organically developed, though this cosmic sanction for grammatical forms has been consistently obscured by grammarians who will not break from the leading-strings of logic.

Fenollosa thus takes the forms of grammar very seriously; Hulme takes them seriously enough to want to debar them from poetry as seriously pernicious. Far more common is the view that they are not serious at all, and therefore that the poet may retain them or abjure them as he chooses. Susanne Langer and most symbolist theorists think he might as well maintain them since he can use them for his own purposes, which are not, however, those of the grammarians. He can make music out of them.

We have to agree that the forms of grammar certainly can be used in this way by the poet; and we owe a great deal to the symbolist theorists, and to a post-symbolist like Mrs Langer, for making us aware of this resource available to the poet. For it illuminates some effects achieved, not only by symbolist and post-symbolist poets, but by many pre-symbolists also. On the other hand there is a limit to this kind of thing; some poets retain the forms of grammar while emptying them of their articulating function, and yet do not provide articulation of any other kind. This seems to me vicious, for here syntax has been perverted to no end. We have lost the syntax, and got no music in exchange.

But I am particularly concerned to rebut those critics who, proceeding from a position like Mrs Langer's, assume that whenever traditional syntactical forms appear in poetry, they are *necessarily* emptied of their grammatical function, *inevitably* less than serious, a phantasmal play on the surface of the poem. 'Syntax as music' explains much; it does not explain all the parts that syntax may play in building up poetic effect. More apposite to some kinds of poetry is Fenollosa's view that the syntax of the transitive sentence obeys a law of nature. Or again, in other kinds of poetry, syntax renders a 'form of thought' more faithfully than the logician does, and with a flexibility that Fenollosa did not dream of.

In fact, I distinguish five kinds of poetic syntax, as follows: (i) subjective, (ii) dramatic, (iii) objective, (iv) syntax like music, (v) syntax like mathematics. But before I go on, I had better define at this point what I mean by 'poetic syntax'. When we speak of 'poetic imagery', we do not usually mean 'all imagery that appears in poetry'; we even allow that 'poetic imagery' can occur in prose. It is just the same with my 'poetic syntax'; and if I take my examples mainly from poetry, that is merely to suit my own convenience.

Most people, if they think about the syntax of poetry at all, regard it as something neutral, in itself neither favourable nor unfavourable to poetry, a mere skeleton on which are hung the truly poetic elements, such as imagery or rhythm. Even when syntactical neatness is acknowledged as giving pleasure, there is a reluctance about admitting that this pleasure is poetic. But a skeleton obviously has a great deal to do with the beauty or ugliness of the body it supports. And, in fact, on second thoughts we may wonder whether the syntax of poetry can ever be aesthetically neutral, a matter of indifference. It can, however. It can be unremarkable, like a human frame that is neither close-knit nor loose-limbed, neither well- nor ill-proportioned, but just normal. Much syntax in poetry is of this kind, and is therefore not poetic syntax as I understand it. For that matter, poetry, it seems, can be invertebrate, as at the end of *The Waste Land* or in much of Pound's *Cantos*, where the poet does without not just conventional syntax but any syntax at all – though never, I think, without loss.

For my own part I affirm that syntax in poetry can be itself a source of poetic pleasure. And it is only to distinguish between the several pleasures it can give, and not (perish the thought) in hopes of furnishing a new gleaming piece of critical machinery, that I have put forward provisionally the fivefold classification which I now want to explain and develop.

(ii) *Subjective Syntax*

POETIC syntax is *subjective* when its function is to please us by the fidelity with which it follows the 'form of thought' in the poet's mind. There has recently appeared an admirable poem by Robert Graves which drives this point home because it pushes this capability of poetic syntax to an extreme. The piece is in fact a *tour de force*:

LEAVING THE REST UNSAID

Finis, apparent on an earlier page,
With fallen obelisk for colophon,
Must this be here repeated?

Death has been ruefully announced
And to die once is death enough,
Be sure, for any lifetime.

Must the book end, as you would end it,
With testamentary appendices
And graveyard indices?

But no, I will not lay me down
To let your tearful music mar
The decent mystery of my progress.

So now, my solemn ones, leaving the rest unsaid,
Rising in air as on a gander's wings
At a careless comma,

There is surely no need to labour the point that the handling of syntax here is a main source of the pleasure we get from the poem. Once we have taken this point, we are in a position to appreciate poetic syntax where its effect is similar but less obtrusive and, just for that reason perhaps, more powerful, as at the beginning of Coleridge's 'Dejection':

> Well! If the Bard was weather-wise, who made
> The grand old ballad of Sir Patrick Spence,
> This night, so tranquil now, will not go hence
> Unroused by winds, that ply a busier trade
> Than those which mould yon cloud in lazy flakes,
> Or the dull sobbing draft, that moans and rakes
> Upon the strings of this Aeolian lute,
> Which better far were mute.

These eight lines slide down a long scale of emotion from something not far short of geniality to a desperate melancholy; this rapid transition is affecting and compelling just because it is all done in the compass of a single complex sentence. And we are sobered and shocked when the mood reaches rock-bottom just because this is acknowledged in a last subordinate clause, as an afterthought, almost under the breath. It is this syntactical arrangement that conveys the poignant impression that this last admission has been wrung out of the poet unwillingly, as if he has said more than he meant to say, having started (this is now the effect of the first two lines) with a determination to keep up appearances.

Obviously, when syntax can do so much as this, it is rendering far more than 'the form of thought' as Richards and the logicians conceive of it. In fact, if we are to retain that expression – 'form of thought' – at all, we must take 'thought' in the very loose sense it always has when we talk of 'poetic thought' in general; what is being rendered to us is a form of *experience*, from which 'thought' in the logician's sense is an abstraction. Here already the poet stands with the grammarian against the logician.

We see this very clearly when we find a poet making play with just those discrepancies between grammar and logic to which Richards draws attention. Richards points out that there are often two or more forms of grammar to render what the logician recognizes as one form of thought; he also points out (and draws upon Jespersen, in doing so) that the opposite case also occurs, where there is available only one form of grammar to cover what the logician sees as many different forms of thought. A good example of a poet exploiting this discrepancy, driving a wedge between grammar and logic, is the attack 'On the Lord Chancellor Hyde', a poem attributed sometimes to Rochester, sometimes to Charles II:

> Pride, Lust, Ambition, and the People's Hate,
> The Kingdom's Broker, Ruin of the State,
> Dunkirk's sad loss, Divider of the Fleet,
> Tangier's Compounder for a barren Sheet . . .

Here the play is all on the ambiguity of the possessive case in English, as in that detective story, 'The Murder of My Aunt', where the murder turns out to belong to the aunt because she committed it, not because she suffered it. So here, the hate belongs to the people because they direct it on Hyde, but also to Hyde because he suffers it; on the other hand, the ruin belongs to the state because the state suffers it, but it belongs to Hyde because he is responsible for it. The loss belongs to Dunkirk, because Dunkirk suffered it, being lost to England when Hyde sold it to France; it belongs to Hyde because, having sold it, 'that was his loss'; Dunkirk has lost Hyde because he is an English subject and she is no longer part of England, but then Hyde is 'no loss' to anyone or anything (and therefore '*sad* loss' is sarcastic); finally, when Dunkirk was sold, that was England's loss, yet also Hyde's because the loss was *his* doing. 'Tangier's Compounder' is more complicated still. Admittedly here the very elaboration of the device takes us a long way from the seriousness of Coleridge; yet the one possessive form, it could be argued, is true to 'the form of thought', in that Hyde is seen throughout as never in possession of himself, but always a tool, in the pay or in the power of some person or institution. He played a different part in each of the situations here glanced at, and in many of those situations he played a disastrously active role, yet (so the construction suggests) he was never in command of any situation, but commanded by it. In the specially abusive seventeenth-century sense he was always someone's or something's 'creature', just as every peerage is some monarch's 'creation'; and the poet goes on, in fact, to call him 'a shrub of gentry', an upstart who can be uprooted as easily as he was planted.

This example from the Restoration period has to do with grammar, but not, strictly speaking, with syntax. For a further instance consider:

> Wandering lonely as a cloud
> That floats on high o'er vales and hills,
> All at once I saw a crowd,
> A host of golden daffodils;
> Beside the lake, beneath the trees,
> Fluttering and dancing in the breeze.

Is there not here an unmistakable loss of poetic pressure? Yet the changes I have introduced – 'Wandering', for 'I wandered', and the omission of 'When' at the start of line three – are surely too slight to account for this loss on the scores of euphony and/or rhythm. The changes made are radical only in one respect, as regards syntax. To make the seeing and not the wandering the main clause of the sentence destroys the effect by which the daffodils, first seen in passing as the poet seems to turn away (his sentence completed, the daffodils acknowledged only in a subordinate clause), expand in unforeseen significance until the wandering mind is focused on them (the main clause forgotten, as the originally subordinate clause renews itself repeatedly in additional phrases). It is not that the poet sees more of the daffodils in a literal sense, catching sight of another bank of the flowers half-obscured by trees, but that he sees more *in* them, catching more and more of the powerful feeling and the significance that emanates from them.

A similar effect is developed on a larger scale by Coleridge in 'This Lime-tree Bower My Prison':

> Well, they are gone, and here must I remain,
> This lime-tree bower my prison! I have lost
> Beauties and feelings, such as would have been
> Most sweet to my remembrance even when age
> Had dimmed mine eyes to blindness! They, meanwhile,
> Friends, whom I never more may meet again,
> On springy heath, along the hill-top edge,
> Wander in gladness, and wind down, perchance,
> To that still roaring dell, of which I told;
> The roaring dell, o'erwooded, narrow, deep,
> And only speckled by the mid-day sun;
> Where its slim trunk the ash from rock to rock
> Flings arching like a bridge; – that branchless ash,
> Unsunned and damp, whose few poor yellow leaves
> Ne'er tremble in the gale, yet tremble still,
> Fanned by the water-fall! and there my friends
> Behold the dark green file of long lank weeds,
> That all at once (a most fantastic sight!)
> Still nod and drip beneath the dripping edge
> Of the blue clay-stone.

The last long sentence takes off from the 'I have lost' of the one before. The poet defines this sense of loss by following in his imagination the friends he cannot accompany, whom he 'never more may meet again', as they pass on to pleasures that he cannot share. But, just as in the Wordsworth stanza, this main statement, apparently completed, refuses to draw to a close, prolonging itself instead in subordinate constructions, each borrowing its impetus from the one before, the dell leading to the ash tree, the tree through its tremulous leaves to the water-fall, and the water-fall through the water weeds to 'the blue clay-stone'. When the poet thought all had been said, it turned out that nothing had been said; in calling to mind the pleasures he cannot share, his imagination permits him to share them. This refers back to the paradox which gives the poem its title. How can a bower of lime-trees be a prison? And, even as he begins to show how this can be, he proves that it cannot be, since the imagination cannot be imprisoned; and the poet goes on to acknowledge, at the end of the poem, that the prison is no prison, and the loss no loss. The syntax, continually finding new stores of energy where it has been affirmed that no more is to be found (the sentence, once the main verb has been introduced, seems ready to draw to a close), mimes, acts out in its own developing structure, the development of feeling behind it.

It is worth while to digress for a moment into prose fiction and into a foreign language:

Even the weather had obligingly accommodated itself to the setting: the day was neither bright nor gloomy, but of a kind of bluey-grey tint such as is found only upon the worn-out uniforms of garrison soldiers, for the rest a peaceful class of warriors except for their being somewhat inebriate on Sundays.

This comes from Gogol's *Dead Souls*. And Vladimir Nabokov, in his brilliant book on Gogol, analyses it in terms which could be used, with minor modifications, of the sentence considered above from Coleridge:

It is not easy to render the curves of this life-generating syntax in plain English so as to bridge the logical, or rather biological hiatus between a dim landscape under a dull sky and a groggy old soldier accosting the reader with a rich hiccup on the festive outskirts of the very same sentence. Gogol's trick consists in using as a link the word '*vprochem*' ('for the rest', 'otherwise', '*d'ailleurs*'), which is a connection only in the grammatical sense but mimics a logical link, the word 'soldiers' alone affording a faint pretext for the juxtaposition of 'peaceful'; and as soon as this false bridge of '*vprochem*' has accomplished its magical work these mild warriors cross over, staggering and singing . . .'[1]

1 Vladimir Nabokov, *Nikolai Gogol* (Editions Poetry, 1947), pp. 81, 82.

Here too, on Mr Nabokov's showing, we see the poet siding with the grammarian against the logician. Of course this sort of thing may be no more than a trick, an eccentric *tour de force.* Every time it occurs, whether in a poem or (at all frequently) in a novel, it has to be shown to be in accord with the burden of the whole. In Browning's 'By the Fire-side', for instance:

> For the drop of the woodland fruit's begun,
> These early November hours,
>
> That crimson the creeper's leaf across
>   Like a splash of blood, intense, abrupt,
> O'er a shield else gold from rim to boss
>   And lay it for show on the fairy-cupped
> Elf-needled mat of moss,
>
> By the rose-flesh mushrooms, undivulged
>   Last evening – nay, in today's first dew
> Yon sudden coral nipple bulged,
>   Where a freaked fawn-coloured flaky crew
> Of toadstools peep indulged.

Here, the toadstools, the mushrooms, the moss, the shield, the creeper grow each out of the one before like Coleridge's water weeds, his water-fall, and ash tree, long after the main verb of the sentence ought to have spent its force. These forms of life in both poems, like the minor characters in Gogol's novel, 'are engendered by the subordinate clauses of its various metaphors, comparisons and lyrical outbursts.' But it is not at all so clear in Browning's baffling poem as in Coleridge's that this syntactical pattern acts out a train of feeling significant to the burden of the whole.

Further examples would be tedious. I will mention only:

> Surprised by joy – impatient as the Wind
> I turned to share the transport – oh! with whom
> But Thee, deep buried in the silent tomb,
> That spot which no vicissitude can find?

(Here certainly versification is very important, for the pauses at line endings fall absolutely right. Still, the heartbreaking poignancy comes with the syntactical shift over from statement to question.) It will be remarked that this example comes from Wordsworth, and, in fact, for illustrations of what I have called 'subjective' syntax, I have drawn very heavily indeed on Wordsworth and Coleridge. I do not think this is mere coincidence. It is in these poets that I have found most often what I was looking for, and I am led to think that Sir Herbert Read, who also starts his search with these poets, may have been on the same trail when he sought 'the true voice of feeling'. If so, then he went wrong, I think, when he looked for 'the true voice' in terms of the audible rhythms of versification rather than the inaudible rhythms of syntax. In that case he is right to insist upon blank verse and free verse as the natural vehicles of the true voice, but only because in those forms the articulations of rhythm can be broken down enough for the articulations of subjective syntax to take over.

This sort of poetic syntax, in fact, seems to me an aspect of what Coleridge and De Quincey call 'eloquence', as distinct from 'rhetoric' – a distinction, incidentally, which avoids the cruder, originally Platonic opposition between poetry and rhetoric, over which so many modern critics find themselves irreconcilably at loggerheads. De Quincey holds that both rhetoric and eloquence are or can be poetic, and that, although eloquence is superior, the one often shades into the other. And Coleridge remarks, 'Eloquence itself – I speak of it as habitual and at call – too often is, and is always like to engender, a species of histrionism.' He goes on to hope that he has avoided this histrionic shallowness of feeling, while yet rendering it with eloquence; and to give his grounds for hoping this. One of his reasons is as follows:

. . . my eloquence was most commonly excited by the desire of running away and hiding myself from my personal and inward feelings, *and not for the expression of them*, while doubtless this very effort of feeling gave a passion and glow to my thoughts and language on subjects of a general nature, that they otherwise would not have had. I fled in a Circle, still overtaken by the Feelings, from which I was evermore fleeing, with my back turned towards them . . .

This fleeing in a circle, and being overtaken by the feelings from which the poet flees, is just the pattern to be found in the passage from 'Dejection' and that from 'This Lime-tree Bower My Prison'; and in each case, even as this happens, the syntax, assisted by but in command of the rhythm, acts it out for the reader.

(iii) *Dramatic Syntax*

POETIC syntax is *dramatic* when its function is to please us by the fidelity with which it follows the 'form of thought' in some mind other than the poet's, which the poet imagines. This second kind of syntax is so obvious a corollary of the first that it may seem pedantic to distinguish them. However, if I am right, Wordsworth's passage beginning 'Blest the babe', from Book II of *The Prelude*, is dramatic in this way, and a critic so scrupulous as Dr Leavis, overlooking this, was led to misjudge the poet's intentions.[1]

We should not suppose that the syntax of poetic drama is always, in this sense, dramatic. Now that we no longer look at each play by Shakespeare as a gallery of character studies, we no longer hear the claim made that every figure in every play is subtly differentiated by the rhythms and imagery of the speeches put into his mouth. Even when Shakespeare plainly is attempting to present a firmly delineated individual character, such as Polonius, he still does so more by rhythm and imagery than by

1 See *post*, pp. 294–305.

syntax. Still syntax does play a part, as in the speech on 'Commodity' by the Bastard Faulconbridge, in *King John* (II.i):

> Mad world! mad Kings! mad composition!
> John, to stop Arthur's title in the whole,
> Hath willingly departed with a part:
> And France, whose armour conscience buckled on,
> Whom zeal and charity brought to the field
> As God's own soldier, rounded in the ear
> With that same purpose-changer, that sly devil,
> That broker, that still breaks the pate of faith,
> That daily break-vow, he that wins of all,
> Of kings, of beggars, old men, young men, maids,
> Who, having no external thing to lose
> But the word 'maid', cheats the poor maid of that,
> That smooth-faced gentleman, tickling Commodity,
> Commodity, the bias of the world,
> The world, who of itself is peisèd well,
> Made to run even upon even ground,
> Till this advantage, this vile-drawing bias,
> This sway of motion, this Commodity,
> Makes it take head from all indifferency,
> From all direction, purpose, course, intent:
> And this same bias, this Commodity,
> This bawd, this broker, this all-changing word,
> Clapp'd on the outward eye of fickle France,
> Hath drawn him from his own determined aid,
> From a resolved and honourable war,
> To a most base and vile-concluded peace.
> And why rail I on this Commodity?
> But for because he hath not woo'd me yet:
> Not that I have the power to clutch my hand,
> When his fair angels would salute my palm;
> But for my hand, as unattempted yet,
> Like a poor beggar, raileth on the rich.
> Well, whiles I am a beggar, I will rail
> And say there is no sin but to be rich;
> And being rich, my virtue then shall be

> To say there is no vice but beggary.
> Since Kings break faith upon commodity,
> Gain, be my lord, for I will worship thee.

In the last dozen lines of this speech, the syntax is the snip-snap of sharp distinctions which we have already recognized from earlier soliloquies as the characteristic utterance of the Bastard's cynical honesty. In the first scene, for instance, we heard:

> For he is but a bastard to the time
> That doth not smack of observation;
> And so am I, whether I smack or no;
> And not alone in habit and device,
> Exterior form, outward accoutrement,
> But from the inward motion to deliver
> Sweet, sweet, sweet poison for the age's tooth:
> Which, though I will not practise to deceive,
> Yet, to avoid deceit, I mean to learn;
> For it shall strew the footsteps of my rising.

The diatribe against Commodity rises suddenly out of what should have been the second member of just such another tart antithesis:

> John, to stop Arthur's title in the whole,
> Hath willingly departed with a part:
> And France, whose armour conscience buckled on . . .

We expect a fourth line to round home pat with a stinging parallel to 'willingly departed with a part'. Instead we are made to wait for over a score of lines, while the speaker rings the changes on the theme of expediency. The motive behind this partakes of righteous indignation, but far more of exuberance. The indignation is more than half assumed, whipped up; we know this not only from the relapse at the end into succinct propositions and distinctions, but also from the way the long sentence, every time it totters like a slowing top, is whipped up again with:

> . . . tickling Commodity,
> Commodity, the bias of the world,
> The world, who of itself is peisèd well . . .

The repetitions – 'Commodity, Commodity' and 'the world, the world' – are like two lashes of the whip to set the top spinning rapidly once more.

Doubtless similar examples could be found without much difficulty elsewhere in Shakespeare and in other poetic dramatists. Another obvious place to look would be in the poets of the dramatic monologue, such as Browning and Kipling. Yet I think that this kind of poetic syntax is rare, for verse that is in any way dramatic is aimed at the ear, as syntax is not. Besides, so many other devices are available. Pope, for instance, when he puts direct speech in the mouths first of a Baconian scientist, then of a Cartesian, distinguishes one from the other very clearly, but not by syntax, nor by rhythm either, but pre-eminently by rhyme. The couplet, in fact, at least as used by Dryden and by Pope, is capable of rendering only one sort of movement through the mind; it is committed by its very nature to a syntax of antithesis and razor-sharp distinctions. That may be one reason why all the Romantic poets, except Byron, eschewed it.

(iv) *Objective Syntax*

YET one of the glories of the heroic couplet at its best is the syntactical nicety it permits and even demands. This syntax, however, aspires to and achieves quite different effects from those already considered. I call it *objective*. Poetic syntax is objective when its function is to please us by the fidelity with which it follows a form of action, a movement not through any mind, but in the world at large. This definition is unphilosophical, of course, for any form or movement observed in the external world is, in the process of observation, taken into the poet's mind and must dwell there until it is bodied forth in his writing. Nevertheless, common sense sees an obvious distinction between the movement of a feeling through a man's mind and the movement of destiny through his life, as through the life of Camillus, the Roman patriot, who was, as Thomas Sackville says, 'banisht by them whom he did thus detbind'. It is in relation to this kind of syntax that one can most readily speak, as H. M. McLuhan and Hugh Kenner do, of a sentence as having a plot. Mr McLuhan has even said that if, according to Fenollosa, every sentence has a plot, then the heroic couplet lends itself to something like 'the double-plot of the Elizabethans'.

The easiest 'plot' to distinguish is the potentially tragic one of 'time brings in his revenges':

> And Time that gave doth now his gift confound.

In this Shakespearian line the syntax is unremarkable. There is no tragic reversal on the relative pronoun as in the line from Sackville, or in this, from Cowper, on the poplars felled:

> And the tree is my seat that once lent me a shade . . .

– or in this from Pope:

> The thriving plants ignoble broomsticks made
> Now sweep those Alleys they were born to shade.

Here the relative – '*that* they were born to shade' – must be understood; such omissions are common in Pope, and give not only a conversational tone, but a characteristic syntactical closeness and rapidity, which is delightful and significant in its own right. But this is to anticipate; for the moment, we are concerned with syntactical features not in their own right but according as they mime a pattern of action. Closeness and rapidity of syntax may be virtues in their own right; here we approve them for the vision they convey of human life constantly subject to vicissitudes which appear and develop so suddenly that they are at all times all but uncontrollable. Pope sees human life as a matter of breathless haste and wild energy, whether the patterns he discerns in it are tragic, as above, or heroically affirmative, as when he sums up the Drapier's Letters controversy:

> The Rights a Court attack'd, a Poet sav'd,

– where, again with an omitted relative, he reduces a chapter of history to one clear and rapid narrative line.

It is this above all that marks Blake as a poet of the eighteenth century. In his poems destiny appears as the moral law that works itself out. As Coleridge, in 'Dejection', casts analysis and argument into the narrative of a changing mood, so Blake gives to his narratives a syntax as of the proposition, so as to bring out the logic of the moral law that informs his stories and gives them their symbolic meanings:

> Pity would be no more
> If we did not make somebody Poor;
> And Mercy no more could be
> If all were as happy as we.
>
> And mutual fear brings peace,
> Till the selfish loves increase:
> Then Cruelty knits a snare,
> And spreads his baits with care.
>
> He sits down with holy fears,
> And waters the ground with tears;
> Then Humility takes its root
> Underneath his foot.
>
> Soon spreads the dismal shade
> Of Mystery over his head;
> And the Catterpiller and Fly
> Feed on the Mystery.
>
> And it bears the fruit of Deceit,
> Ruddy and sweet to eat;
> And the Raven his nest has made
> In its thickest shade.

The Gods of the earth and sea
Sought thro' Nature to find this Tree;
But their search was all in vain:
There grows one in the Human Brain.

In the first stanza of four lines, the effect is very like that of four lines of Pope:

The mind, in Metaphysics at a loss,
May wander in a wilderness of Moss;
The head that turns at super-lunar things,
Pois'd with a tail, may steer on Wilkins' wings.

In reading Pope's lines, as in reading Blake's, the movement of the mind through the first couplet is checked on the rhyme, retracts, and goes through the same motions all over again. The chief difference is that Blake's world is not in such a state of emergency as Pope's is; in Pope's world the mills of God turn much faster. Blake's punctuation is very interesting. Each of his stanzas except the last consists of two complete sentences with a colon or semi-colon between them. This syntactical similarity between the first stanza and those that follow it conveys to us, before we are aware of it, one of the main points Blake wants to make – that each step in his narrative can be reduced to the propositional paradigm or 'abstract' framed at the outset. By the same means Blake slides us into narrative before we are aware of it. The second stanza seems to repeat the syntactical pattern established by the first – a pattern, that is, of two sentences parallel in syntax, rhythm, and meaning. It is only after we have already passed on from the second stanza that we realize that the second sentence of that stanza, while parallel to the first in metre and syntax, is not parallel in meaning, for it has started a narrative upon which we are now fully launched. And that is not the whole story either, for we now perceive that the third sentence is already halfway to narrative, in that, while it repeats the sense of the two sentences in stanza 1, it does not, as they do, put the cart before the horse, looking back from the good things (Pity, Mercy) to the bad things which are the preconditions of their existence, but moves forward in narrative time from the bad thing to the good thing that comes out of it. It is already narrative in that it is putting first things first, not looking back on them, as the opening stanzas did, from the standpoint of 'second things', consequences. Pope, in his line about Swift, makes an abstract of one chapter of Irish history, stripping it of all its contingent factors and drawing out of it one simple diagram of forces – the poet saving what the court attacks. Blake does the same, but not for one chapter of human history, rather for the whole of human life – virtues growing from vices. This, I think, is the meaning of his title, 'The Human Abstract'.

A similar, only less elaborate, case is 'A Poison Tree':

> I was angry with my friend;
> I told my wrath, my wrath did end.
> I was angry with my foe:
> I told it not, my wrath did grow.
>
> And I water'd it in fears,
> Night and morning with my tears;
> And I sunned it with smiles,
> And with soft deceitful wiles.
>
> And it grew both day and night,
> Till it bore an apple bright;
> And my foe beheld it shine,
> And he knew that it was mine,
>
> And into my garden stole
> When the night had veil'd the pole:
> In the morning glad I see
> My foe outstretch'd beneath the tree.

Mr H. Coombes, discussing this, remarks: 'In a poem of sixteen lines there are some sixteen clauses (not one to each line however), and nearly every line is in a sense self-contained, yet so perfectly does the action "grow" out of the initial terse but easily natural "logic" that the poem is a most forcefully coherent whole.'[1] It is obvious that one reason why the action grows so easily out of the logic is that, as in 'The Human Abstract', each stanza, whether narrative or not, contains two syntactical members, so that every stanza seems to parallel every other one, in syntax as in metre and in rhyme. But the 'growth' is easy ('fatally easy', we might say, for the growth of the narrative is also the growth of the dreadful tree) in another way. For in a sense the poem never moves out of the realm of its initial terse logic. The second line of the poem seals off the first; and the fourth, by virtue of the period after it, appears in just the same way to seal off the third. But in fact it needs the whole of the rest of the poem to lay the demon raised by the third line, as the demon raised in the first was laid in the second. That is, after all, what the poem is about – the delay and the difficulty in exorcizing a passion that is allowed to rankle. Hence the peculiar terse syntax given to the narrative is not just a sleight of hand; it is true to the fact that the implications of the initial 'logic' are still being worked out. From this point of view it can be seen that Blake makes great play with the difference between colon and semi-colon. In 'A Poison Tree', as in 'The Human Abstract', a colon marks the start of the narrative and also the end of it. In 'The Human Abstract' the narrative begins after the sixth line and finishes one line from the end. In 'A Poison Tree' the narrative begins after the third line and finishes two lines from the end (its conclusion further emphasized by a change to the present tense in the last two lines). It seems that the period, marking off a stage of the narrative inside this frame of colons, is less of a full stop than the colon is. For Blake, it seems, human life obeyed a rigorous logic, but this logic could only be seen as it worked itself out in the course of life; hence it had to be cast in narrative form. Yet since the course of life was in no way 'chancy' or unpredictable,

1 H. Coombes, *Literature and Criticism*, (Chatto, 1953), p. 95.

the narrative itself quite properly fell into logical form. Hence his syntax, neither narrative nor propositional, but partaking of both.

It will be remarked that with Blake we are already much nearer than with Pope to the symbolist poem that '*is* what it *says*'. We come nearer still, with Keats:

> As when, upon a trancèd summer-night,
> Those green-robed senators of mighty woods
> Tall oaks, branch-charmèd by the earnest stars,
> Dream, and so dream all night without a stir,
> Save from one gradual solitary gust
> Which comes upon the silence, and dies off,
> As if the ebbing air had but one wave:
> So came these words and went . . .

This falls into the same category as Pope and Blake because the syntax mimes an action outside the mind. The action is seen in smaller compass, that is all – it occupies a few minutes, not a lifetime or many lifetimes or several years. But the mimesis here is of a peculiarly close and vivid kind. The clause which tells of the gust is itself 'gradual', for we have to wait for its verb, and the clause which tells of the ebbing air is itself 'ebbing air', for the reader is, or feels as if he were, out of breath.

(v) *Syntax like Music*

THIS is much more difficult. And I am not at all happy about drawing a sharp line between Keats's kind of syntax, in the lines just considered, and the syntax that is or aspires to be 'like music'. But in theory, at any rate, the distinction is sharp enough, if we remember Mrs Langer's judgement, 'what music can actually reflect is only the morphology of feeling', and her remark, 'Articulation is its life, but not assertion; expressiveness, not expression.' If Mrs Langer is right, then poetry of this kind (for her there is no other kind) presents human feelings as they are born, develop, gather momentum, branch, subdivide, coalesce, dwindle and die away. This of course is just what Coleridge does in 'Dejection', but with this difference, that he there commits himself to defining not only the course of the feeling but its nature, so that he shall be seen to deal with one feeling – dejection – rather than with others. Now, as Mrs Langer points out, music does not do this, and all the many attempts to treat it as if it did, by saying this music is sad in such and such a way, this other piece is sad in another way, have come to grief. What sounds sad to one person sounds merry to another. And so Mrs Langer is forced to say that a sad feeling and a merry feeling may have the same morphology; and that, in music, 'The actual function of meaning, which calls for permanent contents, is not fulfilled; for the *assignment* of one rather than another possible meaning to each form is never explicitly made.' Hence we have to say that poetic syntax is like music when its function is to please us by the fidelity with which it follows a 'form of thought' through the poet's mind, ***but without defining that thought.*** (Here our earlier definition of what we mean by 'thought' in this context is of the first importance; the 'thought', we said, in poetry, is 'the experience'. Hence it includes, if indeed it is not the same as, Mrs Langer's 'feeling'.)

Now in poetry it is not so easy as in music to articulate without asserting, to talk without saying what one is talking about. But, as is well known, this difficulty was circumvented by the use of the objective correlative, the invention of a fable or an 'unreal' landscape, or the arrangement of images, not for their own sakes, but to stand as a correlative for the experience that is thus the true subject of a poem in which it is never named. It is true that Mr Eliot, who put the expression 'objective correlative' into currency, speaks as if the function of the correlative is to define, better than by naming, the experience, the feeling, for which it stands. But in the light of Mrs Langer's distinction, we have to say that it defines the morphology of the feeling, not its distinctive nature. In any case this convention has healed or blurred the distinction I have used, between 'subjective' and 'objective' syntax: poems written in this mode employ a syntax that seems to be subjective and objective at once.

What it amounts to can be shown most clearly perhaps by Kenneth Burke's remarks on 'The Lost Son', a poem by Theodore Roethke. In the first place all the poet will say of this poem is that it is 'in a sense a stage in a kind of struggle out of the slime; part of a slow spiritual progress, if you will; part of an effort to be born.' This fits in with Mrs Langer's remark about music, that 'the actual function of meaning, which calls for permanent contents, is not fulfilled.' All the poet offers to give us is the movement through one stage of a struggle, the tensions and resolutions in one part of a progress, the efforts made. To what end they are made, towards what the struggle and the progress are directed – all this can be answered only 'in a sense', only 'if you will'.

Mr Burke quotes and examines the nine lines of section two of the poem:

> Where do the roots go?
>   Look down under the leaves.
> Who put the moss there?
>   These stones have been here too long.
> Who stunned the dirt into noise?
>   Ask the mole, he knows.
> I feel the slime of a wet nest.
>   Beware Mother Mildew.
> Nibble again, fish nerves.

Mr Burke comments:

... much is done by a purely Grammatical resource. Thus, the underlying assertion of the first couplet (this mood is like roots, like under-the-leaves) is transformed into a kind of 'cosmic' dialogue, split into an interchange between two voices. The next restatement (it is like moss-covered stones) is broken into the same Q-A pattern, but this time the answer is slightly evasive, though still in the indicative ('These stones have been here too long' – a 'vatic' way of suggesting that the mood is like stones sunken, and covered heavily). The third couplet (it is like the sound of moles burrowing) is introduced by a slightly longer and more complex question . . . Also the answer is varied by a shift into the imperative ('Ask the mole').

And he sums up:

. . . the Grammatical shifts, by dramatizing the sequence of topics, keep one from noting that the stanza is in essence but a series of similarly disposed images (symbolizing what Roethke, in a critical reference, has called 'obsessions').[1]

I should prefer to say that the images serve to indicate roughly the area of experience that the poet is dealing with; they limit the number of possible answers to the question, 'What is the poet talking about?' But a wide range of possible answers remains, and the poem does nothing to narrow this choice any further. Instead it defines, largely by syntactical arrangements and changes, the extent to which the nameless experience is a search, to what extent it is a surrender, to what extent an agony, to what extent a waiting, and so on. As the poet traces the development of the experience, we can see how at one time the element of passive agony, at another the element of active surrender, at another time the waiting, at another time the searching, predominates in the total experience behind the writing. But that experience is never defined, since we are never told to what it surrenders, what it seeks, what it is waiting *for*. Hence this poem seems to me of just the sort that Miss Langer envisages, and the vital part played in it by syntax seems to be, on her showing, 'like music'.

A subtler case occurs in the first lines of 'Gerontion':

> Here I am, an old man in a dry month,
> Being read to by a boy, waiting for rain.
> I was neither at the hot gates
> Nor fought in the warm rain
> Nor knee deep in the salt marsh, heaving a cutlass,
> Bitten by flies, fought.

1 *Sewanee Review*, Winter 1950, p. 89.

The repeated 'nor' in these lines makes 'neither' look rather silly, but that is not my point, which is rather the last word, the repeated 'fought'. In terms of the prose sense of this passage, there is no need for this word at all. Its presence certainly gives an interesting twist to an otherwise rather facile rhythm. But I have too much respect for Mr Eliot to think this his sole reason for tagging on the word. (He has, of course, in his criticism, seemed to deplore such dictation by merely rhythmical considerations.) The word, coming where it does, has the further effect of acting out through syntax the dwindling and the diminution, the guttering frustration and waste, which is the arc of feeling here being presented. The verb, energetic in meaning, and in the active voice, is held up by the three phrases ('knee deep in the salt marsh, heaving a cutlass, bitten by flies'), and this postponing of the issue builds up a tension which the verb would, in the ordinary way, resolve with all the more vigorous éclat, a powerful reverberation. But this it cannot do, having been negated from the first by that 'nor' from which it is now so far removed. Hence it has the effect almost of parody, of a shrill and cracked vehemence, like:

> I will do such things,
> What they are yet, I know not, but they shall be
> The terrors of the earth.

Lear's windy threatening is a fine piece of dramatic syntax; Gerontion's is unlike it, because we are not to take him as a person but only a *persona* – he is given a phantasmal life only provisionally, not fully bodied forth. Hence, though this is a tricky case, I regard Eliot's lines as an example of syntax like music.

It is important to realize, however, that, although 'objective correlative' and 'syntax like music' are principles only recently formulated in poetic theory, both can be found in the poetic practice of poets writing much earlier. Much pre-symbolist verse can be made to toe a symbolist or post-symbolist line. For instance, this seems to be the place to consider what Hopkins called 'the figure of grammar'. He found it pre-eminently in Hebrew poetry:

A figure of grammar can be shifted to other words with a change of specific meaning but keeping some general agreement, as of noun over against noun, verb against verb, assertion against assertion, etc., e.g. Foxes (A) have (B) holes (C) and birds of the air (A') have (B – not B' here) nests (C'), or more widely even than this/with a change of words but keeping the grammatical and logical meaning – as/Foxes have holes and birds of the air have nests (that is/Beasts have homes to live in) but the Son of Man has not where to lay His head (that is/Man has not a home to live in): the subjects of the clauses being changed the one does no more than say yes, the other no.

This passage is quoted by Sir Herbert Read in the book I have referred to already. He applies it to the verse of Whitman and of Lawrence and, by arguing that they are rhetoricians not poets, seems to want to huddle away the Figure of Grammar out of poetry into rhetoric. But even though we agree in calling Whitman a rhetorician in some pejorative sense, it may not be the Figure of Grammar that makes him so. Hopkins, for instance, spoke of Whitman's 'rhythm run to seed', and Allen Tate, when he follows Hopkins in this, does so with the specific intention of showing how the Figure of Grammar need not involve this sort of rhythmical decadence. According to Tate it does not do so for St-John Perse, whose verse is only superficially like Whitman's. In Perse's poetry, according to Tate, 'the very grammar ... becomes itself a principle of organization.'[1] And if I understand the critic, this means that Perse's poetry is based upon what Hopkins called the Figure of Grammar, and that its syntax is 'like music'.

For an example of this in English, we can go to Eliot again, to the beginning of 'Ash Wednesday':

1 Allen Tate, 'Homage to St-John Perse', *Nine*, No. 3 (1949–50), p. 79.

1. Because I do not hope to turn again
2. Because I do not hope
3. Because I do not hope to turn
4. Desiring this man's gift and that man's scope
5. I no longer strive to strive towards such things
6. (Why should the aged eagle stretch its wings?)
7. Why should I mourn
8. The vanished power of the usual reign?
9. Because I do not hope to know again
10. The infirm glory of the positive hour
11. Because I do not think
12. Because I know I shall not know
13. The one veritable transitory power
14. Because I cannot drink
15. There, where trees flower, and springs flow, for there is nothing again.

I have numbered these lines for ease of reference. Now if we compare lines 8, 10 and 13, it will be observed that 10 and 13 are tied together by an end-rhyme, but that 8 and 10 are tied together no less closely by similarity of grammar. What we have here, in fact, is a sort of parity of esteem between rhyme and metre and grammar or syntax. Every line in the second section, except for the last of all, 'rhymes' with some one or more lines in the first section. Thus 9 is linked with 8 by end-rhyme, but, as I have remarked, 10 no less 'rhymes' with 8 by virtue of grammar. 11 rhymes by syntax with 2. 12 rhymes with 3 by virtue of metre and a certain syntactical similarity, but also by syntax with 5 ('Know I shall not know' echoing 'strive to strive'). 13 rhymes through 10 with 8. And 14 rhymes, by metre and syntax, with 2. The two lines left over are 4 and 15, and one could even argue, though this might be straining a little, that these 'rhyme' together, simply by virtue of being each the odd one out (though each is linked by end-rhyme with another line in its own section).

This use of syntax as rhyme is certainly nearer to 'syntax like music' than to any of the other varieties so far considered. But I confess I am uncertain whether it does not constitute another category again; and to this I now turn.

(vi) *Syntax like Mathematics*

I MAKE this category on the authority of Valéry, speaking of Mallarmé's interest in syntax:

In this – and I told him so one day – he approached the attitude of men who in algebra have examined the science of forms and the symbolical part of the art of mathematics. This type of attention makes the structure of expressions more felt and more interesting than their significance or value. Properties of transformations are worthier the mind's attention than what they transform; and I sometimes wonder if a more general notion can exist than the notion of a 'proposition' or the consciousness of thinking no matter what.[1]

In the light of this we have to say that *poetic syntax is like mathematics when its function is to please us in and for itself.*

Now while in practice it may be (indeed it is) very difficult indeed, quite often, to distinguish syntax like music from syntax like mathematics, in theory it is very easy indeed. For the widest possible gulf yawns between this last category and not only the one before it, but all those so far considered. For all those were alike in appealing for their justification to something outside themselves, which they mimed. All were at bottom *mimetic*, or aspired to be. The syntax of Mallarmé appeals to nothing but itself, to nothing outside the world of the poem.

Hence my hesitation over 'Ash Wednesday', where the use of syntax as rhyme (if I may be permitted to use once more that extravagant expression) seems to be merely a part of the poem's internal economy, purely a structural device. It may be only that. But I do not think it is. I prefer to think – and after all this is

1 *Variété III*, p. 28, quoted Sewell, *The Structure of Poetry*, pp. 151, 152.

not a sheer act of faith – that, when identical syntactical arrangements recur in 'Ash Wednesday', they do so not just to knit the poem together, but because the curve of experience presented in the poem has at that point come round upon itself. Hence the syntax of 'Ash Wednesday' can, after all, be shepherded into the mimetic fold.

In fact it is hard to find in English any counterpart to Mallarmé from this point of view. I think I have found one, however, in the 'Epistle to a Patron' of that most unjustly neglected contemporary F. T. Prince:

> My lord, hearing lately of your opulence in promises and your house
> Busy with parasites, of your hands full of favours, your statutes
> Admirable as music and no fear of your arms not prospering, I have
> Considered how to serve you and breed from my talents
> These few secrets which I shall make plain
> To your intelligent glory. You should understand that I have plotted
> Being in command of all the ordinary engines
> Of defence and offence, a hundred and fifteen buildings
> Less others less complete: complete, some are courts of serene stone
> Some the civil structures of a war-like elegance as bridges
> Sewers, aqueducts, and citadels of brick with which I declare the fact
> That your nature is to vanquish. For these I have acquired a
> knowledge
> Of the habits of numbers and of various tempers and skill in setting
> Firm sets of pure bare members which will rise, hanging together
> Like an argument, with beams, ties and sistering pilasters:
> The lintels and windows with mouldings as round as a girl's chin;
> thresholds
> To libraries; halls that cannot be entered with a sensation as of myrrh
> By your vermilion officiers, your sages and dancers. There will be
> chambers
> Like the recovery of a sick man, your closet waiting not
> Less suitably shadowed than the heart, and the coffers of a ceiling
> To reflect your diplomatic taciturnities . . .

And so this splendid poem goes on. There is no reason why it should ever stop, for it is plain that under the guise of architect speaking to patron the poet is speaking to his reader, and speaking about his poem even as he writes it. For the building is 'like an argument', and the chamber in it 'not less suitably shadowed than the heart'. The poem does not even explore the relationship, actual or ideal, of poet and reader; the poem is the poem's subject – that is all. And this of course is significant. For if the structures of expression are to be more interesting to the reader than the structures of experience behind them, the only way to induce the right sort of attention in the reader is to have nothing behind them at all, that is, to have poems that are meaningless. The only alternative is to have poems that talk about themselves, as Prince's does.

But this is true only so long as the poet is determined to make his poetry 'pure' and 'absolute' for in Valéry's formula it is not necessary that the structure of expressions should be *the only* source of interest in the poem, only that this should be more interesting than anything else. And even Valéry's formula is too narrow, for there is no reason why this sort of syntax, any more than any of the other sorts, should be more than one source of pleasure among many others. It is *poetic syntax* in that it gives poetic pleasure, and it differs from other kinds of syntax only in this, that the pleasure it gives has nothing to do with mimesis. On these terms any amount of older poetry can be seen to employ syntax-like-mathematics and indeed this category becomes more crowded than any of the others. In particular the Augustan age sends up one candidate after another:

Within the couplet the poet worked out as many contrasts and parallels as he could, providing the maximum number of internal geometrical relationships. Denham's lines on the Thames had fascinated later poets with the possibilities of this kind of configuration. They were frequently imitated – too frequently for Swift's pleasure. Their kind of verbal manipulation was improved on, until in Pope a couplet will often suggest a difficult figure in Euclid, its vowels and consonants, its sense-oppositions and sense-attractions, fitted together like arcs and lines.

> A Fop their Passion, but their Prize a Sot;
> Alive, ridiculous, and dead, forgot![1]

The Euclidean reference here is exact. This is a syntax like mathematics, as is Mallarmé's. I have given examples from Pope to illustrate another category of poetic syntax which I have called 'objective', and I think there is some danger that the high shine of artifice over the surface of the best Augustan verse will lead readers to think of their syntax as 'like mathematics' when in fact it has a more mimetic function, clinging closely to the experience behind it. Still, it cannot be denied that it is in the eighteenth century that we find most of this Euclidean syntax.

Yeats may seem to speak of the same thing, though he compares it with mechanics rather than mathematics, when he writes to H. J. C. Grierson in 1912:

> The over childish or over pretty or feminine element in some good Wordsworth and in much poetry up to our date comes from the lack of natural momentum in the syntax. This momentum underlies almost every Elizabethan and Jacobean lyric and is far more important than simplicity of vocabulary. If Wordsworth had found it he could have carried any amount of elaborate English. Byron, unlike the Elizabethans though he always tries for it, constantly allows it to die out in some mind-created construction, but is I think the one great English poet – though one can hardly call him great except in purpose and manhood – who sought it constantly.[2]

But here there is the difficulty of what Yeats means by 'natural'. He opposes it to 'mind-created', which is obviously much the fitter word for the constructions of Denham and Pope. Fenollosa too was much concerned, in his remarks on syntax, for its 'momentum'; and if Yeats intended to give to 'natural' the full and ambitious sense that Fenollosa gave to it, then his view of syntax would become, in my terms, 'objective'. This is unlikely, however. In view of Yeats's lifelong preoccupations and of his

1 *Times Literary Supplement*, Jan. 4, 1936.
2 *Encounter*, No. 2 (Nov. 1953), p. 20.

reference to Wordsworth, it is more probable that he means by 'natural' something like 'in close touch with living speech'. If so, then he esteems momentum in syntax because it assists in the miming of the living speech of those persons (Yeats was quite precise about who they were) who in his view were models of poetic utterance; and in that case the syntax he asks for is 'dramatic'.

VIII

Syntax in English Poetry and in French

I

It is obvious that any attempt to make a hard and fast rule about what poetic syntax is or ought to be depends upon an equally stringent rule about poetic language, about what words are or ought to be in poetry. This is true of both Hulme and Fenollosa, who insist that words in poetry are or ought to be like 'things'. This is nonsense, of course; yet useful nonsense. Words are not things, nor can any one word be shown to be more of a thing than any other; but the fact remains that in reading poetry we do feel some words or some arrangements of words to partake of the nature of the things they stand for, in a way that other words and arrangements of words do not. All the same, common sense must be allowed to have its say. And common sense forces us to ask why the words of poetry should be thought to be all of one kind. The commonsense position is that words are of different kinds, and that the old-fashioned grammatical classification into 'parts of speech' does correspond roughly to the different feelings we have about these different kinds. Hulme and Fenollosa assume that words in poetry are all of one kind; and this assumption rests upon another, that words outside poetry are of only two kinds. They seem to assume that all words are either abstract or concrete, and that by and large concrete words are good for poetry where abstract words aren't. To be sure they refine on this, since Fenollosa in particular insists that the most abstract words are concrete at bottom, and can be shown to be so in a poetic context. Perhaps they would agree that a word is abstract or concrete not in itself, but only relative to the context in which it occurs. Nevertheless it is not unfair to say that for both of them a word, when it appears, is either abstract or concrete. Is this in fact the case? Must we either pick away at the base of one of Fenollosa's pyramids or else leap nimbly from one apex to another? Is there no halfway house? And if there is, what is the significance of that for poetry in general and syntax in particular?

In order to answer these questions it is instructive to look at a foreign language. St-John Perse reports on his friendship with Gide:

> He told me of the attraction that an exhaustive study of the English language was beginning to exert over him. I, for my part, deplored the denseness of such a concrete language, the excessive richness of its vocabulary and its pleasure in trying to reincarnate the thing itself, as in ideographic writing; whereas French, a more abstract language, which tries to signify rather than represent the meaning, uses words only as fiduciary symbols like coins as values of monetary exchange. English for me was still at the swapping stage.
>
> There was some nodding and shaking of the head. That was precisely, if he was to be believed, just what he most needed at the moment: to take on weight and mass in the language of Newton.[1]

There is no need to point out that Perse favours a view of language quite at odds with what Hulme and Fenollosa and Pound, in their different ways and with varying degrees of sophistication, have urged upon the English poet and his readers.

This too, like all theories of syntax, turns out to rest upon a philosophy, an inclusive attitude towards human life and human knowledge:

> French literature, born in a civilization of courts, of salons, cliques, and of philosophers' garrets, and thus eminently social, anti-metaphysical and anti-poetic, is rediscovering its infinite in the very depths of the

1 St-John Perse, 'André Gide: 1909', tr. Mina Curtiss, *Sewanee Review*, LX, 4, p. 601.

well of the human heart, as unfathomable as any other for the Frenchman, who is by nature an analyst and a psychologist. English literature sprang from a more material civilization and, more enamoured of nature, is rediscovering its infinite in the cosmic abyss![1]

This too fits in very well with much we have observed already. Mr Kenner, as a champion of 'ideographic writing', sneers at 'the Cartesian thinkers' hatred of things outside themselves'; this may serve as a gloss on what is meant here by 'psychologist'. Similarly, if the Frenchman is 'by nature an analyst', he will obviously find himself on the other side of the fence from Hulme, for whom analysis is only a form of the 'extensive manifold' with which, he says, poetry has nothing to do – 'The intellect always analyses – when there is a synthesis it is baffled. That is why the artist's work seems mysterious.'

This is a view of poetry at the opposite extreme from Mr Kenner's:

> Looking about the world, we know *things*. On a page of poetry there are set in motion the intelligible species of *things*. Words are solid, they are not ghosts or pointers. The poet connects, arranges, defines, *things*: pearls and eyes; garlic, sapphires and mud.[2]

On this showing to speak of words as 'fiduciary symbols' is to make of them ghosts or pointers.

2

Of course to speak of the nature of French language, the nature of English, is hopelessly unscientific. But the contrast between French and English on this point is useful and suggestive. Dryden, for instance, indebted as he was to French models in

1 St-John Perse, op. cit., p. 600.
2 Kenner, *Poetry of Ezra Pound*, p. 77.

Corneille, Boileau, St Evremond, compared French with English in just the same terms: the language of the French, he said, 'is not strung with sinews like our English; it has the nimbleness of a greyhound, but not the bulk and body of a mastiff.' Dryden's 'bulk and body' corresponds to the French writer's apprehension of 'weight and mass'. The Earl of Roscommon, Dryden's contemporary, made the comparison thus:

> But who did ever in French authors see
> The comprehensive English Energy?
> The weighty Bullion of one Sterling Line,
> Drawn to French Wire, would thro' whole Pages shine.

And this brings us closer to Fenollosa, for whom 'weightiness' and 'energy' go together; the weight and mass do not or need not make the verse inert, quite the contrary. On the other hand, it may make it short-winded: Roscommon's contrast between the 'one Sterling Line' and the 'whole pages' corresponds perhaps to Fenollosa's vindication of only the briefest and simplest of syntactical forms. But this is to read too much into one slender clue.

Hofmannsthal remarks, in the *Book of Friends*, 'French prose at its highest level is more sensual in the intellectual field and in the sensual more intellectual than the German at its present level.' And again, 'One advantage of the French language is that it can form spontaneously the plural of sensual *abstracta: les fatigues, les vides, les noirs*.'[1] This last is obviously an example of how French is 'sensual in the intellectual field'. English can form such plurals: 'leaden-eyed despairs', 'to suffer woes which Hope thinks infinite'. I have not seen it remarked how English Romantic poets, disliking the personifications of the Augustans, evaded them by merely tacking an 's' on the end. This could be taken as an amusing revelation of their hypocrisy. But that would be wrong. The addition of the 's' makes a world of difference:

1 Hofmannsthal, *Selected Prose*, pp. 371, 373.

when abstractions appear in the plural they are no longer to the same degree abstractions. When an eighteenth-century poet writes 'Woe' or 'Despair', we are restive, feeling how many different human experiences have been 'stunned', deprived of all their painful immediacy and uniqueness, in order to come under the one abstracted term. With Keats's 'despairs' and Shelley's 'woes', we do not feel this. The poet, by using the plural, acknowledges that there are many kinds of despair, many kinds of woe; if he does not choose to dwell on them now, it is not that he does not know of them – he asks us to let the word serve for the moment, as we read. What we have in fact is a word that is neither abstraction nor concretion, but something in between. And this may be what our French authority means by 'fiduciary symbols'. If Hofmannsthal is right in saying that French sensualizes the intellectual and intellectualizes the sensual, he may be saying that the tendency of the language is towards words as symbols *in this sense*. Concretions are milked of their concreteness, abstractions are flushed with sense, until both sorts of word can live together on a common symbolic level. Perhaps this corresponds to our intuition of what happens as we read a passage of French.

This is the most important point I want to make, and I want to develop it. But first this is the place perhaps to dispose of a possible confusion. The passages I have quoted come from some fugitive recollections by a French poet, St-John Perse, of a French novelist, André Gide. Now it is a fact that the movement in English poetry that drew upon the authorities of T. E. Hulme and Ernest Fenollosa was also characterized by appeals to French prose as a model. Ezra Pound is the case in point: '... no man can now write really good verse unless he knows Stendhal and Flaubert.' This appears to make against our case that the tendency of French, at least of French prose, is away from the 'ideographic writing' that Pound has developed in his verse. But the point can be cleared up if I appeal, yet once more, to Hugh Kenner:

What Flaubert actually did was arrange not primarily words but things; or words as *mimesis* of things. Out of an odour, a waft of talk, a plume of smoke, the flare of gaslight, the disposition, relative to the carpet and windows, of certain furniture in a certain room, the world of Frédéric Moreau emerges with palpable and autonomous immediacy. The significant action of the novel, in contradistinction to the diagrammable 'plot', obstructed by dull descriptions, that emerges from a poor translation, consists in the interactions of, the tensions set up between, these items. That is the meaning of *le mot juste*.[1]

This is clearly a response to Flaubert very different from Proust's, when he observes, 'The conjunction "*et*" has nowhere in Flaubert's works the purpose assigned to it by grammar. It marks a pause in a rhythmical measure and divides a picture', or, 'That whole second page of *L'Éducation sentimentale* is made of imperfects, except when a change intervenes, an action of which the protagonists generally are things.'[2] Proust seems more interested in the exact nature of the tensions and interactions than in the things thus related. Pound too is interested in these relations, yet he does not use syntax to present them, but rhythm instead. It may be objected of course that this is just the difference between prose and verse; in which case one goes on to argue that authentic syntax has no place in poetry. At any rate this shows how it could come about that a master of French prose syntax was adopted as a model by English poets who were destroying syntax nearly altogether.

3

ST-JOHN PERSE wants words to be 'fiduciary symbols'. 'Fiduciary', says the dictionary, 'held or given in trust; relating to a

1 Kenner, *Poetry of Ezra Pound*, p. 256.

2 Quoted in the Introduction to J. L. Hevesi (ed.), *Essays on Language and Literature* (Wingate, 1948).

trustee.' What is in question plainly is a sort of contract entered into tacitly by speaker and hearer, writer and reader: a convention which both observe. This would be anathema to Fenollosa, for whom the only contract the poet should honour is that between himself and 'nature'. Hulme goes further and says that the contracts normally in being between speaker and hearer are only a hindrance to the poet. Hence critics who follow Hulme's lead (and that is to say most of the critics influential today) lay great stress upon the poet's task in breaking down the reader's 'stock responses', getting through or behind the existent conventions, flouting the established contract in order to enter into another. By this course of reasoning one arrives at the notion that in order to become a reader of poetry the individual must go through a period of strenuous training and rehabilitation. St-John Perse envisages another possibility, that of the poet communicating with his readers in terms of contracts to which the reader is accustomed. As all readers are most accustomed to various sorts of prose, it seems likely that on this view poetry and prose will differ only in degree, where to proponents of the other argument they will differ in kind.

What is the nature of the contract that obtains between the poet and his reader? Or rather (since the whole idea of 'contract' is now being challenged), what has been the nature of such poetic contracts in the past? One obvious clue is the idea of 'genre': the poet, by advertising that his poem is to be elegy or epistle or satire or epic, asks of his reader a certain kind of attention and promises him in return a certain kind of profit. This advertisement may appear even in a title, or else it can emerge from certain easily recognized features of the verse as soon as the reading begins; such are metrical forms, for instance, traditionally connected with one genre rather than another, such as the elegiac stanza; or they can take the form of a certain pitch of tone (epic diction is 'lofty'); or there are such features as the epic simile. C. S. Lewis, when he defends Milton against Dr Leavis, says in effect that, when Dr Leavis reads *Paradise Lost*, he refuses to honour the contract proper to the heroic poem; he gives the wrong sort of attention and expects the wrong sort of profit. On the other hand Dr Leavis can retort that ultimately every poem is unique, and therefore every poem requires a contract valid only for itself. Every poem, even within the convention of its genre, establishes its own convention; and he can argue that, when he says Milton asks too much of his readers, he means that he asks more than even other epic poets have asked for. The contract involved in *Paradise Lost* (he may say) is an unacceptable one, quite unjustly weighted in favour of the poet and against the reader. The poet asks too much and gives too little in return.

But the contract we speak of here is one that is common to the reading of poetry in general, to each and every poem, anterior to the more specific contracts of genre. It concerns something that the reader must grant to the poet before he begins to read any poetry at all. At least one provision of that contract rests upon the nature of reading as an activity taking time: 'The nature of any particular semantic reaction, or any part of a total semantic reaction, is conditional on what precedes and follows it. As all speech signs are presented in a certain time-order, this is a very important point.'[1] In the less rebarbative language of criticism this means no more than the well-worn truth that any word is defined by its context. But it has the advantage of emphasizing that this is not peculiar to those arrangements of language traditionally known as 'literature'. It is a feature of all forms of linguistic communication:

It is almost comic to note the difficulty with which we are confronted when we try to establish the *precise* meaning of a word which, in the ordinary routine of life, we use daily to our complete satisfaction. Take, for instance, the word Time. Caught on the wing, it is perfectly lucid, defined and honest. It fulfils its purpose faithfully, so long as that purpose is to form part of a conventional statement, so long as he who

1 Pollock, *The Nature of Literature*, pp. 42, 43.

employs it has something definite to say. But isolate it, clip its wings, and it turns and takes its revenge . . . It is something entirely different from what it was, an enigma, an abyss, a source of mental torment. The same is true of the word Life, and of many other words.[1]

This, then, is one of the provisions in the contract between poet and reader. The reader undertakes not to tear a word from its context and scrutinize it in isolation. The poet reserves the right to use at any point a word that may seem, by its appearance, to have little or no meaning; he engages, in return, to give it meaning in the context of the whole. This, as we saw, is the contract implicit in Keats's 'leaden-eyed despairs'.

None of this is very startling or novel, until we pause to ask what is meant by 'context'. What is the contextual unit? If we say that by 'in its context' the poet means 'in the context of the whole poem', then we are faced with Ezra Pound's *Cantos*, a poem of enormous length, which has appeared in snatches during the past twenty-five years and is still incomplete. If we are baffled by the significance of any word that has appeared in the sections so far published, we can be told to wait until we see it in the context of the whole poem.

For the ideographic writers who seem in other respects contemptuous of the whole idea of the contract ('You need grant me nothing', they seem to say, 'the thing is there on the page, embodied; the process is there, enacted') turn out to insist rigorously on the form of contract that insists on reading in context – 'Everything will fall into place in the context of the whole.' How does this reading of the contract differ from Valéry's?

Chiefly in this: that Valéry's poet gives us the articulation as he goes along, but asks us to wait till the end for the meaning of the things articulated; Pound is a poet who gives the 'things' as they go along, but asks us to wait till the end before we see the

1 Paul Valéry, 'Poetry and Abstract Thought', tr. Gerard Hopkins, in Hevesi (ed.), *Essays*, pp. 73, 74.

connection between them. This is clear from Valéry's insistence that 'Time' is manageable enough, so long as we take it as 'part of a conventional statement'. It becomes unmanageable only when we take it 'apart from its neighbours . . . in isolation from its momentary function'. It is when we take the words in isolation that they become, as they became for Lord Chandos, 'congealed into eyes which stared at me and into which I was forced to stare back – whirlpools which gave me vertigo and, reeling incessantly, led into the void.' Pound can retort that he never takes a word 'apart from its neighbours'; on the contrary, to give a word three or four selected neighbours is the clue to the ideographic method. On the other hand it certainly cannot then be said 'to form part of a conventional statement'. Valéry's poetry can plainly find room for at least the forms of conventional syntax, where Pound's cannot.

IX

Syntax in the Blank Verse of Wordsworth's Prelude

I

We have to understand that when St-John Perse speaks of the Englishman as enamoured of 'nature', he means the 'nature' of Isaac Newton. If the clue to Newton had not been given, we might have gone astray. We might have thought first of Wordsworth. For it is Wordsworth who springs most readily to mind as the sort of English poet that the Frenchman finds alien, the poet 'enamoured of nature' and 'rediscovering (his) infinite in the cosmic abyss'. But the abyss, we now realize, is not what evoked in Wordsworth 'fleeting moods of shadowy exultation'; what the French poet means is 'a world of atoms in motion, devoid of all secondary sense qualities, such as colour, scent, taste and sound, ordered by causal laws and explicable only in terms of mathematics'[1] – in short, the world of abstract 'matter' in which the early experimenters seemed to find themselves when they followed out the implications of their conscientiously 'concrete' experiments.

Far from making against Wordsworth, Perse's view of poetic language, I shall suggest, is the one best fitted to account for some of Wordsworth's verse. Only in terms of words as 'fiduciary symbols' can Wordsworth's blank verse in *The Prelude* be properly appreciated. In those passages of *The Prelude* where Wordsworth is trying to convey most exactly the effect of the natural world upon himself, his words ('ties' and 'bonds' and

1 R. L. Brett, *The Third Earl of Shaftesbury: A Study in Eighteenth-century Literary Theory* (Hutchinson, 1951), p. 14.

'influences' and 'powers') will carry the reader only (as Valéry says) so long as he does not loiter, so long as they are taken, as coins are taken, 'as values of monetary exchange'. Wordsworth's words have meaning so long as we trust them. They have just such meaning, and just as much meaning, as Perse and Valéry suggest.

We can make a start by pointing out that Wordsworth's world is not pre-eminently a world of 'things'. His language has not, in St-John Perse's sense, 'weight and mass'. It is not concrete. Because in the Preface to *Lyrical Ballads* Wordsworth castigated some earlier poets for giving no proof that they had ever truly *looked* at natural phenomena, it is often supposed that his own verse is full of such phenomena rendered in all their quiddity and concreteness. But this is a sort of optical illusion. What Wordsworth renders is not the natural world but (with masterly fidelity) the effect that world has upon him. He is at all points a very long way from 'trying to reincarnate the thing itself, as in ideographic writing'. As Lionel Trilling remarks, 'Wordsworth never did have the special and perhaps modern sensibility of his sister or of Coleridge, who were so aware of exquisite particularities. His finest passages are moral, emotional, subjective; whatever visual intensity they have comes from his response to the object, not from his close observation of it.'[1] On the contrary I have heard more than one student complain of Wordsworth's diction that it is too 'abstract'. I shall argue that the diction of *The Prelude* is neither abstract nor concrete, but something between the two.

This gives me the chance to introduce a very weighty objection to Ernest Fenollosa's theory of poetic language. It will be remembered that, according to him, 'At the base of the pyramid lie *things*, but stunned, as it were.' T. C. Pollock, however, sees in this view the fallacy of 'Misplaced Concreteness':

1 Lionel Trilling, *The Liberal Imagination* (Secker, 1951), p. 133.

If an abstract term is the sign of an abstraction from an individual experience (E) or a group of individual experiences (E), a non-abstract or a concrete term would be the sign of that from which the abstraction was drawn, the non-abstract individual experience (E) or the non-abstract individual experiences (E) in the group of experiences (E). The opposite of an abstract term would therefore be, not the name of a specific or 'concrete' object, but the sign of a total or concrete *experience* (E). The error arises because of the assumption that the abstraction is from *objects*, instead of from *experiences* (E). (On the contrary, what we call 'objects' are psychologically abstractions from *experiences* (E).)

As Pollock goes on to show,[1] this statement is only the counterpart in linguistic theory of a fact of linguistic history, the fact established by Jespersen that originally words stood for whole *experiences*, which were only subsequently broken down into 'seen' things and 'unseen' feelings about them, or significances in them. Fenollosa's account of metaphor is at odds with Jespersen, as his account of abstraction is at odds with Pollock.

Now if Wordsworth was concerned to render his responses to the natural world, he was concerned with experiences, and these were 'concretions' from which he did not care to abstract (as his sister and Coleridge did) that part of them which we call 'objects' or 'things'. It follows that ideographic writing, in which words embody things, is *more abstract than* writing in which words are fiduciary symbols for elements of an experience.

This view of words as symbols is advanced by Coleridge in a famous passage from *Biographia Literaria*:

The best part of human language, properly so called, is derived from reflection on the acts of the mind itself. It is formed by a voluntary appropriation of fixed symbols to internal acts, to processes and results of imagination, the greater part of which have no place in the consciousness of uneducated man; though in civilized society, by imitation and passive remembrance of what they hear from their religious instructors

1 Pollock, *The Nature of Literature*, p. 62.

and other superiors, the most uneducated share in the harvest which they neither sowed nor reaped.

This statement is made when Coleridge is objecting to Wordsworth's recommendation of rustic language, on the grounds that such language can provide only poor and meagre syntax:

> The rustic, from the more imperfect development of his faculties, and from the lower state of their cultivation, aims almost solely to convey insulated facts, either those of his scanty experience or his traditional belief; while the educated man chiefly seeks to discover and express those connections of things, or those relative bearings of fact to fact, from which some more or less general law is deducible. For facts are valuable to a wise man, chiefly as they lead to the discovery of the indwelling law, which is the true being of things, the sole solution of their modes of existence, and in the knowledge of which consists our dignity and our power.

Coleridge points out, what Perse and Valéry have led us to expect, that if a language is deficient in 'fixed symbols' for 'internal acts', it will also be deficient in syntax. I shall proceed to show that Wordsworth, when he abandoned rustic diction and took to rendering 'internal acts', 'processes and results of imagination', used for the purpose an elaborate syntax, and that an important part of his vocabulary is neither abstract nor concrete, but made up of fixed fiduciary symbols.

In *The Prelude* the syntax is elaborately correct:

> I deem not profitless these fleeting moods
> Of shadowy exultation: not for this,
> That they are kindred to our purer mind
> And intellectual life; but that the soul,
> Remembering how she felt, but what she felt
> Remembering not, retains an obscure sense
> Of possible sublimity, to which
> With growing faculties she doth aspire,
> With faculties still growing, feeling still
> That whatsoever point they gain, they still
> Have something to pursue.

Dr Leavis comments on this passage:

> It would be difficult to suggest anything more elusive than this possibility which the soul glimpses in 'visionary' moments and,
>
> Remembering how she felt, but what she felt
> Remembering not,
>
> retains an 'obscure sense' of. Perhaps it will be agreed that, though Wordsworth no doubt was right in feeling that he had something to pursue, the critic here is in a different case. If these 'moments' have any significance for the critic (whose business it is to define the significance of Wordsworth's poetry), it will be established, not by dwelling upon or in them, in the hope of exploring something that lies hidden in or behind their vagueness, but by holding firmly on to that sober verse in which they are presented.[1]

I may be misreading Dr Leavis, but it seems to me that what is recommended here is what Perse and Valéry recommend: taking the verse at a run, not pausing on the nouns for fear they congeal into the staring unfathomable eyes that appalled Hofmannsthal, but attending rather to the syntactical weave. If this is what Dr Leavis means, the testimony is all the more valuable as coming from a reader who in other cases (on Milton, for instance, as we have seen) is cautious not to grant the poet all that he asks for. What Wordsworth asks for here is for all his words to be considered only in their context. Yet it is different from what Pound asks for in the *Cantos*. These moods, exultations, senses, sublimities and faculties will be no clearer at the end of *The Prelude* than they are here; and yet the poem will not be a botch, for what will be clear at the end is the relationship between them, the articulation. The nouns are not concrete; but the verbs are, and may be lingered over. In short, this is poetry where the syntax counts enormously, counts for nearly everything.

1 F. R. Leavis, *Revaluation* (Chatto, 1936), pp. 173, 174.

Earlier, however, in his chapter on Wordsworth, Dr Leavis has remarked of this blank verse:

> Wordsworth in such passages as are in question produces the mood, feeling or experience and at the same time appears to be giving an explanation of it. The expository effect sorts well with – blends into – the characteristic meditative gravity of the emotional presentment ('emotion recollected in tranquillity'), and in the key passages, where significance seems specially to reside, the convincing success of the poetry covers the argument: it is only by the most resolute and sustained effort (once it occurs to one that effort is needed) that one can pay to the argument, as such, the attention it appears to have invited and satisfied.[1]

And Dr Leavis directs us to William Empson to see how ill the argument stands up to scrutiny, once one gives attention to it.

On this showing the syntax of *The Prelude* is not doing what it offers to do. It seems to be explaining, while in fact it is meditating, ruminating, at all events *experiencing* more fully than one does when one explains. But I am not sure that Wordsworth even pretends to explain. Elsewhere Dr Leavis makes the point like this:

> Even if there were not so much poetry to hold the mind in a subtly incompatible mode of attention, it would still be difficult to continue attending to the philosophic argument, because of the way in which the verse, evenly meditative in tone and movement, goes on and on, without dialectical suspense and crisis or rise and fall. By an innocently insidious trick Wordsworth, in this calm ruminative progression, will appear to be preoccupied with a scrupulous nicety of statement, with a judicial weighing of alternative possibilities, while actually making it more difficult to check the argument from which he will emerge, as it were inevitably, with a far from inevitable conclusion.[2]

Here the expression 'an innocently insidious trick' sends us back

1 Ibid., p. 159.
2 Ibid., p. 162.

to the idea of Wordsworth's syntax as somehow conjuror's patter. On the other hand the 'movement' that 'goes on and on without dialectical suspense and crisis or rise and fall' is, it seems, one of the elements that work against argument. And this movement (this is my point) is as much a movement of syntax, a movement of the mind, as it is a movement in the ear. 'Dialectical' admits as much. The syntax therefore presents what is really going on, meditation, not argument; and it is therefore authentic, not a play of misleading forms. This confirms me in my original explanation: that this is largely a poetry of verbal symbols which must be taken on trust (almost but not quite like notes or chords in music), for the sake of the articulations jointed between them.

2

MR EMPSON and Dr Leavis, I suggest, were wrong to think that this poetry aimed at even the effect of philosophic argument. That Wordsworth thought, at Coleridge's instigation, that he might be a philosophic poet is here beside the point; we are speaking of what the poetry does, not of what the poet intended it to do. And in any case this is the prelude to a philosophic poem, not the poem itself. When that poem appeared, the poetry was not of this kind, as Dr Leavis acknowledges – 'The doctrinal passages of *The Excursion* . . . are plain enough.'

The critics were misled not by the syntax of *The Prelude*, but by its vocabulary, which appears to be 'abstract'. It is certainly more 'abstract' than a great deal of English poetry, but, as I have argued, it is not abstract in any strict sense. Its verbs are concrete, and its nouns are verbal symbols, neither concrete nor abstract. That it was the vocabulary that got in Dr Leavis's way is proved, I think, by his admission that, for him, the Hartleian poem of 1805–6 gives more the effect of philosophic argument than the revised version of 1850. Dr Leavis presents what he calls 'a representative improvement', by printing a passage in both the versions. At the risk of being tedious, I shall present both passages, and consider Dr Leavis's comments on them. First, the version of 1805–6 (lines 237–66):

Bless'd the infant Babe,
(For with my best conjectures I would trace
The progress of our Being) blest the Babe,
Nurs'd in his Mother's arms, the Babe who sleeps
Upon his Mother's breast, who, when his soul
Claims manifest kindred with an earthly soul,
Doth gather passion from his Mother's eye!
Such feelings pass into his torpid life
Like an awakening breeze, and hence his mind
Even [in the first trial of its powers]
Is prompt and watchful, eager to combine
In one appearance, all the elements
And parts of the same object, else detach'd
And loth to coalesce. Thus day by day,
Subjected to the discipline of love,
His organs and recipient faculties
Are quicken'd, are more vigorous, his mind spreads,
Tenacious of the forms which it receives.
In one beloved presence, nay and more
In that most apprehensive habitude
And those sensations which have been deriv'd
From this beloved Presence, there exists
A virtue which irradiates and exalts
All objects through all intercourse of sense.
No outcast he, bewilder'd and depress'd:
Along his infant veins are interfus'd
The gravitation and the filial bond
Of nature, that connect him with the world.
Emphatically such a Being lives,
An inmate of this *active* universe.

In 1850 this becomes (lines 233–54):

Blest the infant Babe,
(For with my best conjecture I would trace
Our Being's earthly progress) blest the Babe,
Nursed in his Mother's arms, who sinks to sleep
Rocked on his Mother's breast; who with his soul
Drinks in the feelings of his Mother's eye!
For him, in one dear Presence, there exists
A virtue which irradiates and exalts
Objects through widest intercourse of sense.
No outcast he, bewildered and depressed:
Along his infant veins are interfused
The gravitation and the filial bond
Of nature that connect him with the world.
Is there a flower, to which he points with hand
Too weak to gather it, already love
Drawn from love's purest earthly fount for him
Hath beautified that flower; already shades
Of pity cast from inward tenderness
Do fall around him upon aught that bears
Unsightly marks of violence or harm.
Emphatically such a Being lives
Frail creature as he is, helpless as frail,
An inmate of this active universe . . .

Dr Leavis remarks, 'No one is likely to dispute that the later version is decidedly the more satisfactory.' However, I mean to dispute it.

I prefer the earlier version in the first place because it does more to deserve that 'active' which in 1805 got italics denied to it in 1850. Not only are there more active verbs in the first version, but they are more energetic. In 1805 the child *claims* kindred and *gathers* passion, where in 1850 he 'drinks in' feeling. His mind *spreads*, is eager to combine, tenacious and *apprehensive*. (The Latinate pun delivers the muscular grasp of the policeman apprehending the lag.) The later version is mawkish, emphasizing the frailty of the child, his weakness. In the first version the Mother's love is an energy, comparable with the force of gravitation and the chemical force that stirs the torpid life. ('Torpid', of course, was a technical term of eighteenth-century science.) In the later version the Mother's love is presented as tenderness, and even then as combined or confused with pity. The 'gravitation', which survives into the later version, is out of place there, in a context of imagery that is predominantly and weakly visual ('*shades* of pity'), where at first it had been muscular and dynamic. The pseudo-syntax of the rhetorical question ('Is there a flower . . .?') goes along with this pervasive slackening of tension, this retarded and unsteadied movement.

If I ask myself what grounds Dr Leavis can have for preferring the later version, I can only suppose he is attracted by the relative concreteness (heaven knows it is phantasmal enough) of the flower and even the 'Unsightly marks of violence or harm'. I would sum up the difference between these two versions by saying that, in the earlier draft, Wordsworth is rendering the experience of being a child at the mother's breast. He is doing this in the only way possible, from inside the child's mind, by rendering in his verse the movements of the child's consciousness, stirring here, checked or sluggish there, drawn this way by powerful currents, dammed back somewhere else. In the later version the poet is sometimes inside the child's mind, sometimes inside the mother's, sometimes inside the spectator's; and by thus shifting his point of view he denies himself the chance of rendering with fidelity the movements in the child's mind or the mother's or the spectator's. Undoubtedly the language of the earlier version appears more abstract, but it is not therefore ratiocinative. It seems to me that its strength is all in its energetic verbs, and the nouns that attend them ('powers', 'elements', 'parts', 'forms', 'sensations', 'objects') are correspondingly thin and general. And of course this energy in representing movements of the mind fits in with the fact that Hartley, Wordsworth's master here, was the last of the mechanic psychologists such as influenced Pope, who explained the movements of the mind in terms drawn ultimately from mechanics.

Mr John Jones, in his very valuable book on Wordsworth,[1] has lately insisted on the extent to which Wordsworth always thought in these eighteenth-century terms:

There is . . . a conservatism in the context of Wordsworth's thought. He is not in revolt against the Great Machine, the master-image of eighteenth-century science and philosophy. Only the phrase is unwordsworthian (though there is enough of pure eighteenth-century poetic in him to allow a reference to his wife's spirit, in relation to her body, as 'the very pulse of the machine'): he would prefer something more supple, like 'this universal frame of things'. His complaint is that nobody has as yet observed its component parts with sufficiently devoted care, or experienced fully the power and beauty of its movement.

In *The Prelude*, Wordsworth uses the word 'things' with astonishing frequency. The Concordance reveals that the 1850 text alone accounts for about one-third of its occurrences in the entire bulk of his poetry. 'I looked for universal things'; 'I conversed with things that really are'; Wordsworth will make his verse 'deal boldly with substantial things' – the word is clearly and consistently referred to the main theme of the poem. His search for universal things is on one side a search for particularity: in his insistence upon constancy, boundedness, irreducibility, he betrays the imaginative impression of a traditional English materialism. But he is more than a materialist, in that he enquires not only for the particular but for the powerful. Here his resources are heavily taxed. In order to express essential energy, he is too often led to personify spirit, motion, power itself, in a context of vague declamation . . .

But Wordsworth can do better than that. In passages such as the one just considered, of 1805, he conveys the power as well as the particularity, the different kinds of pulse in the natural machine, by the precisely discriminated energies of his verbs, which

1 John Jones, *The Egotistical Sublime: A History of Wordsworth's Imagination* (Chatto, 1954), pp. 34, 35.

concretely act out the powers he is speaking of. In him perhaps one may applaud what Fenollosa applauded in Shakespeare, his 'persistent, natural, and magnificent use of hundreds of transitive verbs'.

X

Berkeley and Yeats: Syntax and Metre

I

HUGH KENNER, writing of the damage done to poetry by Descartes and Locke, comments as follows:

> When the mind no longer lays hold of things, when it does no more than construct its own world according to the hints afforded by sensation, when it knows nothing but its own 'ideas', poetic modes of statement, which work by the juxtaposition of objects, are immediately relegated to the status of day-dream ... The poem affords nothing real.[1]

It is easy, indeed it is normal, to connect Berkeley with the movement in philosophy that Mr Kenner objects to. Berkeley, it is usually supposed, pressed one stage further the process started in England by Locke, away from 'things' towards 'ideas'. (It is important, of course, to keep the quotation marks round 'ideas', as Mr Kenner does; by 'ideas' Berkeley means 'sense-impressions' – the 'thing' is only the origin of the impression, the impression itself is something else, an 'idea'.) Locke, we say, moved the so-called secondary qualities out of apparently 'external' reality into the mind; colour, for instance, became a function of the optic nerves. Berkeley points out that, having done so much, Locke might as well do the rest and move into the mind the so-called primary qualities also, such as extension. Hence Berkeley takes his place in the line of succession from Locke to Hume, and becomes the father of European idealism.

1 Kenner, *Poetry of Ezra Pound*, pp. 95, 96.

All this is perfectly true. That the idealists learnt from Berkeley is a matter of fact. But in arguing like this we confuse Berkeley's strategy with his ultimate objective. If the mind is a bag into which Locke put a lot of apparently external 'things', then Berkeley gathers up the things that Locke left outside and pops them in also. But this is to halt midway. Having got everything into the bag, he puts his fist to the bottom; the bag turns inside out and there everything is, outside the bag again, once more an external reality.

This is not offered as an argument, only as the statement of a position. The case has been argued elsewhere.

In any case we have found difficulties in the way of accepting Hugh Kenner's generalization, based on Fenollosa, that 'poetic modes of statement ... work by the juxtaposition of objects.' It turned out that Wordsworth's blank verse, for instance, did not work in this way. It may be, therefore, that Berkeley's view of language can be shown to be more sympathetic to the poet than Mr Kenner would lead us to think. And it is as a philosopher of language that I shall consider him.

Berkeley invites this sort of attention. He is generally acknowledged to be a master of English prose, and it would be odd if so able a practitioner should be unacceptable as a theorist. In fact, as he hints very broadly himself, some of his central arguments could with profit be put into linguistic terms. His criticism of Locke's 'material substance', for instance, would then appear to be a recognition by Berkeley of a submerged metaphor (the table that 'stands under' the knives and forks) coming covertly to life in the middle of Locke's argument. But this again is not my business here. I aim only to put together a number of observations by Berkeley on the nature of language, and to see what they imply as regards the nature and the function of syntax in poetry.

We may observe, to begin with, that Berkeley is as fierce an enemy of 'abstraction' as Hulme or Fenollosa:

For example, the mind having observ'd that *Peter*, *James* and *John*, etc. resemble each other, in certain common agreements of shape and other qualities, leaves out of the complex or compounded idea it has of *Peter*, *James*, etc. that which is peculiar to each, retaining only what is common to all; and so makes an abstract idea wherein all the particulars equally partake, abstracting intirely from and cutting off all those circumstances and differences, which might determine it to any particular existence. And after this manner it is said we come by the abstract idea of *man* or, if you please, humanity or humane nature, wherein 'tis true, there's included colour, because there is no man but has some colour, but then it can be neither white, nor black, nor any particular colour; because there is no one particular colour wherein all men partake. So likewise there is included stature, but then 'tis neither tall stature, nor low stature, nor yet middle stature, but something abstracted from all these; and so of the rest . . .

Whether others have this wonderful faculty of *abstracting their ideas*, they best can tell: for my self I dare be confident I have it not. I have indeed a faculty of imagining, or representing to my self the ideas of those particular things I have perceiv'd and of variously compounding and dividing them. I can imagine a man with two heads or the upper parts of a man joyn'd to the body of a horse. I can consider the hand, the eye, the nose each by itself abstracted or separated from the rest of the body. But then whatever hand or eye I imagine, it must have some particular shape or colour. Likewise the idea of man that I frame to my self, must be either of a white, or a black, or a tawny, a streight, or a crooked, a tall or a low, or a middle-sized man. I cannot by any effort of thought conceive the abstract idea above described. And it is equally impossible for me to form the abstract idea of motion distinct from the body moving, and which is neither swift nor slow, curvilinear nor rectilinear; and the like may be said of all other abstract general ideas whatsoever.

We can compare with this Fenollosa's example, with which Pound makes play, of 'rose – flamingo – iron rust – cherry' as the components of the Chinese ideogram for 'red'. Berkeley agrees with Fenollosa that it is absurd to think we 'see' the thing common to roses, flamingos, iron rust and cherries, and then label this abstraction 'red'; we *see*, not a quality common to these things, but *all these things, by virtue of what is common to them.* Similarly when we say 'man' we do not see the abstraction what-all-men-have-in-common; we *see* a particular man (a tall one, perhaps, a straight and tawny one) standing as a sign for *all* men *by virtue of what they have in common.* When for the purposes of a theorem we have to imagine 'triangle', we do not see an abstraction that is not scalene nor isosceles nor yet equilateral; we see a particular triangle (scalene, perhaps) serving as a sign for all triangles by virtue of what all triangles have in common.

Berkeley draws out the implications of this for language, or, as he prefers to put it (and here perhaps he *is* Cartesian), the way in which language has misled men into the doctrine of abstractions:

> But to give a farther account how words came to produce the doctrine of abstract ideas, it must be observ'd that it's a receiv'd opinion, that language has no other end but the communicating our ideas, and that every significant name stands for an idea. This being so, and it being withall certain, that names, which yet are not thought altogether insignificant, do not always mark out particular conceivable ideas, it is straightway concluded that they stand for abstract notions. That there are many names in use amongst speculative men, which do not always suggest to others determinate, particular ideas, or in truth anything at all, is what no body will deny. And a little attention will discover, that it is not necessary (even in the strictest reasonings) significant names which stand for ideas shou'd, every time they are us'd, excite in the understanding the ideas they are made to stand for: in reading and discoursing names being for the most part used as letters are in *algebra*, in which thô a particular quantity be mark'd by each letter, yet to proceed right it is not requisite that in every step each letter suggest to your thoughts, that particular quantity it was appointed to stand for.

At this point we have come full circle on to T. E. Hulme: 'In prose as in algebra concrete things are embodied in signs or counters which are moved about according to rules, without being visualized at all in the process . . . One only changes the X's and the Y's back into physical things at the end of the process.' Berkeley agrees, but he points out that 'signs or counters' (he uses the counter metaphor himself elsewhere) are not 'abstractions'. On the contrary it is only when we see language as largely composed of such 'counters' that we do away with the need for supposing a faculty of abstraction at all. Hence we can agree with Hulme that the language of poetry should not be 'abstract', without having to agree that therefore it cannot be symbolic, like the language of algebra. A mathematical symbol is one thing; an abstraction is another.

What we get, in fact, from Berkeley, is just what St-John Perse asked for in the language of poetry, a way of using words 'as fiduciary symbols like coins as values of monetary exchange'. And as we moved from Perse to Valéry's remarks about taking words on the run, having faith in them for the sake of articulating a context, so in Berkeley we find the same observation:

In the ordinary affairs of life, any phrases may be retain'd, so long as they excite in us proper sentiments, or dispositions to act in such a manner as is necessary for our well-being, how false soever they may be, if taken in a strict and speculative sense. Nay this is unavoidable since, propriety being regulated by custom, language is suited to the received opinions which are not always the truest. Hence it is impossible even in the most rigid, philosophic reasonings, so far to alter the bent or genius of the tongue we speak, as never to give a handle for cavillers to pretend difficulties and inconsistencies. But a fair and ingenuous reader will collect the sense, from the scope and tenor and connexion of a discourse, making allowances for those unaccurate modes of speech, which use has made inevitable.

This injunction to collect the sense, from 'the scope and tenor and connexion of a discourse', seems very like Dr Leavis's advice not to dwell in or upon the exultations and influences and visionary 'moments' of Wordsworth, but to keep hold of 'that sober verse in which they are presented'. And by 'connexion' in a discourse, Berkeley must mean, among other things, syntax. As Coleridge saw, syntax can have a place in poetry only when poetry makes use of what Hulme denied to it, a language of counters, of fiduciary symbols.

Berkeley of course, in his observations on language, never offers an opinion on the peculiar sort of language (if it *is* peculiar) required for poetry. And we may well feel, as we surely must, that not all the words in a poem should be 'fiduciary symbols'. Indeed we have found ourselves in the position of applauding nouns which are of this sort only because they allow of the use of verbs which vividly and distinctly mime the operation of an energy. But again, we do not want all the nouns in our poetry to be like Wordsworth's 'powers' and 'influences'; we want, for objects as for actions, words which partake of the denseness and the tang of the things they stand for. Such words, or groups of words, having this function are loosely but usefully called, in our criticism, 'images'. And now that we have got rid of the bogey of 'abstraction', finding that most apparently abstract words are in fact symbols, to be taken on trust, we are naturally led to wonder whether in poetry there may not be a right or normal ratio between words which are 'signs' ('symbol' might be misleading here) and words which are 'images'.

Hulme and Fenollosa in effect admit into poetry no words that are not whole images or parts of images. This is one of the reasons why they tend to exclude syntax, for syntax always needs some words sheerly as signs. On the other hand older poets and critics often insisted on the necessity for spacing images, sewing them carefully into language of another sort. As I have argued elsewhere, this is what I take Landor to mean when he tells the poet:

> In every poem train the leading shoot;
> Break off the suckers. Thought erases thought,
> As numerous sheep erase each other's print
> When spungy moss they press or sterile sand.
> Blades thickly sown want nutriment and droop,
> Although the seed be sound, and rich the soil;
> Thus healthy-born ideas, bedded close,
> By dreaming fondness perish overlain.

Since Hulme and Fenollosa represent an influential tendency in the writing of verse, a tendency which their own influence in turn has helped to promote, it is now pertinent to examine the effect on poetic syntax of their refusal to countenance any words that are not 'concrete'. What happens to 'the scope and tenor and connexion' of a poem when the poet labours to give to every word the maximum concreteness?

2

AMONG the words that looked like abstractions but were really fixed symbols, Berkeley included the word 'I':

Euphranor. Pray tell me, Alciphron, is not an Idea altogether inactive? *Alciphron*. It is. *Euphranor*. An Agent therefore, an active Mind, or Spirit cannot be an Idea or like an Idea. Whence it shou'd seem to follow, that those Words which denote an active Principle, Soul, or Spirit do not, in a strict and proper Sense, stand for Ideas: And yet they are not insignificant neither: since I understand what is signified by the term *I*, or *my self*, or know what it means although it be no Idea, nor like an Idea, but that which thinks and wills and apprehends Ideas and operates about them.

It is easy to see that this conviction that the spiritual world is a world of action goes very deep with Berkeley, informing his own prose style. It is what has recommended him to some modern thinkers, and it is what Yeats liked him for. In the wayward but very valuable Introduction that Yeats wrote for a book on Berkeley,[1] he declares, 'Only where the mind partakes of a pure activity can art or life attain swiftness, volume, unity; . . .' And it is in the light of this that he makes the well-known comment on some of his contemporaries: 'One thinks of Joyce's *Anna Livia Plurabelle*, Pound's *Cantos*, works of an heroic sincerity, the man, his active faculties in suspense, one finger beating

1 J. M. Hone and M. M. Rossi, *Bishop Berkeley: His Life, Writings and Philosophy*, (Faber, 1931), pp. xv–xxix.

time to a bell sounding and echoing in the depths of his own mind . . .' One brings this down to earth by rephrasing thus: the mind that is active produces poetry that finds room for verbs and hence (other things being equal) for syntax; when the active faculties are in suspense, the mind produces poetry that is crowded with 'things', that finds little room for verbs, and either abjures syntax or retains only its empty forms.

This is a brutal simplification but it seems to work. Rosemond Tuve points out that Yeats differs from other poets of his generation precisely in the use he makes of syntax:

> Yeats's images are often more traditional than other modern poets' in method, as though in spite of his Symbolist alignments he felt the need of pointing a reader toward the significance 'meant to be seen' – but few modern poets quite like to do this. This is one reason why there are few difficult images in Yeats in which the syntax does not repay study; syntax is the most unobstrusive of all methods of clarification, the closest one can come to the paradox of saying something tacitly.[1]

It is natural to connect this with Richard Ellmann's comment on Yeats, in the light of his observation just quoted, about Joyce and Pound: 'His own way did not lie in the suspension of the active faculties; to the end he remained stubbornly loyal in his art to the conscious mind's intelligible structure.'[2] There is a road plainly open from the intelligible structure of the conscious mind to the intelligible structure of the sentence.

George Barnes supplies an example of Yeats's concern for syntax in his own work, when he recalls the poet's behaviour at a rehearsal for the broadcast reading of his poetry:

> . . . at the rehearsal of a later programme when Baddeley read the first lines of 'Sailing to Byzantium':
>
> That is no country for old men. The young
> In one another's arms; birds in the trees . . .

1 Tuve, *Elizabethan and Metaphysical Imagery*, p. 177.
2 'Joyce and Yeats', *Kenyon Review*, VII, 4, p. 636.

Yeats exclaimed 'Stop! That is the worst bit of syntax I ever wrote', and promptly changed it to:

> Old men should quit a country where the young
> In one another's arms; birds in the trees . . .[1]

This is a change which would have warmed the heart of Ernest Fenollosa. The copula and the negative are replaced by the energetic verb 'quit'. The syntax of the first version was correct enough; but by the revision the poem is given from the first line a backbone, a head and a tail, a drive to carry through the clutter of images that follow.

Just as Yeats abjured 'free' syntax, so he abjured free verse. And this was inevitable. For if Landor was right in thinking that images in a poem must be 'spaced', then, if the poet abandons the spacing he can get by syntax, he has to find some other means. Eliot and Pound find typography; the pause at the ends of lines or spaces in the middle of lines represent the interval which must be left by the reader between the impact of one image and the impact of another. Abolish syntax and you tend to abolish metre: free verse becomes a necessity.

This is clearly seen if we examine a poet who crowds his images one upon another while retaining metre:

> Time, milk and magic, from the world beginning,
> Time is the tune my ladies lend their heartbreak,
> From bald pavilions and the house of bread
> Time tracks the sound of shape on man and cloud,
> On rose and icicle the ringing handprint.

These verses are quoted by Elizabeth Sewell, in a discussion of Rimbaud. She takes it as an example in English of what Rimbaud was doing in *Les Illuminations*:

1 Quoted by Joseph Hone, *W. B. Yeats, 1865–1939* (St Martin's Press, 1942), p. 456.

Coleridge ... says that images may have the function of 'reducing multitude to unity, or succession to an instant'. This fits well here, for Rimbaud, by the closely packed images of *Illuminations*, achieves that very thing, making the reader's mind discard its usual organization of words and images in small separate units, so that a new and far greater unity can be produced, a unity where everything in the cosmos runs into everything else in one enormous oneness, and in place of succession and similarity there only remain simultaneity in space-time, and identification.[1]

This means, in the terms we have been using, that Dylan Thomas exploits a pseudo-syntax. Formally correct, his syntax cannot mime, as it offers to do, a movement of the mind. If the effect is simultaneity and identification, these sentences that seem to drive forward in time through their verbs in fact do no such thing. The verb 'tracks' is completely void of meaning. What appears to be narrative ('Time', the agent, transfers energy through 'tracks' to the object 'sound') is in fact an endless series of copulas: 'Time is tracking which is sound which is shape ...' and so on. That the metaphors could in fact be broken down into successive meanings is irrelevant; even when the breaking down has been done for us, we cannot hold on to it when we return to reading the poem. This explains why Dylan Thomas's good poems are all written in complicated stanza forms, where the varying lengths of line break down the images into 'small separate units' which can be digested by the reader. In *A Refusal to Mourn the Death, by Fire, of a Child in London*, the stanza in print affords the same typographic breathing-spaces as a passage of free verse. It goes without saying, of course, that, in poems of any worth, the arrangement of type corresponds to an arrangement of rhythms. In free verse and in Dylan Thomas's complicated metrical stanzas the articulation and spacing of images is done by rhythm instead of syntax; Thomas's sonnets, I think, show that to do this the rhythms need to be far more various

1 Elizabeth Sewell, *The Structure of Poetry*, p. 131.

and more strongly marked than is possible in the decasyllabic line of the traditional sonnet.

Revealing in this connection are two comments on Rimbaud's syntax which Miss Sewell puts side by side. C. A. Hackett observes:

> One could claim that the poet deliberately suppresses the verbs to lighten the sentence and give more of a lift to his thought.[1]

And François Ruchon:

> The imagery with Rimbaud . . . always envisages reality under the appearance of mobility; that is to say, the verb plays a predominant role in it.[2]

There is no contradiction here, if one critic is speaking of the authentic syntax *behind* the verse, the other of the pseudo-syntax it in fact employs. 'Mobility', too, is significant. This verse is often applauded for its energy, its 'dynamic activity'; and this is just. But the energy is 'wild', undifferentiated; its verbs, any and all of them, are spurts or scurries of activity, a restless fidget. Miss Sewell, endorsing this comment by Ruchon, connects the 'restlessness and mobility' of Rimbaud's verse in *Les Illuminations* with a characteristic of the images of dream, the way they resist any effort to hold them clear and steady. The dream image is constantly changing. This suggests the further observation that a sonnet by Dylan Thomas is unacceptable even on Hulme's terms. When concrete images are crowded upon each other, they lose their concreteness. The milk is soured by the magic, the bread has lost its tang and the cloud its volume. The things will not stand still, but fluctuate and swim like weeds in a stream. A poem, it seems, can give way under the weight of the 'things' that are crowded into it. Broken-backed, the poem can then no longer move; it can only twitch and

1 Sewell, op. cit., p. 127.
2 Ibid., p. 128.

flounder. Not only that; the things, tumbled pell-mell together, can no longer be identified:

> Thus healthy-born ideas, bedded close,
> By dreaming fondness perish overlain.

The poet who sets out to use only words partaking of the hardness and opacity of 'things' finds in the end that the things have gone transparent and yielding. 'Concreteness' itself, if we take it in its current signification, demands in metrical verse a language of 'fixed symbols'.

With free verse the case is different. Here rhythm is set to do the work that syntax does in prose. But we can usefully recall here the notion of a contract between poet and reader. For syntax to be used in verse, the reader has to grant something to the poet – he has to agree to let some words pass in the reading, in the faith that their articulated context will give them the meaning they seem to lack in isolation. A poet who abandons syntax makes no such claim. But he makes another infinitely larger:

> . . . I believe in an absolute rhythm. I believe that every emotion and every phase of emotion has some toneless phrase, some rhythm-phrase to express it.
>
> (This belief leads to *vers libre* and to experiments in quantitative verse.)[1]

Honest as ever, Pound reveals clearly the terms of the compact he would make with his reader. For it is plain that the reader has to make a like act of faith before he can yield himself to the *Cantos*. In the elaborate stanzas of Dylan Thomas at his best, we are not asked for as much as this. There the rhythms take on significance as they depart from or approach a metrical norm. But in Pound's verse the rhythm steps out alone and we must follow it in blind faith, with no metrical landmarks to assist us. Every reader must decide for himself whether he can make this

1 Ezra Pound, *Gaudier-Brzeska: A Memoir* (John Lane, 1916), p. 97.

act of faith. I confess for my part I cannot, and it seems to me that after scrapping the contracts traditionally observed between poet and reader, a poet like Pound substitutes a contract unjustly weighted against the reader.

But when we recognize Pound's and Eliot's honesty, we can give to that word as much weight as we like. Having banished syntax from their poetry, they do not pretend anything else. They do not mislead their readers by retaining even the empty shells of syntactical form. Such forms appear in their poetry, for instance in the weaving together of linguistic units which yet, in the scheme of the whole poem, stand in non-syntactical relation to other such units (as in *Four Quartets*); and when this happens the syntax is authentic in a way that Rimbaud's is not. Rimbaud's syntax, on this showing, is really a pseudo-syntax, a play of forms without even that recondite truthfulness that Mrs Langer claims for her syntax like music. Pseudo-syntax of this kind appears to me to be radically vicious, in the sense, at least, that where it appears poetry flies out of the door. Elizabeth Sewell, I gather, would not disagree.

Finally, I think there is force in Peter Allt's suggestion[1] that, where authentic syntax appears in modern poetry, it is a sort of tribute paid by the poet to 'the beautiful humane cities'. Systems of syntax are part of the heritable property of past civilization, and to hold firm to them is to be traditional in the best and most important sense. This seems ungracious to both Pound and Eliot, who have both insisted upon the value of the European civilized tradition, and have tried to embody it in their poems. Nevertheless it is hard not to agree with Yeats that the abandonment of syntax testifies to a failure of the poet's nerve, a loss of confidence in the intelligible structure of the conscious mind, and the validity of its activity.

1 Peter Allt, 'Yeats, Religion and History', *Sewanee Review*, LX, 4.

XI

Syntax, Rhetoric and Rhyme

I

SIR PHILIP SIDNEY maintained that it was the privilege and peculiar glory of poetry to get the best of both worlds, of history on the one hand, of philosophy on the other. This insight has been elaborated as follows by Mr Northrop Frye:[1]

> History gives the example of the hero without the precept; Philosophy the precept without the example; and poetry gives us the poetic image of the hero which combines the two. Or, as we may say, literature, being hypothetical, unites the temporal event with the idea in conceptual space. On one side, it develops a narrative interest which borders on history; on the other, a discursive interest which borders on philosophy, and in between them is its central interest of imagery.
>
> We may thus distinguish three main rhythms of literature and three main areas of it, one in which narrative controls the rhythm, one in which a discursive interest controls it, and a central area in which the image controls it. This central area is the area of poetry; the parietal ones belong to prose, which is used for both hypothetical and descriptive purposes.

Mr Frye then relates each of these 'three main rhythms' and 'three main areas' to one of the three departments of the trivium. Philosophy, with its discursive rhythm based on the unit of the proposition, falls in the department of logic; poetry, with its figurative rhythm (based on 'the arranging and patterning of verbal symbols'), in the province of rhetoric; and history, with its narrative rhythm, in the province of grammar.

1 'Levels of Meaning in Literature', *Kenyon Review*, XII, 2, pp. 246–62.

It is this last alignment, no doubt, that at first appears peculiar. Yet Fenollosa has made it already. For Mr Frye is echoing Fenollosa when he writes: 'As for narrative prose, it is clear that we cannot restrict the conception of narrative to the gross events: the basis of narrative is the temporal order of symbols; in particular, the word order which is the movement of literature. We may, then, suggest a link between narrative and grammar . . .' This is precisely Fenollosa's insight by which every sentence is seen to have a plot. It seems that for Mr Frye this perception is less important than it was for Fenollosa, and it may be that he gives it less importance than he should – a point to which I shall return. On the other hand, his appeal to the trivium (grammar, rhetoric, logic) seems to explain what is wrong with Fenollosa's principles when we try to apply them in criticism. If Mr Frye is right in sending us back to the trivium, then Fenollosa's essay represents an attempt to climb into poetry up one of its props, that of history, narrative and grammar, while taking away the prop on the other side, that of philosophy, the discursive and logical.

For instance we may compare with Fenollosa's dislike of the copula, of what he calls the 'weak' (meaning 'unpoetic') *is*, Mr Frye's reminder about 'the metaphysical structures based on the fact that the verb *to be* implies both existence and identity.' So Jonson starts a poem:

> To know no vice at all and keep true state
> Is virtue and not fate . . .

and we get an effect of tremendous rapidity, as if the sense were a ball-bearing that pelts along a slot and raps upon the metal check of the rhyme. For this effect of energy there is nothing in Fenollosa's essay to prepare us. Innocent of all concretion, and driving through the so-called 'weak' copula, the line should have no energy at all and, in isolation, no poetic value. In fact it seems to me that it has both, and, leaving aside all questions of metre and the tone of address, I find that energy in syntax, pre-eminently in the twin implications of the verb *to be*: the lines have the effect of proclaiming exultantly that this innocence exists, at the same time as they make a predication about it. A verb capable of doing so much must be, for all that Fenollosa says to the contrary, a channel of great energy.

Mr Frye, when he writes that literature 'unites the temporal event with the idea in conceptual space', is, in effect, challenging Fenollosa in Fenollosa's own terms. For the latter's insistence on narrative came from his insistence that all mental experience occurs in the dimension of time and (this is his implication) *in that alone*. Yet while this may be true of our perception of a man seeing a horse ('We saw, first, the man before he acted; second, while he acted; third, the object toward which his action was directed'), is it true of our perceptions of correspondences, identities or incongruities (such as provoke for instance a burst of laughter)? Of these we are accustomed to say that we saw them 'in a flash', and this witnesses to our feeling that these perceptions occur out of time, in no time at all. Every thinker will testify, for instance, to the way in which, having laboured over two bodies of evidence, having followed repeatedly the steps in each of them, having tugged them about and measured them against each other, he sees the connection between them suddenly, 'in a flash'. There is obviously a connection between the process of 'mulling over' and the final recognition. But the connection remains mysterious, and perception in the end seems not a working from the one thing to the other, but rather, a seeing of them simultaneously side by side. They are 'side by side', I take it, in Mr Frye's 'conceptual space', in a dimension of mental activity which is other than Fenollosa's temporal dimension, and one for which his theory finds no room. If we want to transmit our perception to another, we cast it in temporal form, with all the verbs that Fenollosa requires: 'If we pursue this line of argument . . .', 'It follows that . . .', 'We reach the conclusion . . .' But here the time-dimension is a falsification, not a true rendering of the way the perception came to us; for it is characteristic of this type of perception that it comes to us, we do not go after it and seize it.

Mr Frye returns to 'conceptual space' when he writes:

> The link between rhetoric and logic, between the image and the concept, is in the diagrammatic structures underneath our thoughts, which appear in the spatial metaphors we use. 'Beside', 'on the other hand', 'upon', 'outside': nobody could connect thoughts at all without such words, yet every one is a geometrical image, and suggests that every concept has its graphic formula.[1]

This is unsatisfactory, if only because Fenollosa, arguing from Chinese, in which 'the preposition is frankly a verb', has speculated whether, in English too, prepositions are not verbal in origin. At all events, in the examples that Mr Frye gives, 'on the other hand' could well be regarded as shorthand for a movement of turning from one side to another, as 'upon' for an act of placing, and 'outside' for an act of exclusion, the shutting of a door in the stranger's face. In other words these prepositions and prepositional phrases could be the images of actions in time no less than arrangements in space.

But what worries me, in Mr Frye's account of 'the link between rhetoric and logic', is the inference that may be drawn from it that logical discourse is permissible in poetry only when the metaphors it uses, whether spatial and passive, or temporal and active, come to life in the reading. This is an implication common to both Mr Frye and Fenollosa. For the latter, too, language becomes true and poetic only when it brings again to life the metaphors gone dead in abstractions:

> Only scholars and poets feel painfully back along the thread of our etymologies and piece together our diction, as best they may, from forgotten fragments. This anaemia of modern speech is only too well

1 Cf. Bergson: 'We think in terms of space – the insurmountable difficulties presented by certain philosophic problems arise from the fact that we separate out in space, phenomena which do not occupy space' (quoted by Hulme, *Speculations*, p. 178). But contrast P. Wyndham Lewis, *Time and Western Man* (Chatto, 1927), p. 3.

encouraged by the feeble cohesive force of our phonetic symbols. There is little or nothing in a phonetic word to exhibit the embryonic stages of its growth. It does not bear its metaphor on its face. We forget that personality once meant, not the soul, but the soul's mask. This is the sort of thing one cannot possibly forget in using the Chinese symbols.[1]

Of course I agree. I agree that one half of the poet's task 'lies in feeling back along the lines of advance', as I agree with Pound in a footnote that the other half is to 'prepare for new advances along the lines of true metaphor'. But there is also the question of strategy, of where and how to create the new metaphor or re-create the old so that it may have the greatest effect. The right strategy is not to reveal the metaphor, the concretion, in every word used, even in prepositions like 'upon' or 'outside'. This is the strategy of some poets writing today; and the result is only an incessant and intolerable fidget. If all the words we use are dead or dormant metaphors, then in any one poem the poet must permit the greater part of such words to continue sleeping or shamming dead. Only in that way can he bring into prominence the metaphors he has for the moment selected to create or to re-create. The language of logical discourse is chiefly valuable to the poet for providing a store of such words that can be left as 'fiduciary symbols':

> Ev'ry thy haire for love to worke upon
> Is much too much, some fitter must be sought;
> For, nor in nothing, nor in things
> Extreme, and scatt'ring bright, can love inhere;
> Then as an Angell, face, and wings
> Of aire, not pure as it, yet pure doth weare,
> So thy love may be my loves spheare;
> Just such disparitie
> As is 'twixt Aire and Angells puritie,
> 'Twixt womens love, and mens will ever bee.

1 Fenollosa, 'The Chinese Written Character', pp. 74, 75.

Here the only concretion is the image of the aureole of hair – 'ev'ry thy haire . . . extreme, and scatt'ring bright'; and the only re-created metaphor occurs in conjunction with this, in 'extreme'. The words of logical discourse, such as 'inhere' and 'disparitie', or even (given the philosophy Donne has in mind) such words as 'Angell', 'aire' and 'spheare', are not subjected to the same probing beam, but taken at their face value, marshalled rapidly into the analogical structure and used as pegs for the syntactical weave. If Donne had given concreteness to 'spheare', for instance (as of course he was to do in other poems), that would only have got in his way, distracting the reader's attention. If the word 'spheare', had thickened into a thing rather than a fiduciary symbol, it would have grown too dense and heavy, tearing a hole in the web the poet weaves about it.

I am equally unhappy about the other of Mr Frye's 'links':

> The link between grammar and rhetoric appears to be a subconscious paronomasia, or free association among words, from which there arise not only semantic connections, but the more arbitrary resemblances in sound out of which the schemata of rhyme and assonance evolve. *Finnegans Wake* is an attempt to write a whole book on this level, and it draws heavily on the researches of Freud and Jung into subconscious verbal association.

Mr Frye illustrates from Smart's *Jubilate Agno* what he describes as 'the creative process in an interesting formative stage':

> For the power of some animal is predominant in every language.
> For the power and spirit of a CAT is in the Greek.
> The sound of a cat is in the most useful preposition
> *Kat'euchen* . . .

and he goes on:

> It is possible that similar sputters and sparks of the fusing intellect take place in all poetic thinking. The puns in this passage impress the reader as both outrageous and humorous, which is consistent with Freud's

view of wit as the escape of impulse from the control of the censor. In creation the impulse appears to be the creative energy itself, and the censor the force which adapts that impulse to outward expression, a force which might be called the 'plausibility-principle'.

This is undoubtedly well said; one only doubts if this was the place to say it. For we are forced to ask what connection there is between this paronomasia and the 'grammar' we have been invited to see as the province of narrative, of energy transferred from agent through active verb to object. Fenollosa's view of the link between grammar and rhetoric has the advantage of holding close to this perception of plot in the sentence, and I think it is preferable.

I have dwelt upon this essay by Northrop Frye because it seems to me an exceptionally subtle and intelligent statement of a view which is widely held. As Mr Frye rightly maintains, it was held also by the Elizabethans. The argument goes something like this: rhetoric is the province of poetry, as logic is the province of discourse, and grammar the province of narrative; rhetoric touches upon and even overlaps grammar on the one side, logic on the other; but logic and grammar move into the area of rhetoric, history and philosophy move into poetry, *only by shedding their distinctive syntax*. The forms of discursive and narrative syntax may be retained, in accordance with 'the plausibility-principle'; but in that case the forms are empty and fraudulent, for articulation in rhetoric and poetry is not by syntax but by figuration of images.

2

THE case for rhetoric can be made more subtly still. The argument goes as follows. Words are not signs standing for ideas, but it is important to behave as if they were. Fortunately this behaviour and this illusion appear to be endemic in man. The illusion that words are signs for ideas is invaluable, because it means that the mind when it hears a word said will look for an idea to fit it. If it cannot find such an idea to stand as 'meaning' or reference, it will make one. Or so it seems. But in fact the idea must somehow have been there, waiting to be made – as Northrop Frye says, 'The poet's new poem merely articulates what was already latent in the order of words.' Loosely, however, we may say that the word creates the idea, creates its own meaning. And the practical injunction arising from this argument is clear: 'Do not be afraid of using a meaningless word; use it, and the meaning will accrue to it.'

Jean Paulhan gives two striking examples:

> Cilia, when attempting to explain to the doctor what ails her little daughter, comes to realize as she speaks what she really fears, and is astonished at herself. When Atys finds himself saying to Chrysos: 'So you lied', each of them, starting from the word, composes his thought afresh. An idea here serves as a sign to the word, and as a means of sharing it, far from the word being so for the idea. We know, too, of the poet who, cast among words, squeezes them, listens to them, awaits them.[1]

We all know this common experience: 'I had spoken, before I realized what I was saying.' And perhaps most poets can testify to the way an apparently meaningless line of verse will arise in the mind, demanding a context that shall make sense of it.

Here the word is a sign only after it has been uttered; it calls into being the idea to fit it. Hence (so the argument develops), if we make patterns of words, patterns of thought (of experience) will follow. Make a syntactical structure, and a structure in nature, psychical or even physical, will be found to leap towards it. In this way the inconceivable becomes conceivable. Because we want a perfect language, a language fitting words closely to reality, our language becomes perfect even as we use it. And all syntax becomes authentic ('true') as soon as it has been con-

1 Jean Paulhan, 'Jacob Cow the Pirate', Hevesi (ed.), *Essays*, p. 114.

structed. This, I think, is what Rimbaud meant: 'Du reste, toute parole étant idée, le temps d'un langage universal viendra.' Every word *is* an idea. It is not just a sign for an idea. For if there was no idea for it to signify before it was uttered, as soon as it was uttered the idea awoke to meet it.

But there are in language systems of articulation other than syntax. There is, in particular, the articulation indicated by the 'figures auricular' of the old rhetoric books, the relations that words strike up among themselves by similarities of sound or written appearance, relations known to us as metre, quantity, alliteration, assonance, rhyme. If we are to trust words to do our thinking for us (and we have shown that we may and do – by articulating themselves, words articulate thoughts), we must trust them when they make this sort of pattern, no less than when they make the patterns we call syntactical.

So Paulhan writes:

> Much is said of the spell of rhyme: perhaps for want of reasons. It does not disconcert us, but indeed falls exactly in with the line of our comments, that the task of this rhyme should be to provide grounds momentarily for a claim by proximity in sound to proximity in sense – and so to gratify our concern for a perfect language. We should not accuse it on occasion of hindering the meaning if we had not counted on its helping it. We experience this disappointment because we entertained that hope.[1]

Is this really the task of rhyme, and its effect when successful – to persuade us that when words sound alike they must mean alike?

H. M. McLuhan selects two lines by Pope to illustrate how the couplet can contrive a main plot and a sub-plot:

> The hungry judges soon the sentence sign
> And wretches hang that jurymen may dine.

Here there is proximity in sense in so far as (the rhyme suggests)

1 Ibid., pp. 119, 120.

the signing of a death-warrant and eating one's dinner are actions equally momentous to the coarsened and dehumanized mind. But here the rhyme only clinches an effect prepared by the syntax; if the sub-plot is a parallel to the main plot, obviously the climax of the one is likely to resemble the climax of the other. And this is only a particularly obvious example. Professor W. K. Wimsatt, in a sustained and admirable analysis of Pope's rhyming, shows that such an exercise becomes inevitably an analysis of syntax – 'In fact, words have no character as rhymes, until they become points in a syntactic succession.'[1] In other words, articulation by rhyme depends upon syntax as much as articulation by images.

If this were not so, there would be no difference between rhyme and other relationships by sound that the words set up among themselves. Then Smart's lunatic logic (quoted by Mr Frye) would be cogent:

> For two creatures the Bull and the Dog prevail in the English,
> For all the words ending in ble are in the creature.
> Invisi-ble, Incomprehensi-ble, ineffa-ble, A-ble . . .
> For there are many words under Bull . . .
> For Brook is under Bull. God be gracious to Lord Bolingbroke.

All that differentiates this from such an exercise in 'figures auricular' as Sidney's 'Shepherd's Song' is the absence of what Mr Frye calls the 'plausibility-principle'. And that, so we are to understand, is in any case optional, only a sop to the reader's prosaic habits.

Again we perceive that rhetorical theories of poetry demand of the reader an enormous initial act of faith. Jean Paulhan's argument has the effect of giving enormous weight to the first word in the phrase 'fiduciary symbol'. And when we look back at them from this point, St-John Perse and Valéry appear in a

1 'One Relation of Rhyme to Reason', in W. K. Wimsatt, *The Verbal Icon* (University of Kentucky Press, 1954), p. 156.

different light. The possibility now presents itself that when they asked us to have faith in words as symbols, they were asking for far more than Berkeley, for instance, who at one time seemed to echo them.

And yet we have to admit the force of Jean Paulhan's anecdote about Cilia and her little girl who is sick. It is true that a word, once uttered, can evoke a meaning that flies to meet it; that sometimes and quite legitimately in our common speech the word comes first and the idea, the appropriate meaning, only afterwards. C. Day Lewis points out that this is implicit in two well-known manifestos in verse written by poets in English, Edward Thomas's 'English Words', and the passage from 'Little Gidding' which begins, 'So here I am, in the middle way . . .':

> Both poets speak of words as if they had an independent life of their own ('Choose me, you English words': 'one has only learnt to get the better of words'). Both poets are expressing a sense of dedication and of humility: Mr Eliot writes of the 'men whom one cannot hope to emulate'; Edward Thomas asks words to use him 'As the winds use a crack in the wall or a drain'. Both poets consider a poem as an exploration – 'a raid on the inarticulate', Mr Eliot calls it – in which words play the leading part, can discover truths the poet was unaware of or incredulous of – 'as dear as the earth which *you prove* that we love'.[1]

This seems to imply, once again, that no arrangement of words can ever, strictly speaking, be meaningless. And so it reinforces Jean Paulhan's plea for 'the rhetorician', who has faith that words will lead him to truth, as opposed to 'the terrorist', who suspects that words are always ready to baffle and mislead unless he keeps control of them.

Yet Mr Eliot speaks of 'getting the better of words', and he says he proceeds 'By strength and submission' – by submission certainly, but also by strength, by letting the words lead him, but also by making them go where he wants. This, I should say,

1 C. Day Lewis, 'What is Modern Poetry?' *The Listener*, Jan. 22, 1953, p. 148.

is in part what makes Mr Eliot's lines superior to Thomas's. He grasps the paradox of poetic composition, its way of surrendering and conquering all at once. According to Mr Eliot (and of course corroboration can be found), the poet's traffic with the words he uses induces in him a state of mind that is neither passive nor active, but both, and both at once. If this is so, then the distinction between 'terrorist' and 'rhetorician' is false, for the poet, it seems, in the act of composition, is both. And the active positive element in the affair is something more essential than a graceful acquiescence in Professor Frye's 'plausibility-principle'; it is what we come across in Yeats, a declaration of faith in the conscious mind, its intelligible structure and significant activity.

XII

The Grammarian's Funeral

JESPERSEN'S investigations into the historical development of English grammar have been seen to invalidate some of the presumptions about 'concreteness' which are still current among poets and their readers. The upshot of his arguments was that the only ultimate concretion is 'the experience'; and that the 'things', so much prized by many poets and critics for their supposed concreteness, are in fact *abstractions*, abstracted from experiences in which things, and the thoughts and feelings they occasioned, were indistinguishable. T. E. Hulme and his disciples could thereafter continue to ask poetry for 'things', rendered in all their toughness and quiddity; but they could no longer pretend that, in making this demand, they were appealing for a return to nature, to the original and as they thought perennial norms of experiencing, obscured and sophisticated by the refinements of grammarians and logicians. To some of them, at any rate, this had been one of the strongest attractions of the discredited doctrine of 'concretion': its claim to return to the archaic simplicity of a Golden Age which poetry, if it were concrete enough, could re-create.

But Jespersen, in turn, lent himself to just this primitivism. The return to nature was still a possibility, and it could be still peculiarly the province of poetry to effect this return. It was only necessary to change the poetic strategy. Owen Barfield was the first English critic to realize this, and to demand of poetry that it re-create the massive indivisible experiences of primitive man, for whom no distinction was possible between the things he perceived, the significances folded in those things, and the responses they evoked from him. I do not know that any critics have followed Mr Barfield's lead. But certainly some poets have, or, if they have not, they have reached the same position by another route:

AFTERNOON AT HOME

Seeing the earth dry into shoots of summer
And sea dissolve the line of rock in steam
On my garden hill I gather
Impressions of the girl I live in dream

Until the ray that reads this flesh withdraws
Either from rare rainshine or dull moonwater
Drives me to pines with claws
And deserts the mere man who does not dream.

Under this granite bank fall banks of flowers
Lawns of herbs, grazing cubes of sea
Polished from hill to shore by showers
That release zones of new translucency

Where opaque dust, dazzling diamonds lay
Battering my sense to feel no symbol, no time,
Merely hostile rain, sepia spray-water,
In my Irish garden a grove of Japanese trees

Where rhododendron folly and quartz contour
Imposed foreign forms on day
Wrapped the night in snow-coral sea-fog,
Until I am not man or girl or dream

But wake from sleep this afternoon apart
Stretched on my garden rock an eye in words
Alone, to hear my song sung by birds,
Joined to hill, ground and sea, but separate.[1]

The last five lines of this poem, so far as I understand them, come near to admitting that what is attempted in the whole is the re-creation of an experience in which the scene, the circum-

1 Richard Murphy, *The Listener*, April 9, 1953.

stances, and the mind of the protagonist swim into one another, from which nothing, not even the 'I' and the 'not-I', is abstracted.

Mr Murphy dislocates his syntax. But it is perhaps not clear why he had to do so, his objective being what it was. Indeed, have I not claimed to show that Wordsworth's syntax in *The Prelude* was both authentic and poetic, just because he held close by experience, the ultimate concretion, in just this way? But alas, I fear Owen Barfield would not take *The Prelude* on my terms, any more than Ernest Fenollosa would. The thinness of Wordsworth's nouns would be immediately suspect. He too, it might be said, renders, not the experience itself, but an abstraction from it, an abstraction not of 'things', but of everything else, everything that excludes the things. And I suppose I have to agree. Nothing will do, really, but the language of *Finnegans Wake,* or else Fenollosa's dream of an English like Chinese, where nouns are verbs, and verbs are nouns, and all other parts of speech are both and neither.

For if Fenollosa fell foul of Jespersen in the matter of metaphor, this other side of his argument is a surprising achievement of historical anticipation. He anticipates here not the poetic theorists but the grammarians themselves. For the grammarians soon realized, following Jespersen's line of thought, that the traditional English grammar, with its 'parts of speech', could no longer apply. Terms such as 'noun', 'verb', 'adverb', 'preposition', themselves represent a breaking down of the massive compounds of experience into thoroughly misleading 'elements'. They represent the imposition of a Latinate system upon modern European languages, where it does not fit. Hence, for instance, the traditional objection to the split infinitive can no longer be sustained. For 'to walk' is not in any real sense the infinitive form of the verb 'walk'; to regard it so is only a grammarian's convenience.

The whole of traditional grammar was thus thrown into the melting-pot: 'It is very doubtful whether English has a passive voice at all, in any meaningful sense of the term. "Mr X is now being issued with a licence" might be bad Latin, but it is perfectly good English'.[1] It depends what we mean by 'good'. No doubt we have to agree with Mr Hugh Sykes Davies that it is entirely *correct* English (if, that is, as grammar now stands, the terms 'correct' and 'incorrect' still have any meaning at all). But it does not follow that the purist, when he objected to that construction, was moved only by feelings of vindictive superiority. Nor does it follow that the ground has now been cut from under his feet. He feels, perhaps, not the nasty meanness of a pedant, but the same pang of angry discomfort as he feels before any kind of tastelessness – in stone and steel, no less than in words. What matters, surely, is that this construction is ugly, inelegant. Ideas of beauty and elegance differ, no doubt; but mine are not therefore any less real, for me and perhaps for others.

And up to a point they can be rationalized. Beauty is, or it includes, order; ugliness is or includes muddle. 'Mr X is being issued with a licence'; 'rum is being issued with a ladle'. The connection between 'Mr X' and his 'licence' is quite different, in quite another pattern, from the connection between the rum and the ladle. If these two different patterns are cast into one pattern of speech, somewhere there is muddle; and muddle is ugly. It is also dishonest, for a distinction in experience is being denied in the speech that claims to render it.

This is beside the point. If the grammarian has got into the position of condoning muddle, that is the grammarian's funeral. What matters to us is the effect of these trains of thought upon poetry. It has for long been acknowledged that the poet enjoys a special licence in the matter of making nouns do the work of verbs, adjectives of nouns, and so on. There are abundant examples in Shakespeare. But now it can be claimed that this sort of thing is at the very heart of poetry, since it represents a

1 'Thersites', 'Private Views', *The Irish Times*, April 11, 1953.

re-creation by the poet of the natural patterns of experience. Allen Tate begins a poem:

> The idiot greens the meadow with his eyes

And his poem ends:

> the towering weak and pale
> Covers his eyes with memory like a sheet.

The adjective 'green' serves as a verb; other adjectives, 'towering', 'weak', 'pale', serve – some or all of them – as nouns. And of course the device is not uncommon. Richard Murphy's poem represents only a more extreme and less efficient application of the same principle – but with this difference: Allen Tate's poem is about an idiot, and it tries to re-create faithfully the patterns of idiotic experience. To identify the primitive with the natural, and the natural with the genuine, is to imply that the idiot is the only honest man. We reach the point where, to write poetry or to read it, we have to behave like idiots.

XIII

What is Modern Poetry?

WHAT is modern poetry? We cannot say, simply, that all poets who have written since a specific date are thereby modern poets. Or rather we can talk of 'modern poetry' in this sense, but more often we do not. Mr Walter de la Mare is presumably a modern poet in this sense, but his is not the poetry we have in mind when we speak of 'modern' poetry. Usually, when we use the term, we have in mind poetry which has broken with the poetry of our grandfathers in a way that Mr De la Mare's exquisite poetry has not. 'Modern', in fact, has taken over the functions of the now outmoded adjective 'modernist'; modern poetry, as we usually understand it, is something that appears aggressively and consciously different, in important ways, from the poetry of the past. In this sense of 'modern', the modern poet is standing on the near side of a gulf. Very often, indeed, the poet is at some pains to show us that the gulf can be bridged, and he points to the bridges he has crossed. But at any rate the bridges are thrown over in unlikely places; they are not broad and obvious like the bridge that leads back from Mr De la Mare to Keats.

All the same, the bridges are easier to find than is the gulf beneath them. Or rather the gulf is plain when we are 'on the spot', and very deep and wide; but it is hard to find it on the map or to instruct the stranger where to look out for it. There is a distinct break with the past, that we know; there is a gulf to be crossed if we want to move from Tennyson to T. S. Eliot; but when we try to define that break, to chart the gulf, we fall out among ourselves. We have all negotiated the passage, yet it seems we have come by different routes. One party of poets and critics finds the decisive innovation in one place, another in quite another, and so on. And though we feel, viewing the matter from a distance, that all modern poetry hangs together, when we come closer this impression vanishes and we see only a bewildering diversity. Somehow, we acknowledge, modern poetry begins with symbolism. Modern poetry, we say, is post-symbolist poetry. *Post hoc*, certainly, but *propter hoc*? And there we begin to wrangle. It is just there, when we try to explain just *how* symbolism 'started it all', that we fall out.

If the foregoing pages have tended to any one conclusion it is this: the break with the past is at bottom a change of attitude towards poetic syntax. It is from that point of view, in respect of syntax, that modern poetry, so diverse in all other ways, is seen as one. And we can define it thus: *What is common to all modern poetry is the assertion or the assumption (most often the latter) that syntax in poetry is wholly different from syntax as understood by logicians and grammarians.* When the poet retains syntactical forms acceptable to the grammarian, this is merely a convention which he chooses to observe. We may acknowledge that such emptied forms are to be found (and frequently too) in Shakespeare and in Milton. But never before the modern period has it been taken for granted that all poetic syntax is necessarily of this sort.

This is, surely, the one symbolist innovation that is at the root of all the other technical novelties that the symbolist poets introduced. Later poets could refuse to countenance all the other symbolist methods, and still, by sharing, consciously or not, the symbolist attitude to syntax, they stand out as patently 'post-symbolist'. This aspect of the symbolist doctrine – and, as I have pointed out, it is more than just one aspect, it is at the core – has been obscured by the fact that Mallarmé and Valéry talk of syntax, and appear to lay great store by it, in a way that earlier poets did not. But this arises from the use of one word 'syntax', to mean two things which are really widely different. In fact I think we shall find that we need not just two terms, but several, instead of the one. At any rate Mallarmé and Valéry, when they speak of 'syntax', do not mean by it what is meant by the common reader.

Here only blunt common sense will serve:

The point was not that the emotions of, say, Jules Laforgue were necessarily more complicated than those of, say, Catullus in his sequence of poems about Lesbia, but rather that the symbolist poet – instead of disentangling a complex emotion into a series of varying moods or at least, when the mood of a single poem is allowed to change abruptly (as in Catullus's *Illa Lesbia* . . .), of subduing the disordered feeling to the logic of consecutive statement – is in the habit of telescoping the whole thing by a few stenographic strokes. Nor are his feelings necessarily more difficult to render than those, say, of Wordsworth in the most mysterious of his visions of the natural world; but the symbolist – instead of attempting to reduce an unearthly elusive sensation to the lucidity of simple language – invents for it a vocabulary and a syntax as unfamiliar as the sensation itself.[1]

The symbolist poet, we realize, has a choice of two alternatives: either he telescopes his feeling 'by a few stenographic strokes' – that is, he abandons even the appearance of syntactical arrangement and merely juxtaposes images; or else he 'invents . . . a syntax as unfamiliar as the sensation itself' – that is, something that may look like normal syntax but fulfils a quite different function.

As H. M. McLuhan has pointed out, Wordsworth comes nearest to symbolist poetry in such a poem as 'The Solitary Reaper', where he leaves the reader to gather from the poem the feeling, never overtly described, which inspired the poet to write it. This is the poetry of 'the objective correlative', which describes not the emotion itself, but a symbolic landscape or action which may stand as its equivalent.[2] It is sometimes maintained

1 Edmund Wilson, *The Shores of Light* (Farrar, Straus, 1952), pp. 55, 56.

2 Cf. Yvor Winters 'Gerard Manley Hopkins', *Kenyon Review*, II, 1, p. 63: 'In no other literary period, I think, would a poet who was both a priest and a genuinely devout man have thought that he had dealt seriously with his love for Christ and his duty toward Him by writing an excited description of a landscape: this kind of thing belongs to the nineteenth and twentieth centuries, to the period of self-expression and the abnegation of reason.'

that the discovery how to do this was the decisive innovation of the symbolists, and the starting-point for the symbolist movement. But this is not the case, as the reference to Wordsworth serves to show. What is novel in symbolist technique is the way of organizing the items inside the symbolic landscape or the train of symbolic events.

When Edmund Wilson points out that Tennyson 'was nearer to the school of Verlaine than it is likely to occur to us to notice', he is enforcing this point, that the objective correlative is not peculiar to symbolism but can be found in pre-symbolist writing. Tennyson indeed is a crucial case, and H. M. McLuhan has treated him at some length from this point of view, arguing that he anticipates the Symbolist expedient of '*le paysage intérieur* or the psychological landscape':

> This landscape, by means of discontinuity, which was first developed in picturesque painting, effected the apposition of widely diverse objects as a means of establishing what Mr Eliot has called 'an objective correlative' for a state of mind . . . Whereas in external landscape diverse things lie side by side, so in psychological landscape the juxtaposition of various things and experiences becomes a precise musical means of orchestrating that which could never be rendered by systematic discourse. Landscape is the means of presenting, without the copula of logical enunciation, experiences which are united in existence but not in conceptual thought. Syntax becomes music, as in Tennyson's 'Mariana'.[1]

'Syntax becomes music'; and this is plainly the 'music' of St-John Perse, which is best fitted for 'joining without binding, and gathering together without fettering'. It is the music of Susanne Langer, in which 'The actual function of meaning, which calls for permanent contents, is not fulfilled; for the *assignment* of one rather than another possible meaning to each form is never explicitly made.' And if our earlier analysis was

1 H. M. McLuhan, 'Tennyson and Picturesque Poetry', *Essays in Criticism*, I, 3, pp. 270, 271.

correct, this means a syntax that is a shadow-play, a lifting of non-existent weights, a dance that ends where it began.

It will have been noticed that Wilson and McLuhan differ at one point, radically. For the latter the symbolist sort of syntax is justified because by it the poet may communicate or embody 'that which could never be rendered by systematic discourse'. And this is something that Wilson goes out of his way to deny. Laforgue, he insists, could have been as systematic as Catullus; he chose not to be:

> Symbolism, at its most successful, contrives to communicate emotions by images whose connection with the subject and whose relevance to one another we may not always understand ... These images could probably have been conveyed in a perfectly conventional manner – as Dante, describing a state of mind surely not less unusual and difficult, would write in the *Paradiso* of the fading from his memory of the divine vision, 'so the snow is unsealed by the sun, so the light leaves of the Sybil's message are scattered by the wind.'[1]

If Wilson is right, then McLuhan's case for symbolism comes out of a loss of faith in conceptual thought. It testifies to a loss of nerve, as with Hofmannsthal's Lord Chandos. And this was general. As Richard Ellmann says, Yeats stands almost alone in the post-symbolist generations as 'stubbornly loyal in his art to the conscious mind's intelligible structure'. For that, we see again, is what it amounts to: where there is authentic syntax in poetry (syntax, that is, not wholly different from the syntax of logician and grammarian), the poet retains hope of the conscious mind's activity; when he has lost that hope, his syntax is either dislocated altogether, or else turns into music.

H. M. McLuhan distinguishes between 'picturesque' and 'symbolist' poetry, though only as phases in the development of one tradition. He distinguishes between them as follows:

1 Wilson, loc. cit.

The picturesque artists saw the wider range of experience that could be managed by discontinuity and planned irregularity, but they kept to the picture-like single perspective. The interior landscape, however, moves naturally towards the principle of multiple perspectives as in the first two lines of *The Waste Land* where the Christian Chaucer, Sir James Frazer and Jessie Weston are simultaneously present. This is 'cubist perspective' which renders, at once, a diversity of views with the spectator always in the centre of the picture, whereas in picturesque art the spectator is always outside. The cubist perspective of interior landscape typically permits an immediacy, a variety and solidity of experience denied to the picturesque and to Tennyson.[1]

Now this, too, immediately recalls Yeats, speaking of Joyce, of Pound and of Proust:

This new art which has arisen in different countries simultaneously seems related . . . to that form of the new realist philosophy which thinks that the secondary and primary qualities alike are independent of consciousness; that an object can at the same moment have contradictory qualities. This philosophy seems about to follow the analogy of an art that has more rapidly completed itself, and after deciding that a penny is bright and dark, oblong and round, hot and cold, dumb and ringing in its own right; to think of the calculations it incites, our distaste and pleasure at its sight, the decision that made us pitch it, our preference for head or tail, as independent of a consciousness that has shrunk back, grown intermittent and accidental, into the looking-glass . . .

If you ask me why I do not accept a doctrine so respectable and convenient, its cruder forms so obviously resurrected to get science down from Berkeley's roasting-spit, I can but answer like Zarathustra, 'Am I a barrel of memories that I should give you my reasons?'; somewhere among those memories something compels me to reject whatever – to borrow a metaphor of Coleridge's – drives mind into the quicksilver.[2]

1 McLuhan, loc. cit., pp. 281, 282.

2 Hone and Rossi, *Bishop Berkeley*, pp. xxiv, xxv.

There is an obvious relation between McLuhan's cubist perspective offering 'at once, a diversity of views', and the new realist philosophy indicated by Yeats, according to which 'an object can at the same moment have contradictory qualities'. Where McLuhan speaks of 'the spectator always in the centre of the picture', Yeats talks, here and elsewhere, of a consciousness withdrawn into the quicksilver at the back of the mirror. The critic and the poet are speaking of the same thing, and in very similar imagery, though from different points of view.

Yeats's appeal to Coleridge is just:

In disciplining the mind one of the first rules should be, to lose no opportunity of tracing words to their origin; one good consequence of which will be, that he will be able to use the *language* of sight without being enslaved by its affections. He will at least save himself from the delusive notion, that what is not *imageable* is likewise not *conceivable*. To emancipate the mind from the despotism of the eye is the first step towards its emancipation from the influences and intrusions of the senses, sensations and passions generally. Thus most effectively is the power of abstraction to be called forth . . .[1]

This is the Coleridge who admonished Wordsworth that the best part of human language comes from the allocation of fixed symbols to internal acts of the mind. All this side of Coleridge's thought flies in the face of modern poetic theory, symbolist or imagist. And from his point of view such modern theory is grounded upon the delusion that what cannot be imaged cannot be conceived. According to Coleridge conceptual thinking outstrips thinking in images; for H. M. McLuhan, as for most symbolist and post-symbolist theorists, the truth is just the other way round – images, if cunningly arranged, can get beyond concepts. At this point the alignment of forces, for and against authentic syntax in poetry, is particularly clear.

1 Quoted by Herbert Read, *The True Voice of Feeling*, p. 179.

2

LET us try, for the last time, to focus the point at issue in particular examples. To be fair we need to compare two whole poems. Here is Pound's 'The Gypsy':

That was the top of the walk, when he said:
'Have you seen any others, any of our lot,
With apes or bears?'
    – a brown upstanding fellow
Not like the half-castes,
    up on the wet road near Clermont.
The wind came, and the rain,
And mist clotted about the trees in the valley,
And I'd the long ways behind me,
    gray Arles and Biaucaire,
And he said, 'Have you seen any of our lot?'
I'd seen a lot of his lot . . .
    ever since Rhodez,
Coming down from the fair
    of St John,
With caravans, but never an ape or a bear.

A similar experience lies behind Wordsworth's 'Stepping Westward':

'*What, you are stepping westward?*' – '*Yea.*'
– 'Twould be a *wildish* destiny,
If we, who thus together roam
In a strange land, and far from home,
Were in this place the guests of Chance:
Yet who would stop, or fear to advance,
Though home or shelter he had none,
With such a sky to lead him on?

The dewy ground was dark and cold;
Behind, all gloomy to behold;
And stepping westward seemed to be
A kind of *heavenly* destiny:

I liked the greeting; 'twas a sound
Of something without place or bound;
And seemed to give me spiritual right
To travel through that region bright.

The voice was soft, and she who spake
Was walking by her native lake:
The salutation had to me
The very sound of courtesy:
Its power was felt; and while my eye
Was fixed upon the glowing sky,
The echo of the voice enwrought
A human sweetness with the thought
Of travelling through the world that lay
Before me in my endless way.

Wordsworth's poem is one I am very fond of; yet it is difficult to deny that Pound's is much superior. On the other hand I do not think its superiority can be defined in terms of concretion over against abstraction, objective correlative against subjective disquisition.

It is apparent in the first place that Pound's apparently 'free' versification is incomparably stricter than Wordsworth's apparent regularity. Consider only 'spiritual right', and the choking elision to be given to the last three syllables of 'spiritual'. Wordsworth's italics, on 'wildish' and 'heavenly', ask the reader for an emphasis that Pound would have forced upon him by an arrangement of rhythms; and they testify also, I think, to Wordsworth's embarrassment, his sense of insecurity, about the colloquialisms he employs. Then, too, Pound is so much more concise. The poems are really strikingly similar. The impression of illimitable horizons, of 'something without place or bound' (Wordsworth lends himself to quotation, Pound does not – that is part of the difference), receives, in both poems, a slanting ray of other feeling, towards the end. Wordsworth's 'human sweetness' means a recognition that the ardent wanderlust is provided for and sanctioned by popular feeling – the folk know that sort of yearning and acknowledge it as human. Pound's last cadence, 'but never an ape or a bear', throws an oblique ray in just the same way, mingling with the predominant emotion a feeling, this time, of wistfulness, even frustration. A very similar arc of feeling is followed in both poems, but by Pound with a far finer economy. And undoubtedly Pound's is a musical syntax, where Wordsworth's is not. For consider: who is 'up on the wet road near Clermont'? The authentic Romanies? Or the half-castes with whom they must not be confused? Or the poet himself, and the man he has encountered? We do not know, and it does not matter. For all that is required at this moment in the poem is the 'up' and the 'on', the release, like the call of a horn, into distance and altitude. Or when was it that 'the wind came, and the rain'? Was it when he saw the half-castes, or when he saw the full-blooded gypsies, or in between his meeting either of these and his meeting with the man who addressed him; or finally, did the squall come while he and the man were talking? And again, it doesn't matter. This is a rattle on the percussion as the other was a call of the horn; syntax has become music.

But, if Pound's poem is better than Wordsworth's, it is not better because it is more 'concrete' or because its syntax has become music. If it is more concise, it is not for these reasons. On the contrary, what pads out Wordsworth's poem and makes it blowsy is just that part of it where he tries to be specific and to provide 'images':

> The dewy ground was dark and cold;
> Behind, all gloomy to behold . . .

But, in any case, this is not the point. Is 'Stepping Westward' poetry at all? According to McLuhan it cannot be. For its language is most distinguished and affecting just where it is most abstract and conceptual:

> The echo of the voice enwrought
> A human sweetness with the thought

> Of travelling through the world that lay
> Before me in my endless way.

A new quality ('human sweetness') enters into the poet's thinking; nothing could be much more 'abstract' than that. But, when all is said and done, Wordsworth's poem is more original than Pound's. That there is a wistfulness at the heart of the wanderlust is no new idea; and that need not matter when the old idea is expressed so memorably as it is by Pound. But Wordsworth's recognition that the wanderlust is acknowledged by traditional sentiment, and that that acknowledgement makes it all the more attractive – that is the sort of idea that could have occurred only to Wordsworth; it is something far more strange and novel.

'Stepping Westward' offends against other canons of modern criticism. It tells us about an experience, instead of presenting it; what happened is described, not embodied. The question whether this is legitimate in poetry is one that has been much debated. And it might seem that the question of poetic syntax is bound up with this; that, in order to find room for authentic syntax in poetry, we have to admit that poetry may talk about, describe, comment explicitly on the experiences it presents. As a matter of fact I *would* admit that. But it is important to realize that there is no need to do so, that the issue here debated is *not* the same as that between 'talking about' and 'presenting'. On the contrary, a case for syntax other than symbolist syntax in poetry can be made to rest upon just these grounds – that a movement of syntax can render, immediately present, the curve of destiny through a life or the path of an energy through the mind. It is true that the emphasis on presentation rather than description has tended to exclude authentic syntax from poetry. But that is another matter; in my view the enthusiasts for presentation, for embodiment, have been ill-advised in ignoring the part that authentic syntax can play in bringing about all that they hope for, by miming a movement of the mind or of fate.

There is a muddle in the offing here, about the word 'discursive'. Mrs Langer uses it precisely, when she discriminates between discursive and presentational symbolism; by 'discursive' she means what moves from point to point. Literary critics frequently use it loosely, to mean an apparently casual musing or meditation, something not far short of 'rambling'. In Mrs Langer's sense of the word, the verse of *The Prelude* is discursive; for a poetry depending so much on nicely distinguished verbs must move through them, from point to point in time. It is often called 'discursive' in the looser sense also; but my disagreement with Dr Leavis turned on just that point – in the first version, at any rate, the verse of *The Prelude* does not describe or discuss an experience; it renders it in mime.

This cannot be said of the syntax in 'Stepping Westward', a poem which is discursive, I think, in the looser sense. There the comparison with 'The Gypsy' was in terms of conciseness. And the point to be made is that Wordsworth comes nearest to the conciseness of Pound at just the point where his language is most conceptual and his syntax correspondingly most rapid.

When all is said and done there is no way of deciding which is the better poem – 'Stepping Westward' or 'The Gypsy'. In the end we have to admit that there is no comparison. Certainly there is a sense in which one can say Pound's poem is much better *as a poem*. But then it is a queer understanding of 'poem' which obliges us, when we judge it as such, to leave out of account all the originality and profundity in what the poem says. This is, however, what we are forced to do, if we believe with Mrs Langer that 'it is not a proposition, but the entertainment of one' which we should attend to. On this showing, the quality of what is entertained cannot enter into our judgement of the poem as poem. And however handy this may be when we deal with a poet like Yeats, who seems to entertain some very queer customers indeed, it blinds us to the greatness of a poet like Wordsworth, which often resides just in his capacity for making novel discoveries about human sentiment. His entertainment may be shabby, but the company is of the best; yet this, it seems, is just what we have to leave out of account.

It was De Quincey who made much of Wordsworth's faculty for sheer 'discovery':

A volume might be filled with such glimpses of novelty as Wordsworth has first laid bare, even to the apprehension of the *senses*. For the *understanding*, when moving in the same track of human sensibilities, he has done only not so much. How often must the human heart have felt the case, when there are sorrows which descend far below the region in which tears gather; and yet who has ever given utterance to this feeling until Wordsworth came with his immortal line:

Thoughts that do often lie too deep for tears?

This sentiment, and others that might be adduced (such as 'The child is father of the man'), have even passed into the popular heart, and are often quoted by those who know not *whom* they are quoting.[1]

This is trite and homely stuff beside the refinements of symbolist aesthetics, but it brings us back to a point made earlier about a line of Shakespeare, 'Uneasy lies the head that wears a crown.' This is another line that has 'passed into the popular heart', and the point made then was that the pursuit of concretions would banish such a line (for visualize the image or, more properly, make an image of it, and it is ludicrous). Now, coming upon a similar instance from a quite different direction, we find such a line debarred from poetry once again. Just those lines that have gone over into folk wisdom are stigmatized as unpoetical. The folk, of course, can pervert a poetic statement by tearing it from its context; there is the notorious case, 'One touch of nature makes the whole world kin.' Yet this is the exception, not the rule. And there must surely be something wrong with theories that banish from poetry all that part of it which is taken up into popular wisdom. Mrs Langer is forced to do this, because the folk, when they seize upon a line of poetry, make what is for her the cardinal error of supposing that the poet means just what he

1 *De Quincey's Literary Criticism* (ed. Darbishire, 1909), p. 240.

says, that the poetic statement he makes is not wholly different from the statements they make themselves, and that the syntax of his statement is not wholly different in function from the syntax they are used to elsewhere.

XIV

The Reek of the Human

It will be apparent that the impulse behind all this writing is conservative. But it is, I hope, a rational conservatism. When a poem abjures even the forms of syntax, or when it retains those forms but perverts their function to make syntax into music, or when it uses syntax only incidentally, articulating rather through images spaced by rhythms – when any of these things happen in a poem, I do not say, 'This is not poetry at all', or, 'This is not poetry as I understand it.' I have risked such a sweeping judgement only once, on the sort of poetry represented by the sonnets of Dylan Thomas. I am concerned only to make room, in our understanding of what poetry is, for all of the varieties of poetic syntax which I have tried to distinguish. And it is my contention that there is not room for all of them in any one of the theories of poetry which I have considered.

If I am most anxious to show the inadequacy of the symbolist and post-symbolist tradition, it is because that is still the prevailing tradition in criticism and poetic theory (though not any longer, I think, in English poetic practice). By comparison, Fenollosa, though he certainly pushes his insights too far, is thoroughly conservative in spirit, and provides indeed the best antidote to the symbolist excesses.

The tendency of all symbolist theories is to make the world of poetry more autonomous. Most of them, like Mrs Langer's, stop short of making the world of poetry wholly self-sufficient, and keep open some avenue, however narrow and winding, by which the world of poetry can communicate with the outside world, through mimesis. But some theorists – those, perhaps, who see poetic syntax as mathematics rather than music – seem prepared to cut poetry loose altogether. And here I will use Mr Northrop Frye, once again, as whipping-boy:

> The assumption in the word 'universe', whether applied to physics or to literature, is not that these subjects are descriptive of total existence, but simply that they are in themselves totally intelligible. No one can know the whole of physics at once, but physics would not be a coherent subject unless this were theoretically possible. The argument of Aristotle's *Physics*, which treats physics as the study of motion in nature, leads inexorably to the conception of an unmoved mover at the circumference of the world. In itself this is merely the postulate that the total form of physics is the physical universe. If Christian theology takes physics to be descriptive of an ultra-physical reality or activity, and proceeds to identify this unmoved first mover with an existent God, that is the business of Christian theology: physics as physics will be unaffected by it. The assumption of a verbal universe similarly leads to the conception of an unspeakable first word at its circumference. This in itself is merely the postulate that literature is totally intelligible. If Christian theology identifies this first word with the Word of God or person of Christ, and says that the vision of total human creative power is divine as well as human, the literary critic, as such, is not concerned either to support or to refute the identification.[1]

I go so far as I can in understanding this passage by setting it beside Elizabeth Sewell's very suggestive notion of systems in the mind, some 'open' and some 'closed', an idea which comes by analogy from mechanics.

Miss Sewell observes that 'The mind has a choice of systems within which it can work.' She quotes, 'The primary control of the concepts of mathematics is that contradiction should not be involved.' And she goes on:

> Nightmare works in reverse, including all that is disorder and excluding all that is order. In the one system there is the certainty of the expected, in the other the certainty of the unexpected, but in neither system is there any room for probability or uncertainty.[2]

1 Frye, 'Levels of Meaning in Literature', *Kenyon Review*, pp. 260, 261.

2 Elizabeth Sewell, *The Structure of Poetry*, p. 64.

It should now be plain that Mr Frye's rhetoric converts language from an open system into a closed one. In literature, on his view, there is the certainty of the intelligible, and there is therefore no room in it for probability or uncertainty. Literature is certain to find what it seeks because its conclusions are implicit in its postulate. But then our mistake is in thinking that it seeks anything. It does not seek, it constructs:

The poet's new poem merely articulates what was already latent in the order of words, and the assumption of a single order of words is as fundamental to the poet as the assumption of a single order of nature is to the natural scientist. The difficulty in understanding this arises from the confusion of language with dictionary language, and of literature with the bibliography of literature. Language in a human mind is not a list of words with their customary meanings attached, but a single interlocking structure, one's total power of expressing oneself. Literature is the objective counterpart of this, a total form of verbal expression which is re-created in miniature whenever a new poem is written.[1]

This emphasis on 'articulation', on 'a single interlocking structure', rather than on 'words with their customary meanings attached', seems to promise well for poetic syntax. But a moment's thought will reveal that these expressions make a case for syntax on still other grounds than the several we have discussed already. For if the words in poetry are to be considered in their relations with each other, not in their relations to 'their customary meanings', syntax in the same way is to be considered not in its relation to anything outside the realm of language, but in relation to 'a total form of verbal expression'. This syntax articulates, not 'the world', but 'the world of the poem'.

It is quite natural, therefore, for Mr Frye to pronounce:

The relation of literature to factual verbal structures has to be established from within one of the latter. Literature must be approached centrifugally, from the outside, if we are to get any factual significance out of it ... One begins talking about *Lycidas*, for instance, by

1 Frye, loc. cit., p. 260.

itemizing all the things that *Lycidas* illustrates in the non-literary verbal world: English history in 1637, the Church and Milton's view of it, the position of Milton as a young poet planning an epic and a political career, the literary convention of the pastoral elegy, Christian teachings on the subject of death and resurrection, and so on. It would be quite possible to spend a whole critical life in this allegorical limbo of background, without ever getting to the poem at all, or even feeling the need of doing so.[1]

Lycidas is an apt example, of course. But take Wordsworth's 'Complaint of a Forsaken Indian Woman'. The whole point of this poem lies in its truth to human nature; and is it really true that, to get its factual significance as presenting the feelings of a woman separated from her child, we need to come at it from within a 'factual verbal structure', that is, presumably, through a treatise on the psychology of mother and child? We need, it is true, to have some humanity ourselves; but is that searching of our own hearts an 'allegorical limbo of background'? And when we come out of that limbo and get to the poem, what is left for us to get to? Once we have taken the truth of the poem to a human predicament, there is nothing left; for diction, metre, rhyme, imagery, all are made transparent for the truth to shine out through them. This poem is not a world, like the world of a symbolist poem, 'closed and self-sufficient, being the pure system of the ornaments and the chances of language.' It takes on meaning only as it is open to another world; unless it refers to that other 'real' world, it is meaningless. Its syntax articulates not just itself, not only its own world, but the world of common experience.

The appeal of theories such as Mr Frye's is manifest in the loaded words that their promoters use in recommending them. A poetry in which the syntax articulates only 'the world of the poem' is said to be 'pure', 'absolute', 'sheer', 'self-sufficient'. Wordsworth's poems are 'impure' because they have about them

1 Ibid., p. 250.

the smell of soil and soiled flesh, the reek of humanity. Their syntax is not 'pure' syntax because it refers to – it mimes – something outside itself and outside the world of its poem, something that smells of the human, of generation and hence of corruption. It is my case against the symbolist theorists that, in trying to remove the human smell from poetry, they are only doing harm. For poetry to be great it must reek of the human, as Wordsworth's poetry does. This is not a novel contention; but perhaps it is one of those things that cannot be said too often.

APPENDIX

Hulme, Mrs Langer and Fenollosa on the Relation of Poetry to Science

IT is instructive to compare my three main authorities – Hulme, Fenollosa and Mrs Langer – from the point of view of the attitudes they adopt to scientific thought.

Hulme takes scientific explanation as the type of 'the extensive manifold'. According to him, because the scientist is committed to explanation of this sort, he is satisfied only when he finds it, and the phenomena which are of the other, intensive, sort are not acknowledged, merely because they do not suit the mental machinery. Hulme takes 'as an example of the kind of thing the intellect does consider perfectly clear and comprehensible' the image of pieces on a draughtboard:

> You find as a matter of fact that any science, as it tends towards perfection, tends to present reality as consisting of something exactly similar to this draughtboard. They all resolve the complex phenomena of nature into fixed separate elements changing only in position. They all adopt atomic theories, and the model of all the sciences is astronomy. In order to get a convenient nomenclature one calls all complex things which can be resolved into separate elements or atoms in this way 'extensive manifolds'.[1]

But later, when he discusses the Bergsonian concepts of time and change, he changes his image for the scientific outlook, from draughts to billiards:

> One can get a picture of the type in terms of which the mind insists on conceiving change by thinking of the motion of billiard balls on an

1 Hulme, *Speculations*, pp. 176, 177.

ideally smooth table where there is no friction. It would be impossible here to discover or conceive the existence of freedom. There is in fact no change at all. You can predict with certainty the position of the balls at any future moment, for you have a fixed number of elements moving under fixed laws.

But – and here comes one of the most important elements for the understanding of what Bergson is getting at – this is only a true account of change if you admit that everything can in reality be analysed into separate elements like the balls on the table. If it can, then the future must be determined; but we have just seen that mental life at the level of the fundamental self cannot. It is an interpenetrating whole: it is not composed of elements. It changes, but the way in which it changes will not fit into the kind of conception which the intellect forms of change.[1]

This conception of the scientific outlook was already outdated in Hulme's time, but its obsolescence was only later brought home to the general reader, by Eddington:

The recognition that our knowledge of the objects treated in physics consists solely of readings of pointers and other indicators transforms our view of the status of physical knowledge in a fundamental way. Until recently it was taken for granted that we had knowledge of a far more intimate kind of the entities of the external world . . . The Victorian physicist felt that he knew just what he was talking about when he used such terms as *matter* and *atoms*. Atoms were tiny billiard balls, a crisp statement that was supposed to tell you all about their nature in a way which could never be achieved for transcendental things like consciousness, beauty, and humour.[2]

It will hardly be supposed that Eddington's world will recommend itself to Hulme any more than the world of the Victorian physicist. A pointer-reading is even more 'abstract' than an atom. On the other hand, to a theorist for whom words are verbal symbols, Eddington's science recommends itself at once.

1 Hulme, *Speculations*, p. 192.

2 Sir A. S. Eddington, *The Nature of the Physical World* (CUP, 1932), pp. 258, 259.

For Hulme Eddington only widens the gap between poetry and science; but for Susanne Langer he has closed it, for the pointer-readings of the physicist are seen to be a language of symbols interposed between him and experience, just as a language of non-verbal symbols is interposed for the mathematician and the musician.

As for Fenollosa, his attitude to science emerges from his attitude to the traditional grammarians and their backers, the logicians:

> Of course this view of the grammarians springs from the discredited, or rather the useless, logic of the Middle Ages. According to this logic, thought deals with abstractions, concepts drawn out of things by a sifting process. These logicians never inquired how the 'qualities' which they pulled out of things came to be there. The truth of all their little checkerboard juggling depended upon the natural order by which these powers or properties or qualities were folded in concrete things, yet they despised the 'thing' as a mere 'particular', or pawn. It was as if Botany should reason from the leaf-patterns woven into our tablecloths. Valid scientific thought consists in following as closely as may be the actual and entangled lines of forces as they pulse through things. Thought deals with no bloodless concepts but science watches *things move* under its microscope.[1]

This seems quite close in places to Hulme's Bergsonian distinction between intensive and extensive manifolds; the qualities, powers and principles that for Fenollosa are 'folded in concrete things' are the things that for Hulme and Pound are 'unfolded' in the extensive manifold of syntax, though Hulme thinks that some of them resist that process. But there is the significant difference that, according to Fenollosa, the scientist stands for 'the thing', along with the poet, over against the logician.

This is no doubt a necessary correction of Hulme's emphasis.

1 Physics is not the only science. Fenollosa here appeals to botany. And it is notable that when Pound restates Fenollosa's position for him, he finds his example in biology, a science still far from pointer-readings and mathematics.

The continually renewed hostility between the experimental scientist and the rationalist is a fact of history for which Hulme and others like him, who put a gulf between science and poetry, make no provision. But Fenollosa does not stop here. Hating abstraction as fiercely as Hulme, he flies in Hulme's face to assert that, wherever else abstraction is found, it is not found in the literature of science. Having castigated, through a couple of harsh and brilliant pages, the methods of medieval logic, he blames this habit of mind, as Hulme had blamed the 'extensive manifold' habit, for the difficulty that was found in accommodating the idea of evolution: 'It is impossible to represent change in this system or any kind of growth. This is probably why the conception of evolution came so late to Europe. It could not make way *until it was prepared to destroy inveterate logic of classification.*' So, for Fenollosa, the acceptance of the idea of evolution represents a triumph for the scientist over the logician: 'Science fought till she got at the things.' And a few lines later: 'In diction and in grammatical form science is utterly opposed to logic. Primitive men who created language agreed with science and not with logic. Poetry agrees with science and not with logic.' Plainly, this position is miles away from Hulme's.

It may now be clear how Fenollosa's Augustan air is so revealing. Though he is as averse as Hulme to endorsing the 'billiard-balls' of the Victorian physicist, he is even further than Hulme from endorsing Einstein's and Eddington's world of 'pointer-readings'. His view of science, and his affection for it, go back to the very dawn of modern natural philosophy, further than Newton, back to the world of Robert Boyle and the Royal Society, a world of 'things' that act upon one another, the heyday of experimental optimism. Boyle and his fellows were fierce anti-Rationalists, who set up Bacon in opposition to Descartes. That distinction fell to the ground with Newton: 'It is true that Newton, a tireless experimenter and a distruster of theories, astonished his age, but his principal work represented a triumph for Descartes and the mechanical philosophy more than for experimental science.'[1] And the billiard-balls of the Victorian physicist were in sight as soon as Locke distinguished between primary and secondary qualities, and posited the abstract 'substance', matter. This point is worth making because it explains, I think, why Fenollosa's views of poetic language and syntax are particularly helpful to the reader of the poetry of just Boyle's period; and also because it helps to explain why, in Chapter X, I thought that I had to establish the relevance of Berkeley, Locke's most powerful critic.

1 R. F. Jones, 'The Background of the Attack on Science in the Age of Pope', in James L. Clifford and Louis A. Landa (eds.), *Pope and His Contemporaries: Essays Presented to George Sherburn* (OUP, 1949), p. 111.

Acknowledgements

Some parts of *Purity of Diction in English Verse* have previously appeared in *The Cambridge Journal*, *Hermathena* and *Essays in Criticism*. My thanks are due to the editors of these journals for permission to reproduce material which first figured in their pages.

Some parts of *Articulate Energy* have appeared in rather different form in *The Twentieth Century* and in *Essays in Criticism*; and I thank the editors of these journals for permission to reprint this material.

D.A.D.

'Leaving the Rest Unsaid' by Robert Graves (from *Collected Poems 1975*), which appears on p. 255, is reproduced by permission of A. P. Watt Ltd on behalf of The Trustees of the Robert Graves Copyright Trust.

Index

Index